PERSPECTIVES

IN

ECONOMICS

Readings in Economics and Economic History

PERSPECTIVES

IN

ECONOMICS

Readings in Economics and Economic History

—SECOND EDITION—

Edited by

John W. Snow, Ph.D., J.D.

Assistant Professor of Economics
University of Maryland

**The Interstate
Printers & Publishers, Inc.**

Danville, Illinois

PREFACE

There are various approaches to the teaching of elementary economics. The purpose of this book of readings is to complement a course in elementary economics that uses an historical or institutional approach to introduce the student to the world of economics. Such is the approach which we have taken here at the University of Maryland where the elementary course serves to combine an historical and analytical introduction to economics. This book is an outgrowth of my experience in teaching this introductory course.

The readings are designed to introduce the student to economics as a social science and to supply the student with a key to comprehension and analysis of important aspects of European and American economic history such as unemployment and modern technology, the rise of big business and unions, international trade and tariffs, the development of markets, economic growth, the rise of big government, fiscal policy, money, economic instability, and the Federal Reserve System.

Each reading is a self-contained essay which elucidates the fundamental problem under consideration and provides the student with a framework with which to think more clearly and carefully about that particular aspect of economics.

These readings will therefore serve to complement an historical introduction to economics in which the student is required to put economics and economic problems into an institutional or historical perspective, drawing upon economic analysis to isolate and think carefully about the economic forces at work. The advantage of such an approach is that it maintains the essential social science characteristics of economics, continuously demonstrating to the student the changing nature of the economic problem and economic institutions and calling upon and equipping the student to think about his economic system—what it is, what it has been, and what it will be.

I am greatly indebted to the contributors of articles and to the publishers of works included in this volume. As for the book itself, I hope the reader will find it a welcome addition to his library, a book which can be turned to again and again for assistance in understanding the complexity of the economic world about us.

University of Maryland
January, 1969

TABLE OF CONTENTS

Section III

INTERNATIONAL TRADE
AND EXCHANGE

Section IV

MONEY AND MONETARY POLICY

Section IX

ECONOMIC SYSTEMS

GLOSSARY

Section I

INTRODUCTION TO ECONOMICS

THE ECONOMIC PROBLEM

Marvin M. Phaup, Jr.

Introduction

It may seem extremely presumptuous to title an article "The Economic Problem." After all, anyone exposed to today's mass media cannot help but be aware of the existence of a variety of social problems that involve economics. There is the farm problem, the monopoly problem, the poverty problem, the balance-of-payments problem, and the unemployment problem, to mention only a few.

Unlikely though it may seem, the fact is that there is a *the* economic problem which lies at the bottom of all other economic issues. The student must grasp this fundamental issue at the outset of his study of economics if he is to understand the myriad manifestations of the economic problem with which he will be confronted.

The aim of this paper, then, is to provide the student with a reference point, a navigational aid which, it is hoped, will see him through the sometimes treacherous, frequently murky waters of economic analysis. To accomplish this, the economic problem will be defined and explained. Three implications of the economic problem will then be discussed.

The Problem

The economic problem is the simple fact that a society's wants always exceed its ability to satisfy those wants. There can and must be no hedging on this point: The fundamental premise of economics is that things

The author is Assistant Professor of Economics, Roanoke College, and Visiting Lecturer in Economics, University of Lancaster.

of value are not available in the quantity desired. This means that economic goods are scarce. In fact, scarcity and the economic problem refer to exactly the same condition. Stated another way, every society is confronted with the problem of trying to gratify an infinitely large aggregate appetite for goods and services from a larder of resources which is finite in size. This is the economic problem, and it is the reason for economics.

A frequent student reaction to this first article of faith in the economist's creed is skepticism. The student understandably believes that there is considerable evidence that scarcity is not a very widespread, real world phenomenon in the "affluent society." After all, the sight of farmers destroying their crops and dairy products is too recent and too vivid to be conveniently ignored just to humor some economics professor. What is more, complaints are often heard from businessmen that there are far too many firms both at home and abroad producing the same product for the good of this country. Public officials have spoken out that the roads are too crowded with too many automobiles, that the rivers are filled with pollutants, and that there are now or soon will be too many people. If this were not a world of surplus how can we explain things like the annual model change in the automobile industry, throw-away containers, the two-car family or color T.V. Surely then, surplus is what confounds society rather than scarcity. If there is a *the* economic problem, it seems to be that man will bury himself under his own output.

While this is a common reaction, it is not correct.

Reconsider the evidence that is supposed to show that general scarcity does not exist. If the reader is very careful, he will notice that what is actually indicated in each of these instances is that either (1) sellers are dissatisfied with the price they are receiving, i.e., the farmer and the businessman, or (2) there are excess quantities of some particular things, but at the same time there are shortages of other economic goods, i.e., too many motor vehicles, too few modern streets and highways; too much pollution and too few antipollution treatment systems; too many people and too little food, housing, education, recreation, etc., for those many people.

The "evidence" does not indicate the absence of the economic problem. It does not contradict the *general* scarcity of want-satisfying goods relative to the magnitude of our unlimited desires.

There is a simple and widely used method of illustrating the limited productive capacity of an economy and the nature of the economic problem. In graphical form, this explanation is called a production frontier or a transformation curve. The illustration is developed by conceptually considering the case of an imaginary country. Ruritania. This region, like all countries at a particular point in time, possesses fixed amounts of productive resources, i.e., land, labor, capital, and a specified state of technology. By the judicious use of these factors of production, Ruritania is able to produce certain amounts of the goods and services which are desired by its citizens. It will simplify the discussion to assume that the country produces only two goods, e.g., beef and potatoes. (It is just as easy to assume that two types of goods are produced, e.g., consumer goods and industrial goods.) Beef and potatoes, then, are representative of the many goods and services produced and consumed.

Now, suppose that during one year, Ruritania uses all of its land, labor, and capital to produce beef. In this case, no potatoes will be grown, but a large, though finite, quantity of meat will be available. Similarly, if all the country's facilities are devoted to potato production for one year, many potatoes will be grown, but again these will be finite in number. A third possibility is that some resources will be used for potatoes and some for meat production, but nonetheless the resulting output will be a finite quantity. That is to say, production will have an upper bound above which it will be unable to go. In fact, in every case, production is everywhere limited by the availability of resources and the level of technology by which those resources are transformed into economic goods.

Some production possibilities for Ruritania are as follows, with respect to output during a specified time period.

Possible Combinations	Tons of Potatoes Produced per Year	Hundreds of Pounds (cwt.) of Beef Produced per Year
A	100	0
B	75	25
C	50	50
D	25	75
E	0	100

The tabulation indicates that resources are available in Ruritania such that either 100 tons of potatoes *or* 100 cwt. of beef may be produced in one year. It is also indicated that if this economy produces 50 tons of potatoes per year, it may also produce 50 cwt. of beef. Yet, no matter how well Ruritania uses its resources, under present circumstances it is impossible for the country to produce, say, 75 tons of potatoes and 50 cwt. of beef. Resource availability simply does not permit such an output level.

The data contained in the table are presented in graphical form on a two-dimensional axis in Figure 1.[1]

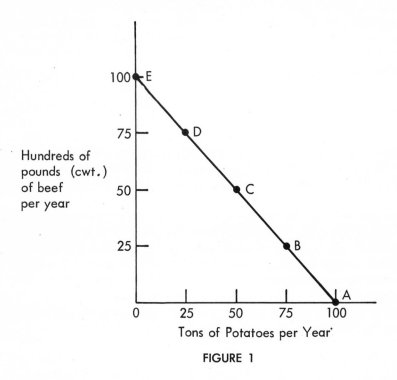

FIGURE 1

Line EA, which is composed of points representing maximum combinations of output, is called a production frontier or a production possibilities curve because it indicates the bounded nature of the productive capabilities of this economy as well as the alternative product combinations that are possible. The economic problem is evidenced here inasmuch as production cannot take place outside the production frontier (EA), while the wants of this society are not similarly limited. A society's wants are literally insatiable and unbounded. Man's reach does exceed his grasp.

---

[1] Note that the two-product limitation was assumed to allow use of a two-dimensional axis for the illustration.

6

The labor leader Samuel Gompers was not alone when, in answer to a question regarding what labor wanted, he replied, "More." The world needs more food, more medical care, more freedom from drudgery, more beauty, more leisure.

To repeat, society cannot have everything it wants, given the limited nature of its productive resources. This is the economic problem; and it is the reason for economics, a study which directs its efforts at finding means for getting the most human satisfaction out of these resources that are scarce.

Implications of the Economic Problem

Careful consideration of the economic problem reveals at least three major implications of the fact that resources are scarce relative to the uses to which they may be put. These implications involve: (1) the desirability of full employment of resources, (2) the desirability of a proper use of available resources, and (3) the inescapable necessity of choice. It will be of value to consider each of these implications in turn.

First, if a society is going to obtain maximum benefit from its resources, it will want to ensure that all the resources are being used. That is, it will be rational to avoid unemployment. Since only a limited quantity of resources are available, it would be foolish to allow some to be wasted in idleness.

The second implication of scarcity and a desire to maximize the benefits which can be derived from the available resources is that the resources should be employed in the most productive fashion. It is not enough that all factors of production be employed; they must be allocated to various uses in the best possible way. As the proverb advises, "There is no point in running if you are on the wrong road."

These first two implications of the economic problem can be illustrated in terms of a game, for example, chess. The object in this game is, of course, to move one's own pieces in such a manner as to capture the opponent's king. In pursuit of this objective, it is only rational to use all of one's resources, i.e., pawns, bishops, knights, etc. It is simple common sense to avoid "unemployment." At the same time, it is essential to use the pieces to best advantage. Similarly, in managing the resources of an economy, it makes sense to use them all and to use them in such a fashion that they will be of most value.

Yet in a game of chess there is, more often than not, a victor and a victory. The objective of one of the players is accomplished. In economics, victory is less recognizable and much less frequent. If the objective in economics was to satisfy all wants, there could be no victory at all. The more modest objective of economics is to do the best that is possible, given the circumstances. Yet the necessity of settling for this lesser goal means that society must choose which wants will be satisfied. Scarcity implies choice. This is the third implication of the economic problem.

Choice is not only the process by which it is decided which wants will be satisfied, for such a decision is simultaneously a decision to deny other wants. The inability to satisfy all wants necessitates gratifying some wants at the sacrifice of other satisfactions. Only at the Big Rock Candy Mountain does choice wane in importance.

In different societies, various methods have been employed to decide the allocation of resources among competing uses. These methods may be conveniently classified into two groups: market and nonmarket solutions to the problem of choice.

Students in the United States are most familiar with the market mechanism as a decision-making system. In such an institutional arrangement, members of the society may engage in economic activity and thereby generate income. Such income is then used to gratify "needs" and wants. Variations in income received, of course, mean that some households will be able to satisfy more of their wants than others. Each family, though, is confronted with the economic problem in microcosm, i.e., each is unable to satisfy all its wants out of its limited income. Hence, households are forced to choose which wants to meet. Choice in a market system is based on the distribution of income and individual preferences.

Alternatives in the market system of choosing are observed in socialist countries where public officials, functioning within a command structure, exert a very strong influence over the allocation of resources. A significant difference between market and nonmarket choice systems is the number of people whose preferences enter into the actual decision making. Obviously, in the case of resource allocation by committee fiat, committee member preferences will be of greater importance than nonmembers' desires. This means that nonmarket choice systems will be very likely to produce a different allocation of resources than market systems.

Yet, no matter what type of institutional structure is involved, the economic problem exists and cannot be ignored. Even if, as rationality dictates, all of the available resources are allocated to their best use, society will still be unable to satisfy its unlimited wants. Goods will be scarce relative to the desire for them. Scarcity means that choices will have to be made by someone regarding which and whose wants are to be satisfied. The economic problem is the most fundamental principle in economics. The student who grasps its meaning now will rarely lose his way on the path to economic understanding.

Questions for Thought and Discussion

1. Keeping in mind the nature of the economic problem, which would you say is more desirable for the welfare of a country, imports or exports? Is this the same answer that you would have given before you began your study of economics?
2. If peace came to the world tomorrow, many workers in defense-related occupations would probably lose the jobs they now hold. Would this be desirable or undesirable from the standpoint of the economic problem? Why?
3. An overweight student walked into a pizza parlor and ate nine family-size pizzas loaded with sausage, peppers, mushrooms, anchovies, etc., after which she was heard to mumble, "I never want another pizza as long as I live." Since the student was able to eat only nine pizzas, does this mean that human wants are not really unlimited?
4. "The rush of technological advance that we observe in the world today will soon make economics obsolete. With the push of a single button, the productive machinery will spring to life, turning out enough goods to satisfy all of man's wants. There will be no economic problem." Do you agree? Is the study of economics a poor use of that most scarce resource—time?
5. A student once argued, "Economics assumes that any and all of our resources or factors of production can be used to produce whatever we want. This is not true. For example, consider two types of factors of production: steelworkers and musicians. Ordinarily, steelworkers produce steel and musicians make music. But suppose society decides it wants more music and less steel. Steelworkers can no more make music than musicians can produce steel. No matter how hard we try, we cannot have more music." What do you think about this? Are resources flexible with respect to the purpose for which they are used?

9

THE METHODOLOGY OF ECONOMICS

Charles J. Goetz

What is "economic research"? Although there is no simple or completely precise answer to that question, the average layman does tend to have a somewhat inaccurate picture of the economist's activities.

Four distinguishable elements constitute principal activities in economic research: (1) description, (2) theory, (3) inductive estimation, and (4) prediction. In practice, any particular piece of economic research usually combines two or more of these elements. Nonetheless, by treating them separately, it is possible to gain a better appreciation of the problems encountered in economic research. Finally, we can point out how and why the tools of economic research are much broader in applicability than is commonly realized, extending into such offbeat fields as the analysis of nuclear weapons systems and the operation of political parties.

Descriptive Economics

Descriptive economics, as the name suggests, puts primary emphasis on information-gathering. The information may be statistical, such as current or past GNP, consumer prices, wheat production in Kansas, etc. Alternatively, it may be a synthesis of current positions on an issue such as guaranteed annual income. This aspect of economic research is "economic" by virtue of its subject matter, but historians, statisticians, and even journalists may be perfectly competent for many types of descriptive economic research. Large sections of undergraduate economics texts also tend to be descriptive, and properly so, since raw facts

The author is Associate Professor of Economics at Virginia Polytechnic Institute.

are the building blocks of any intellectual skill. It is a mistake to think, however, that a large proportion of the typical economist's research really consists of the type of information collection and synthesis that under-graduate research papers too often represent.

Theorizing in Economics

Let us, then, turn to the economist's function of theorizing. Actually, pure theory is essentially a rigorous, formal system of logical reasoning. Given certain premises, such as profit maximization, the economist *deduces* that a particular set of conclusions either is or is not a logical consequence of the premises. Hence, we can deduce that *if* businessmen maximize profits *then* they must produce the output where marginal costs equal marginal revenue. Of course, in some cases the theorist cannot arrive at determinate and unique conclusions from the premises he employs, but he can at least tell whether certain results are inconsistent with the premises.

If one looks at research in economic theory as an exercise in logic, it is not difficult to understand why such a large percentage of the theory articles in economics professional journals are couched in mathematical language. Mathematics is itself a system of formal logic which lends itself well to the statement of many economic premises which the economist employs.

Lest the advantages of creating logical reasoning methods for certain problems be minimized, a very simple example will suffice to show the way theory helps people avoid errors. A governmental unit in the western United States was attempting to count up the benefits from a new dam for irrigation purposes. In arriving at a valuation, the government officials added together (1) the market value of the increased crop produced on the irrigated land and (2) the increase in market value of the farmland itself. The theorist can tell them that this seemingly reasonable procedure is illogical. The increased value of the land was due to the fact that buyers bid up land prices by an amount exactly equal to the capitalized value of the higher crop yield. The government's procedure actually amounted to double-counting of the higher yield, once as the rights to the yield were transferred in the commodity market and once as the rights to that yield were transferred in the land market!

An important field of economic research, then, is the application of formal logic, of theory, to new problems. Simple applications of theory are contained in all textbooks. More complex economic problems, however, require powerful and sophisticated analysis to make logical order out of the apparent chaos of economic life. It is the theorist's job to reveal the logical order which underlies even the most complicated economic problems.

Although theory is important, its usefulness depends on the accuracy of its premises. Perfectly consistent mathematical theorems can be derived from the premise that $1 + 1 = 3$. Economic theories would, however, have doubtful value if they merely made logical deductions from such unrealistic premises. But a theory is a "theory" and not a "fact," because its premises are not completely certain.

There are always some "primitive" premises which each science takes as given and whose validity is not seriously examined. A good example is that, of all the sciences, only metaphysics questions the causality premise that "every phenomenon has a sufficient cause." However, there are a host of other premises about the workings of the economic system which we may wish to employ as the underpinnings of a theory. How can one know what sorts of relationships are "reasonable" premises for economic theories?

Inductive Research and Estimation

One of the ways the economist supplements his deductive reasoning is by an inductive method, a process of *inference* from the facts. The goal of this inductive process may vary in the degree of exactitude desired. For instance, we may wish to test the premise called the "Law of Demand"—that there is an inverse relationship between price and quantity demanded. In this case, we are interested in only the *direction* of the relationship between quantity and price. For some theories, however, it may be necessary to say something about the *sensitivity* of the relationship, i.e., by how much does quantity change when price changes?

The "Law of Demand" example can be used to show how the researcher attempts to derive conclusions or estimates from observed phenomena. Suppose he can get information on the price of oranges and the quantity demanded in your city over a period of time. When plotted, the observations have the pattern indicated in Figure 1. Do the observations confirm or reject the "Law of Demand" hypothesis?

The difficulty in deriving definitive conclusions from Figure 1 is symptomatic of the problems encountered in this area of economic research. Note, for instance, that observations C and D correspond to *both* higher prices and higher quantities than at observations A, B, and E. If we

13

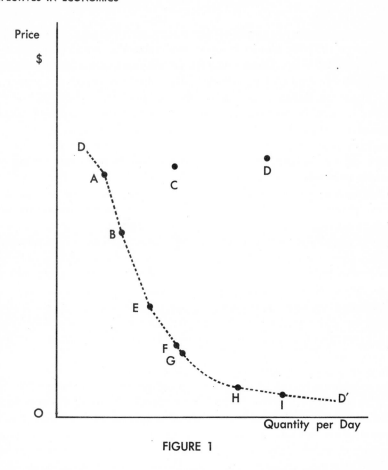

FIGURE 1

knew that, at the time of the various observations, all other relevant influences on demand (such as income, prices of tangerines, etc.) were the same, Figure 1 would not bode well for the reliability of the "Law of Demand." Unfortunately, unlike the chemist or physical scientist, the economist cannot perform laboratory experiments during which the *ceteris paribus*, or "other things being equal," condition is maintained. The effects of the corporation income tax in the United States, for instance, have never been resolved because the only conclusive proof would be to run the twentieth century through twice, once with the tax and once without it!

There is another problem even if we consider Figure 1 without the deviant observations C and D. If the researcher's purpose is estimation of the degree of price-quantity interconnection, the remaining points—A, B, E, F, G, H, I—are consistent with an infinite number of different demand curves. This will be obvious to anyone who takes his pencil and sees how many different curves he can draw to connect the points, subject only to the stipulation that any curve have at least some degree of negative slope at every point. (The line DD' is only one illustration.)

The hypothesis-testing and estimative problems mentioned briefly above are one reason why the economist counts statistical testing procedures among the important tools in his professional bag of tricks. Techniques such as regression analysis and Chi-Square tests are typical of the ways the economic researcher tries not only to "fit" relationships to the phenomena of his uncontrollable real-world laboratory, but also to ascertain the probability limits within which his conclusions can be considered valid.

In this inductive area of economic research, there is a good deal of "art" necessitated in the pursuit of economic science. All too frequently, the researcher finds it impossible to acquire information on the variables which are directly involved in the premise or relationship whose validity he wishes to test. For instance, suppose that information on orange prices in your city has never been collected and cannot be derived from any existing source. It may then be possible to seek a "proxy variable" which is a good measure of the variable which is really directly involved. The U.S. Department of Agriculture may have an index of *national* fruit prices, or the *Fruit Processing Weekly* may publish *wholesale* orange prices by city. The question is: Does one of these proxy variables enable us to form an estimate of retail orange prices in your city which is close enough to be useful?

Ironically, the proxy variable phenomenon can be as much a curse as a blessing. Consider the research on the relationship between getting a college degree and the size of one man's lifetime income stream. If attendance at college is at least to some degree a proxy measure of above average intelligence, a Figure 1 type plot between income and education may fool us into attributing to education some effects which are really attributable, in whole or in part, to native ability.

At root, the inability of the economist to control the conditions of his "laboratory," the economy, is a nagging problem which rarely permits a degree of exactitude really satisfactory to the scholar. Nonetheless, useful statements of tendency or of probabilistic nature can usually be de-

15

rived. If the economist cannot modify his real-world "laboratory" to facilitate his experiments, at least he can exercise his ingenuity and art to process and test his observations from the world environment in a way which frequently permits insights into important problems.

Prediction: Both the Goal and Test of Economic Research

If economists' deductive reasoning and inductive estimates of relationships are successfully carried out, the economic research culminates in a synthesis of theory and the tested empirical relationships in the form of a "model" which explains some set of real-world phenomena. Of course, we must use the word "explain" in a tentative way, admitting that the explanation may later be improved upon or even shown to be incorrect. Indeed, the value of an explanatory model essentially rests upon whether people consider it more "useful" than other currently existing explanations of the same set of phenomena.

Useful for what? Well, simple intellectual curiosity, the sheer urge to know, has been and always will be a motive for much research. It is, for instance, of no pressing practical import to explain the impact of early U.S. canal systems on the economic development of America's nineteenth-century frontier. Still, many people may derive intellectual satisfaction from the results of this type of research.

Clearly, though, the results of economic research frequently do have a great practical importance. This practical utility derives principally from the fact that economic models can be used for *predictive* purposes. What would happen if the United States devalued the dollar? If there is no tax change, what is unemployment likely to be next year? What effect will inflation have on the demand for new residential housing? Both business and political decision makers require answers to such questions in order to weigh the merits of alternative plans they might lay for the future.

Predictions of the future are made by extrapolating from theories which were constructed principally on the basis of past experience. Essentially, we bet that the relationships that we have been able to detect in past situations will give us a good basis for making estimates about the future.

An important test of a good model, indeed, is the fact that it *does* enable us to make good predictions. Some economists go so far as to say that a model or a theory can contain premises which are manifestly unrealistic and still be acceptable if the predictions it leads to are borne out. Extreme adherence to this position leads to curious results. For instance, it has been found that retail sales of clothing and shoes are a good predictor of the demand for electric power in California. Nonetheless, few would seriously maintain that this observation of a relationship should be used to say that apparel demand *explains* anything about the use of electric power. If one is willing to make the necessary qualifications, however, it is easy to see why economists regard predictive accuracy as a good test of their research into the workings of the economy.

At this point, one may feel motivated to ask, "If economic research does yield useful predictions, why does a roomful of economists often generate as many opinions about the course of the economy as there are economists?" The answer is that the quality of economic predictions decreases as the focus of the "model" being used grows wider and encompasses more variables. The models used to explain many of the vast and sweeping problems which occupy the public interest can be "narrowed" by asking the user to prestipulate some of the model's "inputs," such as certain future prices, the interest rate, etc. Hence, people using the same model may reach different conclusions because they disagree about the relevant values of the so-called exogenous, or externally-determined, variables that should be used in the model.

In any event, the day-to-day efforts of a practicing research economist are likely to be on a less grand scale than predicting the level of the stock market in 1975 or whether there will be a recession next year. He is a good deal more likely to be working on some extremely small piece of the economic picture: the effect on drugstore sales of price cuts vs. trading stamps, the response of steel manufacturers to investment credits, the reaction of Savings and Loan banks to mortgage rate changes, etc. Just as physics has its general theories produced by an Einstein or a Newton, economic research occasionally turns out a broad systematic model such as those of Keynes or of Walras. Still, most of the contributions in any science come in single painful inches which, only as they accumulate many times over, ultimately give rise to those great advances which capture the public's imagination.

The Scope of Economic Research

A final thread to be tied in is the question of what makes research "economic." After all, in their own ways all sciences perform the broad functions previously outlined, and the other social sciences even share with economics some of the peculiar difficulties we have cited.

Any student of the principles of economics quickly learns that the salient feature of economics is its concern with *scarcity* and the *satisfaction of preferences*. Another way of putting it is that economics deals with situations in which individuals are seeking to maximize their preferences to the extent that a set of scarcity *constraints* will allow. Of course, trade is the primary process whereby this preference-maximization occurs, and the popularity of economic research into the function of markets and their constituent firms and consumers, therefore, needs no explanation. However, there is another world of economic research which is less familiar.

There are many essentially *nonmarket* processes toward which the research economist is increasingly turning his interest. Consider, for example, the choice of military weapons systems. This is certainly a nonmarket decision process. Nevertheless, note that it corresponds quite clearly to the formal definition given above to a case where preferences are being maximized subject to a scarcity constraint. A major role of the economist in this nonmarket process has been to point out in detail how, within a fixed budgetary allotment (the scarce resources), satisfaction of a preference for, say, more helicopters necessarily means less of something else, such as ICBM's.

Another representative area of nonmarket economic research is that of political decision-making. Unlike the typical civics textbook, the economic researcher has found some good to say about such maligned practices as logrolling in legislatures, earmarking of taxes, nonproportional representation, etc. Although this smacks of professional trespassing on the territory of political science, the fact is that the models and analytic techniques developed by economists for market trading often prove surprisingly adaptable to those "trades" which result from attempts to form political coalitions.

The necessity for economists to develop some ingenuity or "art" in dealing with less-than-satisfactory information, widespread uncertainty, and generally poor experimental conditions is, ironically, one of the reasons why economic analysts' research efforts find increasingly favorable reception in dealing with nonmarket problems faced by the government. The economist is accustomed to conjuring up a number, to fashioning at least some sort of an estimate even in the face of very unsatisfactory information.

The point of these examples is that economic research is not necessarily business- or market-oriented. If the situation can be described as one wherein preferences are being maximized subject to constraints, don't be surprised to find an economist trying to dig into the problem with his special brand of tools.

Conclusion

"Textbook economics" is likely to give a person a distorted view of economic research. The world of the practicing research economist has little of the textbook's color and description and few, if any, of the textbook's broad and sweeping theories. But it does offer the scholar a sense of profound satisfaction if he is clever enough to painfully coax one small, new filament of order out of the tangled threads of the economy.

Questions for Thought and Discussion

1. Is economics a true science? Are there laws of economics? Does economics have predictive capacity?
2. Would a law of economics differ from a law of one of the physical sciences, such as the law of gravity? From a law of the legal system? What distinctions can you see?
3. What role do assumptions perform in economics? Why do economists talk as if variables not being specifically studied in a particular research problem are constants?

THERE ARE NO SIMPLE ANSWERS

TO ECONOMIC QUESTIONS

Paul A. Samuelson

There is much talk about taxes. When I flick on the dial of my radio in the morning, I hear a Congressman quoted on how our high level of taxes is ruining the Nation or a Senator's tape-recorded alarm over the unfair burden the poor man has to carry because the administration has been favoring big business. My morning paper at breakfast brings me the view of its editor that the United States has been pursuing unsound fiscal policy for the last 25 years. Scratch the barber who cuts my hair and you find a philosopher ready to prescribe for the Nation's monetary ills.

This is as it should be. We expect sweeping statements in a democracy. We hope that out of the conflict of extreme views there will somehow emerge a desirable compromise. Yet such sweeping statements have almost no validity from a scientific, or even from a leisurely common-sense point of view: spend as little as a year going over the factual experience of American history and of other economies, devote as little as a month to calm analysis of probable cause and effect, or even spend a weekend in a good economics library—and what will you find? Will you find that there breathes anywhere in the world an expert so wise that he can tell you which of a dozen major directions of policy is unquestionably the best? You will not. Campaign oratory aside, the more assuredly a man asserts the direction along which salvation is alone to be found, the more patently he advertises himself as an incompetent or a charlatan.

From "The New Look in Tax and Fiscal Policy," *Federal Tax Policy for Economic Growth and Stability* (Washington: Joint Committee on the Economic Report, 1955), pp. 229-230. The author is Professor of Economics at Massachusetts Institute of Technology.

The plain truth is this, and it is known to anyone who has looked into the matter: the science of economics does not provide simple answers to complex social problems. It does not validate the view of the man who thinks the world is going to hell, nor the view of his fellow idiot that ours is the best of all possible systems.

I do not wish to be misunderstood. When I assert that economic science cannot give unequivocal answers to the big questions of policy, I do not for a moment imply that economists are useless citizens. Quite the contrary. They would indeed be useless if any sensible man could quickly infer for himself simple answers to the big policy questions. No need then to feed economists while they make learned studies of the obvious. It is precisely because public policy in the tax and expenditure area, for example, is so complex that we find it absolutely indispensable to invest thousands of man-years of scholarly time in scholarly economic research in these areas.

Make no mistake about it. The arguments that we all hear every day of our lives on the burning partisan issues have in every case been shaped by economists—by economists in universities, in business, in Government, and by that rarest of all birds, the shrewd self-made economist. What economists do not know about fiscal policy turns out, on simple examination, not to be known by anyone.

ECONOMICS AND ECONOMIC HISTORY

Jerry Shipley

Economic history is a systematic record of the events relating to the material aspects of human existence; it depicts the eternal struggle mankind has waged against the resource limitations of nature. No single strategy, however, has been universally followed in this struggle. From nomadic existences to national and world economies, the methods which mankind has used to fight scarcity have changed, sometimes dramatically fast, throughout the course of human existence. The methods which man has used and the changes which have occurred in them are the subject matter for economic history. In the remarks which follow, I will suggest some reasons why a study of economic history should be accompanied by an introduction to theoretical economics.[1]

Imagine yourself, for a moment, sitting down to write an economic history. To make your problem more concrete, suppose, unrealistically, that you have *all* the facts of the period about which you will write at your disposal.[2] A little reflection should make it clear that this is a historian's dream world (or nightmare). You will not suffer endless hours in

The author is Assistant Professor of Economics at the University of Maryland.

[1] For a more complete and very readable discussion of the general topic of the relationship of theory to history, see E. H. Carr, *What Is History?* (New York: Alfred A. Knopf, 1962), particularly Chapters 1 and 4. My debt to Mr. Carr in these areas is a very heavy one.

[2] In emphasizing the uses of the economic theory to the historian, it has been assumed that all the facts were available. Unfortunately, this is seldom the case. The historian very often does not know and cannot determine what the facts were at a crucial point in his argument. A formal theory can also be used in a situation such as this to deduce what the facts must have been. See A. Conrad and J. Meyer, *The Economics of Slavery in the Antebellum South* (Chicago: Aldine, 1964), for theoretical essays and applications of this sort of analysis.

dusty libraries and archives searching for elusive facts. Rather, having all the facts at hand, your job is to select pertinent facts from this gargantuan mass of information and to organize these facts into a meaningful history. But selection and organization must be done according to some set of criteria. It is not enough simply to choose every millionth fact and string this list together and call it history. There is more to history than just facts. Criteria and principles by which the facts are selected and organized must precede choosing the facts. Moreover, these criteria can neither be so mindless nor so arbitrary as simple randomness. Here is where theory plays its role. Either consciously or unconsciously, the writer of history must employ a theory of how the facts which he has are related before he can begin to pick and choose among the facts at his disposal.

Theory is the framework of history. In the sense in which it is used here, a theory is a general statement of causality. A theory posits certain particular cause-and-effect relationships between one or several observed events and some other observed event or events. For example, a theory drawn from the field of economics says that the amount which consumers of a particular product demand will decline if the price of that product should rise and if all the other factors affecting the demand for and supply of the product remain unchanged. The foregoing, which is a very elementary proposition in economics, is nevertheless a statement of causality. Stated more generally, it says a change in the amount demanded of a good is *caused* by a change in its price. A theory need not—indeed, to be used as the basis for history, will not—be so simple or limited as this example. But one must construct a set of causal relationships before any selection and organization of facts can be done. A history is differentiated from an almanac by the causal analysis in it. An almanac simply lists a great number of facts; a history discusses those facts, suggesting the ways in which an observed event has been shaped by other events which have preceded it and how that event in turn has caused other events.

In emphasizing the necessity for having a theory before attacking the facts, I do not intend to make the unwarranted inference that facts are unimportant. Theories purport to explain the relationships existing between observed phenomena. When a theory cannot do this—that is, when it is constructed in contradiction to *the facts* it should be explaining—then it is not a good theory and must be discarded. Hence, while facts without a theory to explain them are not history, facts can destroy a theory. It should be clear, however, that without a theory one cannot write history. It verges on the ludicrous to say that one is going to let the facts speak for themselves. Merely by selecting some facts and not others, an interpretation of history has been made by the historian. The facts are evidence which bolster a history, but they themselves are not history. (Of course, no theory, no matter how grandiose, can incorporate all the facts. The undying hope that a new theory explaining more facts will be discovered constitutes the major rationale for maintaining historical archives.)

Admitting the necessity of a theoretical framework, what sorts of theories should be used to write an economic history? The answer to this question may appear absurd in its obviousness. Economic theory should be used to write economic history. (During the past century, historians of all colors have come increasingly to focus on economic forces. More surprisingly, economic historians, whose concerns are primarily the economic developments of the past, have only recently acknowledged the relevance of theoretical economics.[3])

More specifically, I would contend that some model (theory) of economic growth must occupy a central position in the writing of economic history. As a framework for history, as guideposts for selecting and organizing facts, models of economic growth have more pegs on which the facts of history may be displayed than any other conceptualization of economic causality which economists have devised. I wish I might add at this point that there is some particular model of economic growth which is at once (1) capable of explaining all the cases of economic development or non-development which have been observed and (2) sufficiently elegant mathematically to satisfy the most abstract economists; even more, I wish I might claim such a model for my own. Unfortunately, such a model does not to my knowledge exist. In a more general way, however, the fundamental concepts of almost all growth models are the economists' greatest contribution to economic history. It is quite understandable why this should be so. In the area of growth, the concerns of economists and economic historians most nearly coincide. There is very little difference between the questions of the historians who ask about causal processes of a changing economy and the economists who ask about the same things. Their methods have differed traditionally, no doubt because the economic historians have felt less comfortable making the assumptions of unchanging institutions and attitudes which would have been required to use some theoretical and quantitatively oriented techniques than the economists who typically have worked with shorter spans of time.

---

[3] See Dudley Dillard, *Economic Development of the North Atlantic Community* (Englewood Cliffs: Prentice-Hall, 1967), pp. 11-12, for references to this point.

A growth model is an abstract set of relationships depicting the forces at work in the growth of an economy. The central element of any growth model is a production function, which is a technical relationship expressing the quantities of various inputs which are required to produce output. One might be inclined to think of a production function as a recipe for output, but it is something more than this. A production function expresses *all* the recipes for output in a single relationship from which one is chosen, usually on the basis of the costs of inputs to minimize the total cost of some given quantity of output.

Moreover, the production function changes over time, as new ways of producing output are discovered or new forms of organization of the economy develop, making it possible to utilize already known, but previously infeasible, methods of production. Hence, we can say, for example, that the steam engine when finally perfected late in the eighteenth century was a change in the production function, making it possible to produce more output. Many of the events which comprise the industrial revolution can be summarized under the heading of technological progress, by which is meant those changes in the production function yielding more output from a constant amount of inputs. Indeed, a crucial concept in the label "modern economic growth," which many economists apply to economic developments beginning approximately with the first Industrial Revolution in England in the eighteenth century, is the ever-increasing importance of technological progress. An example of the organizational changes which also give rise to changes in the production function is the enclosure movement. By eliminating the feudal practice of dividing fields into many small strips and placing decisions about how a field was to be cultivated in the hands of a single individual, it was possible to introduce methods of cultivation which would not have been possible if agreement between all the parties who had cultivated the fields under the old system had been required. Hence, with the theoretical concept of a production function, the historian can identify increases in output as coming from three distinct sources: (1) the increasing availability of inputs—more people, more materials, more land, and more capital; (2) changes in the production function arising from technological progress; and (3) changes in the production function arising from organizational or institutional change.

These aspects of growth models might be characterized as determining the growth of potential output or supply. Equally important are some other parts of the model which describe the growth of demand for output.

There are different kinds of demand for output. Consumption demand is demand for output which will be used up in a relatively short period of time (theoretically, instantly). Of the highest priority in consumption are the subsistence needs of the population who must be fed and sheltered to sustain life. Investment demand is demand for output which will not be used instantly, but which will be used *as an input into the production process* in subsequent periods to increase output then. Not only the total amount of demand is relevant in the historian's analysis of the economic past but also the composition of demand. In relatively recent periods, some economists have raised the spectre of economic stagnation arising from too little or too slowly growing demand for output. Just the reverse applies to earlier stages of economic development when it was common for subsistence demand to exceed capacity output, leaving no surplus for productive investments which have been responsible for much of the growth of potential output. (It might be noted here that the parts of the model are not independent. Investment, we have just seen, depends on the existence of a surplus of output over subsistence needs; in turn, that investment causes output to grow, further increasing the surplus of output over elemental demands.)

Another determinant of demand—both the total and its composition—is the manner in which output is distributed to individuals. Since investment is critical to growth and depends on the existence of a surplus above subsistence needs, it may be possible for some individuals to have the required surplus if the distribution of output is sufficiently unequal, even if the mass of the population is just at the edge of subsistence. On the other hand, it is frequently alleged that an unequal distribution of income is less likely to lead to investment than to luxurious consumption. Hence, an unequal distribution is not a sufficient condition, perhaps not even a necessary condition, for investment to occur. This notwithstanding, those parts of the growth model which determine the amount and composition of demand play important roles in the historian's analysis of the past.

The list of factors which contribute to economic growth and development could go on almost endlessly, and I have referred to only a very few items on the list. What is important, however, is that all the items can be incorporated in the framework of a growth model, and (my more quantitatively minded colleagues would add) their relative importance can be measured with modern quantitative techniques. In writing or, perhaps more to the point, in reading history, a formal theoretical framework is essential. Without a conceptual apparatus, the facts say nothing; with one, the past comes alive to recall its lessons to the present.

Questions for Thought and Discussion

1. The economist Simon Kuznets has characterized the growth experiences of some of the advanced economies of Western Europe and North America as "modern economic growth." The major attribute of modern economic growth is sustained increases, virtually without interruption, in per capita material welfare, arising out of technological change. Discuss what this means in the framework of the concept of a production function.
2. "Theory is a model of causality." What does this statement mean?
3. Discuss the roles which investment plays in the process of economic growth. Are investment and technological change related?

ROUNDABOUT PRODUCTION

Eugen von Bohm-Bawerk

The end and aim of all production is the making of things with which to satisfy our wants; that is to say, the making of goods for immediate consumption, or Consumption Goods. . . . We combine our own natural powers and natural powers of the external world in such a way that, under natural law, the desired material good must come into existence. But this is a very general description indeed of the matter, and looking at it closer there comes in sight an important distinction which we have not as yet considered. It has reference to the distance which lies between the expenditure of human labour in the combined production and the appearance of the desired good. We either put forth our labour just before the goal is reached, or we, intentionally, take a roundabout way. That is to say, we may put forth our labour in such a way that it at once completes the circle of conditions necessary for the emergence of the desired good, and thus the existence of the good *immediately* follows the expenditure of the labour; or we may associate our labour first with the more remote causes of the good, with the object of obtaining, not the desired good itself, but a proximate cause of the good; which cause, again, must be associated with other suitable materials and powers, till, finally—perhaps through a considerable number of intermediate members—the finished good, the instrument of human satisfaction is obtained.

The nature and importance of this distinction will be best seen from a few examples; and, as these will, to a considerable extent, form a demonstration of what is really one of the most fundamental propositions in our theory, I must risk being tedious.

A peasant requires drinking water. The spring is some distance from

---

Eugen von Bohm-Bawerk, *The Positive Theory of Capital* (1891).

his house. There are various ways in which he may supply his daily wants. First, he may go to the spring each time he is thirsty, and drink out of his hollowed hand. This is the most direct way; satisfaction follows immediately on exertion. But it is an inconvenient way, for our peasant has to take his way to the well as often as he is thirsty. And it is an insufficient way; for he can never collect and store any great quantity such as he requires for various other purposes. Second, he may take a log of wood, hollow it out into a kind of pail, and carry his day's supply from the spring to his cottage. The advantage is obvious, but it necessitates a roundabout way of considerable length. The man must spend, perhaps, a day in cutting out the pail; before doing so, he must have felled a tree in the forest; to do this, again, he must have made an axe, and so on. But there is still a third way; instead of felling one tree he fells a number of trees, splits and hollows them, lays them end for end, and so constructs a runnel or rhone which brings a full head of water to his cottage. Here, obviously, between the expenditure of the labour and the obtaining of the water we have a very roundabout way, but, then, the result is ever so much greater. Our peasant needs no longer take his weary way from house to well with the heavy pail on his shoulder, and yet he has a constant and full supply of the freshest water at his very door. . . .

Yet another example. I am short-sighted, and wish to have a pair of spectacles. For this I require ground and polished glasses, and a steel framework. But all that nature offers toward that end is silicious iron ore. How am I to transform these into spectacles? Work as I may, it is as impossible for me to make spectacles directly out of silicious earth as it would be to make the steel frames out of iron ore. Here there is no immediate or direct method of production. There is nothing for it but to take the roundabout way, and indeed, a very roundabout way. I must take the silicious earth and fuel, and build furnaces for smelting the glass from the silicious earth; the glass thus obtained has to be carefully purified, worked, and cooled by a series of processes; finally, the glass thus prepared—again by means of ingenious instruments carefully constructed beforehand—is ground and polished into the lens fit for short-sighted eyes. Similarly, I must smelt the ore in the blast furnace, change the raw iron into steel, and make the frame therefrom—processes which cannot be carried through without a long series of tools and buildings that, on their part again, require great amounts of previous labour. Thus, by an exceedingly roundabout way, the end is attained.

The lesson to be drawn from . . . these examples alike is obvious. It is—

that a greater result is obtained by producing goods in roundabout ways than by producing them directly. Where a good can be produced in either way, we have the fact that, by the indirect way, a greater product can be got with equal labour, or the same product with less labour. But, beyond this, the superiority of the indirect way manifests itself in being the only way in which certain goods can be obtained, if I might say so, it is so much the better way that it is often the only way!

That roundabout methods lead to greater results than direct methods is one of the most important and fundamental propositions in the whole theory of production. It must be emphatically stated that the only basis of this proposition is the experience of practical life. Economic theory does not and cannot show *a priori* that it must be so; but the unanimous experience of all the technique of production says that it is so. And this is sufficient; all the more that the facts of experience which tell us this are commonplace and familiar to everybody. But *why* is it so? The economist might quite well decline to answer this question. For the fact that a greater product is obtained by methods of production that begin far back is essentially a purely technical fact, and to explain questions of technique does not fall within the economist's sphere. For instance, that tropical lands are more fruitful than the polar zone; that the alloy of which coins are made stands more wear and tear than pure metal; that a railroad is better for transport than an ordinary turnpike road;—all these are matters of fact with which the economist reckons, but which his science does not call on him to explain. But this is exactly one of those cases where, in the economist's own interest—the interest he has in limiting and defining his own task—it is exceedingly desirable to go beyond the specific economic sphere. If the sober physical truth is once made clear, political economy cannot indulge in any fancies or fictions about it; and, in such questions, political economy has never been behind in the desire and the attempt to substitute its own imaginings! Although, then, this law is already sufficiently accredited by experience, I attach particular value to explaining its cause, and, after what has been said as to the nature of production, this should not be very difficult.

In the last resort all our productive efforts amount to shiftings and combinations of matter. We must know how to bring together the right forms of matter at the right moment, in order that from those associated forces the desired result, the product wanted, may follow. But, as we saw, the natural forms of matter are often so infinitely large, often so infinitely fine, that human hands are too weak or too coarse to control them. We are as powerless to overcome the cohesion of the wall of rock when we want building stone as we are, from carbon, nitrogen, hydrogen, oxygen, phosphor, potash, etc., to put together a single grain of wheat. But there are other powers which can easily do what is denied to us, and these are the powers of nature. There are natural powers which far exceed the possibilities of human power in greatness, and there are other natural powers in the microscopic world which can make combinations that put our clumsy fingers to shame. If we can succeed in making these forces our allies in the work of production, the limits of human possibility will be infinitely extended. And this we have done.

Questions for Thought and Discussion

1. What is roundabout production?
2. What examples of roundabout production can you think of in addition to those discussed by Bohm-Bawerk?

DIVISION OF LABOUR AND THE
EXTENT OF THE MARKET

Adam Smith

The greatest improvement in the productive powers of labour, and the greater part of the skill, dexterity, and judgment with which it is any where directed, or applied, seem to have been the effects of the division of labour.

The effects of the division of labour, in the general business of society, will be more easily understood by considering in what manner it operates in some particular manufactures. . . .

. . . . . .

To take an example, therefore, from a very trifling manufacture; but one in which the division of labour has been very often taken notice of, the trade of the pinmaker; a workman not educated to this business (which the division of labour has rendered a distinct trade), nor acquainted with the use of the machinery employed in it (to the invention of which the same division of labour has probably given occasion), could scarce, perhaps, with his utmost industry, make one pin in a day, and certainly could not make twenty. But in the way in which this business is now carried on, not only the whole work is a peculiar trade, but it is divided into a number of branches, of which the greater part are likewise peculiar trades. One man draws out the wire, another straights it, a third cuts it, a fourth points it, a fifth grinds it at the top for receiving the head; to make the head requires two or three distinct operations; to put it on is a

---

Adam Smith, *The Wealth of Nations* (1776).

peculiar business, to whiten the pins is another; it is even a trade by itself to put them into the paper; and the important business of making a pin is, in this manner, divided into about eighteen distinct operations, which, in some manufactories, are all performed by distinct hands, though in others the same man will sometimes perform two or three of them. I have seen a small manufactory of this kind where ten men only were employed, and where some of them consequently performed two or three distinct operations. But though they were very poor, and therefore but indifferently accommodated with the necessary machinery, they could, when they exerted themselves, make among them about twelve pounds of pins in a day. There are in a pound upwards of four thousand pins of middling size. Those ten persons, therefore, could make among them upwards of forty-eight thousand pins in a day. Each person, therefore, making a tenth part of forty-eight thousand pins, might be considered as making four thousand eight hundred pins in a day. But if they had all wrought separately and independently, and without any of them having been educated to this peculiar business, they certainly could not each of them have made twenty, perhaps not one pin in a day; that is, certainly, not the two hundred and fortieth, perhaps not the four thousand eight hundredth part of what they are at present capable of performing, in consequence of a proper division and combination of their different operations.

In every other art and manufacture, the effects of the division of labour are similar to what they are in this very trifling one; though, in many of them, the labour can neither be so much subdivided, nor reduced to so great a simplicity of operation. The division of labour, however, so far as it can be introduced, occasions, in every art, a proportionable increase of the productive powers of labour. The separation of different trades and employments from one another, seems to have taken place, in consequence of this advantage. This separation too is generally carried furthest in those countries which enjoy the highest degree of industry and improvement; what is the work of one man in a rude state of society, being generally that of several in an improved one. . . .

· · · · · ·

This great increase of the quantity of work, which, in consequence of the division of labour, the same number of people are capable of performing, is owing to three different circumstances; first, to the increase of dexterity in every particular workman; secondly, to the saving of time which is commonly lost in passing from one species of work to another; and lastly, to the invention of a great number of machines which facilitate and abridge labour, and enable one man to do the work of many.

. . . . . .

It is the great multiplication of the productions of all the different arts, in consequence of the division of labour, which occasions, in a well-governed society, that universal opulence which extends itself to the lowest ranks of the people. Every workman has a great quantity of his own work to dispose of beyond what he himself has occasion for; and every other workman being exactly in the same situation, he is enabled to exchange a great quantity of his own goods for a great quantity, or, what comes to the same thing, for the price of a great quantity of theirs. He supplies them abundantly with what they have occasion for, and they accommodate him as amply with what he has occasion for, and a general plenty diffuses itself through all the different ranks of the society.

Observe the accommodation of the most common artificer or day-labourer in a civilized and thriving country, and you will perceive that the number of people of whose industry a part, though but a small part, has been employed in procuring him this accommodation, exceeds all computation. The woollen coat, for example, which covers the day-labourer, as coarse and rough as it may appear, is the produce of the joint labour of a great multitude of workmen. The shepherd, the sorter of the wool, the woolcomber or carder, the dyer, the scribbler, the spinner, the weaver, the fuller, the dresser, with many others, must all join their different arts in order to complete even this homely production. How many merchants and carriers, besides, must have been employed in transporting the materials from some of those workmen to others who often live in a very distant part of the country! how much commerce and navigation in particular, how many ship-builders, sailors, sail-makers, rope-makers, must have been employed in order to bring together the different drugs made use of by the dyer, which often come from the remotest corners of the world! What a variety of labour too is necessary in order to produce the tools of the meanest of those workmen! To say nothing of such complicated machines as the ship of the sailor, the mill of the fuller, or even the loom of the weaver, let us consider only what a variety of labour is requisite in order to form that very simple machine, the shears with which the shepherd clips the wool. The miner, the builder of the furnace for smelt-

35

ing the ore, the feller of the timber, the burner of the charcoal to be made use of in the smelting-house, the brick-maker, the brick-layer, the workmen who attend the furnace, the millwright, the forger, the smith, must all of them join their different arts in order to produce them. Were we to examine, in the same manner, all the different parts of his dress and household furniture, the coarse linen shirt which he wears next to his skin, the shoes which cover his feet, the bed which he lies on, and all the different parts which compose it, the kitchen-grate at which he prepares his victuals, the coals which he makes use of for that purpose, dug from the bowels of the earth, and brought to him perhaps by a long land carriage, all the other utensils of his kitchen, all the furniture of his table, the knives and forks, the earthen or pewter plates upon which he serves up and divides the victuals, the different hands employed in preparing his bread and his beer, the glass window which lets in the heat and the light, and keeps out the wind and the rain, with all the knowledge and art requisite for preparing that beautiful and happy invention, without which these northern parts of the world could scarce have afforded a comfortable habitation, together with the tools of all the different workmen employed in producing those different conveniences; if we examine, I say, all these things, and consider what a variety of labour is employed about each of them, we shall be sensible that without the assistance and cooperation of many thousands, the very meanest person in a civilized country could not be provided for, even according to, what we very falsely imagine, the easy and simple manner in which he is commonly accommodated. Compared, indeed, with the more extravagant luxury of the great, his accommodation must no doubt appear extremely simple and easy; and yet it may be true, perhaps, that the accommodation of an European prince does not always exceed so much that of an industrious and frugal peasant, as the accommodation of the latter exceeds that of many an African king, the absolute master of the lives and liberties of ten thousand naked savages.

The Principle Which Gives Occasion
to the Division of Labour

This division of labour, from which so many advantages are derived, is not originally the effect of any human wisdom, which foresees and intends that general opulence to which it gives occasion. It is the necessary, though very slow and gradual, consequence of a certain propensity in human nature which has in view no such extensive utility; the propensity to truck, barter, and exchange one thing for another.

. . . . . .

In civilized society he (man) stands at all times in need of the cooperation and assistance of great multitudes, while his whole life is scarce sufficient to gain the friendship of a few persons. In almost every other race of animals each individual, when it is grown up to maturity, is entirely independent, and in its natural state has occasion for the assistance of no other living creature. But man has almost constant occasion for the help of his brethren, and it is in vain for him to expect it from their benevolence only. He will be more likely to prevail if he can interest their self-love in his favour, and shew them that it is for their own advantage to do for him what he requires of them. Whoever offers to another a bargain of any kind, proposes to do this. Give me that which I want, and you shall have this which you want, is the meaning of every such offer; and it is in this manner that we obtain from one another the far greater part of those good offices which we stand in need of. It is not from the benevolence of the butcher, the brewer, or the baker, that we expect our dinner, but from their regard to their own interest. We address ourselves, not to their humanity but to their self-love, and never talk to them of our own necessities but of their advantages. Nobody but a beggar chooses to depend chiefly upon the benevolence of his fellow-citizens. Even a beggar does not depend upon it entirely. The charity of well-disposed people, indeed, supplies him with the whole fund of his subsistence. But though this principle ultimately provides him with all the necessaries of life which he has occasion for, it neither does nor can provide him with them as he has occasion for them. The greater part of his occasional wants are supplied in the same manner as those of other people, by treaty, by barter, and by purchase. The old cloaths which another bestows upon him he exchanges for old cloaths which suit him better, or for lodging, or for food, or for money, with which he can buy either food, cloaths, or lodging, as he has occasion.

As it is by treaty, by barter, and by purchase, that we obtain from one another the greater part of those mutual good offices which we stand in need of, so it is this same trucking disposition which originally gives occasion to the division of labour. In a tribe of hunters or shepherds a particular person makes bows and arrows, for example, with more readiness and dexterity than any other. He frequently exchanges them for cattle or for venison with his companions; and he finds at last that he can in ·this manner get more cattle and venison, than if he himself went to the field to catch them. From a regard to his own interest, therefore, the making of bows and arrows grows to be his chief business, and he becomes a sort of armourer. Another excels in making the frames and covers of their little huts or moveable houses. He is accustomed to be of use in this way to his neighbours, who reward him in the same manner with cattle and with venison, till at last he finds it his interest to dedicate himself entirely to this employment, and to become a sort of house carpenter. In the same manner a third becomes a smith or a brazier; a fourth a tanner or dresser of hides or skins, the principal part of the clothing of savages. And thus the certainty of being able to exchange all that surplus part of the produce of his own labour, which is over and above his own consumption, for such parts of the produce of other men's labour as he may have occasion for, encourages every man to apply himself to a particular occupation, and to cultivate and bring to perfection whatever talent or genius he may possess for that particular species of business.

The difference of natural talents in different men is, in reality, much less than we are aware of; and the very different genius which appears to distinguish men of different professions, when grown up to maturity, is not upon many occasions so much the cause, as the effect of the division of labour. The difference between the most dissimilar characters, between a philosopher and a common street porter, for example, seems to arise not so much from nature, as from habit, custom, and education. When they came into the world, and for the first six or eight years of their existence, they were, perhaps, very much alike, and neither their parents nor playfellows could perceive any remarkable difference. About that age, or soon after, they come to be employed in very different occupations. The difference of talents comes then to be taken notice of, and widens by degrees, till at last the vanity of the philosopher is willing to acknowledge scarce any resemblance. But without the disposition to truck, barter, and exchange, every man must have procured to himself every necessary and convenience of life which he wanted. All must have had the same duties to perform, and the same work to do, and there could have been no such difference of employment as could alone give occasion to any great difference of talents.

As it is this disposition which forms that difference of talents, so remarkable among men of different professions, so it is this same disposition which renders that difference useful. Many tribes of animals acknowledged to be all of the same species, derive from nature a much more remarkable distinction of genius, than what, antecedent to custom and education, appears to take place among men. By nature a philosopher is not in genius and disposition half so different from a street porter, as a mastiff is from a greyhound, or a greyhound from a spaniel, or this last from a shepherd's dog. Those different tribes of animals, however, though all of the same species, are of scarce any use to one another. The strength of the mastiff is not in the least supported either by the swiftness of the greyhound, or by the sagacity of the spaniel, or by the docility of the shepherd's dog. The effects of those different geniuses and talents, for want of the power or disposition to barter and exchange, cannot be brought into a common stock, and do not in the least contribute to the better accommodations and convenience of the species. Each animal is still obliged to support and defend itself, separately and independently, and derives no sort of advantage from that variety of talents with which nature has distinguished its fellows. Among men, on the contrary, the most dissimilar geniuses are of use to one another; the different produces of their respective talents, by the general disposition to truck, barter, and exchange, being brought, as it were, into a common stock, where every man may purchase whatever part of the produce of other men's talents he has occasion for.

Division of Labour Is Limited by the Extent of the Market

As it is the power of exchanging that gives occasion to the division of labour, so the extent of this division must always be limited by the extent of that power, or, in other words, by the extent of the market. When the market is very small, no person can have any encouragement to dedicate himself entirely to one employment, for want of the power to exchange all that surplus part of the produce of his own labour, which is over and above his own consumption, for such parts of the produce of other men's labour as he has occasion for.

There are some sorts of industry, even of the lowest kind, which can be carried on no where but in a great town. A porter, for example, can find employment and subsistence in no other place. A village is by much too narrow a sphere for him; even an ordinary market town is scarce large enough to afford him constant occupation. In the lone houses and very small villages which are scattered about in so desert a country as the Highlands of Scotland, every farmer must be butcher, baker and brewer for his own family. In such situations we can scarce expect to find even a smith, a carpenter, or a mason, within less than twenty miles of another of the same trade. The scattered families that live at eight or ten miles distance from the nearest of them, must learn to perform themselves a great number of little pieces of work, for which, in more populous countries, they would call in the assistance of those workmen. Country workmen are almost every where obliged to apply themselves to all the different branches of industry that have so much affinity to one another as to be employed about the same sort of materials. A country carpenter deals in every sort of work that is made of wood: a country smith in every sort of work that is made of iron. The former is not only a carpenter, but a joiner, a cabinet maker, and even a carver in wood, as well as a wheelwright, a ploughwright, a cart and waggon maker. The employments of the latter are still more various. It is impossible there should be such a trade as even that of a nailer in the remote and inland parts of the Highlands of Scotland. Such a workman at the rate of a thousand nails a day, and three hundred working days in the year, will make three hundred thousand nails in the year. But in such a situation it would be impossible to dispose of one thousand, that is, of one day's work in the year.

.   .   .   .   .

Questions for Thought and Discussion

1. Do you think labor will be more specialized in a developed or underdeveloped country? Why?
2. If specialization and division of labor are highly developed in some economy, what else would you expect to find?
3. Could specialization have any disadvantages?

Section II

THE PRICE SYSTEM

RESOURCE ALLOCATION IN A MARKET ECONOMY

Marvin M. Phaup, Jr.

Introduction

A fundamental characteristic of a market economy is decentralized decision making. Decentralized decision making means that individual economic units, e.g., consumers, producers, etc., make the necessary choices in the system and, therefore, no single being "runs the whole show." In a market system, resource owners themselves choose if and when to accept offers of employment for those resources. Producers select their inputs and produce goods and services on the basis of their own decisions as to what is appropriate. Consumers buy what they wish and reject what they dislike. A market system, then, is a highly individualistic institution where members do that which *they* choose to do.

Much can be said for the individual freedom implicit in such a situation, but it is *not* immediately obvious how such an undirected economy deals rationally or in an orderly way with the problem of limited resources and unlimited wants.

This explanation of resource allocation in a market economy consists of three parts. First, in order to show that the problem is not trivial, resource allocation in a centrally directed, nonmarket economy is considered. Second, a simple model of a market economy is developed and used to predict what kind of resource allocation may be expected with such an institutional framework. Third, some consideration is given to the role of market prices in allocating resources.

The Allocation of Resources in a Non-Market Economic System

In order to grasp the nature and the immensity of the problem of resource allocation, assume that the market system is replaced with a

43

highly centralized decision-making system in which one person makes all the economic decisions. Suppose, for instance, that you were suddenly selected to direct the U.S. economy, and that economic activity would occur only as a consequence of a specific and direct command from you. Additionally, you will be burdened with the responsibility of directing in accordance with the objective of maximizing the total satisfaction of wants with the limited available resources.

A starting point in this task would be to take stock of (1) the available resources, (2) the state of technical know-how for converting these resources into goods and services capable of satisfying human wants, and (3) the nature of consumer wants and preferences. Statistics must be assembled regarding the availability of land, water, raw materials, labor, energy sources, equipment, factories, transport—in short, all resources. In addition, the lists will have to be highly detailed as to quality and location. For example, it is not sufficient to know how much coal there is; it must be determined what kinds of coal there are and where and how these types of coal are to be found and extracted. This same detailed information must be compiled for *all* inputs. The economic resources of the country will have to be described in detail. Once gathered, such a mass of data will present enormous problems of storage and retrieval, even with the use of modern electronic computer systems.

When this herculean resource inventory has been completed, at a considerable cost in terms of resources expended, you must move on to the assemblage of the second sort of information required—namely, the determination from a technological standpoint of what goods and how many of each can be produced from these resources. This task is equivalent to the determination of the actual shape of the economy's production frontier. However, in this case, you must work in multidimensional space, for there will be a large number of alternative goods which may be produced, e.g., several grades of beef and potatoes, thousands of types of shoes, dresses, recreation, etc.

Finally, in terms of information required, some data must be obtained from the hundreds of millions of people living in the society regarding their wants and preferences within the range of what it is possible to produce. That is, what is now required is to identity that combination of output from the possible range of outputs which will maximize the total satisfactions of the population.

At this point, it is necessary to comment on the possibility of acquiring the information needed. Of the total information required, it is at least conceptually possible that a resource-technology inventory would produce a reasonable estimate of the productive capability of the economy.

There are, however, grave doubts as to whether it is conceptually possible to collect the relevant information on wants. Of course, people can be asked what they want or prefer, and answers can be given. Yet, there remains the problem of giving weights to individual wants. Citizen A wants good X, Citizen B wants good Y, Citizen C wants good Z, *ad infinitum*. If resource availability does not permit the production of X, Y, *and* Z in the amounts desired, but only X *or* Y *or* Z, whose wants are to be satisfied?

One answer is that those wants which are greatest ought to be provided for first, since the aim is to maximize want satisfaction. But here is the difficulty: There is no sure way of comparing the intensity of individual wants. If two citizens claim to have a very intense desire for some product, there is no method available for measuring the extent of either's wants.

An alternative decision-making method is to give each individual's wants equal weight, i.e., devote one-third of the relevant resources to the production of X, one-third to Y, and one-third to Z. Another possibility is to allocate resources to the satisfaction of individual wants on the basis of productivity, i.e., those citizens who are most productive will receive first consideration. This may have the desirable effect of spurring the able worker on to greater effort, but it raises serious moral questions regarding the neglect of the nonproductive members of society. Hence, as director of this economy, you may decide to employ some combination of the equality and productivity roles for the allocation of resources, and ultimately goods, to consumers, thus providing each citizen with some minimum amount of goods and allocating the remainder on the basis of individual productivity.

At last, the decision is made. The possible combinations of output have been determined, and that combination which, by some weighting of individual wants, maximizes total satisfaction is selected.

The next step is to see that this output is produced and distributed to the consumers. Instructions must be prepared and sent to the owners of all factors of production telling them in detail what they are to do. The logistics of transporting resources and intermediate as well as final goods will have to be worked out.

A number of problems can be expected to crop up at this point, including the difficulties of coordination and control. One source of difficulty will arise from the fact that not only must you tell those with control over resources what to do, but also when to do it. Supplies of inputs must not only appear at the proper factory, but they must appear at the proper time. Furthermore, a mistake in coordinating economic activity at one point will inevitably cause repercussions elsewhere. For instance, if a shipment of parts arrives late at a tractor factory, tractor deliveries will be delayed, farm plantings may need to be postponed, agricultural supplies to the consumer and industry may be reduced, and so on. Unemployment may also result if the tractor factories have to wait for key parts in order to complete the machine, and tractor-using sectors are idled waiting the required equipment.

Finally, it cannot be assumed that economic units will respond to directions in precisely the manner envisioned when their instructions were prepared. They may not understand the directive, and, even if comprehension is not a problem, they may choose to act in some fashion other than as they were requested. This means that some sort of control mechanism will need to be devised to insure directive compliance. Again, just as earlier the collecting of information required resources, so also will this control system involve a diversion of scarce resources away from the satisfaction of consumer wants to the administration of economic activity.

After some period of time, resources will have been allocated and some quantity of goods will have been produced and distributed to consumers. But you, as director, cannot rest; you must keep your information regarding resources, technology, and wants up to date, and unless the economy is to be completely shut down from time to time, you must send out a continuous stream of directives. The diversion of resources from direct use in production to the administration of the economy is not a once-and-for-all cost; rather, it is a continuous drain.

In conclusion to this discussion of resource allocation in a centrally directed economy, there are several observations that can be made:

1. The problem of allocating resources so as to maximize satisfaction is immensely complex.
2. The centrally directed approach, though cumbersome, seems fairly scientific. The problem is identified and a step-by-step solution is attempted.
3. The information used in making economic decisions is extremely suspect.
4. In terms of resource diversion, the information is costly to obtain.
5. Further costs are incurred to insure that directives are carried out.

Resource Allocation in a Market Economy: Circular Flow

Although decision making is decentralized in a market economy, this does not mean that the individual decisions will be irrational. In fact, the assumption is just the opposite: If an economic unit is left to determine its own actions, that unit then will act in a fashion so as to maximize its own welfare. It will be helpful to explore carefully the implications of this fundamental premise.

To simplify the exposition, ignore the existence of government and international transactions. This reduces the number of economic units to two, the household and the firm. The household functions as a consumer of goods and services and also as an owner-supplier of factors of production. Subject to the constraint imposed by its income, the rational household will behave in such a way as to maximize its well-being. This involves consuming those goods which maximize its total satisfaction and selling its productive factors (labor, land, etc.) in such a way as to maximize its income.

The firm, on the other hand, includes those units which hire factors of production in order to produce goods for sale to the households. A satisfactory first approximation of the behavior of the firm may be obtained by assuming that the firm's aim of maximum well-being is achieved when the firm is maximizing profits.

The relationship that exists between these two units may be depicted as shown in Figure 1.

This simplified model of the economy is called the circular flow of income, because it shows that expenditures by the households, which are income to the firms, are derived from the firms' expenditures on factors of production; the households may continue to spend and to consume because they continually supply factors to, and receive income from, the firms.

The circular flow of income diagram, Figure 1, can be used to demonstrate how an "undirected" market system allocates scarce resources. The households, in their attempts to obtain maximum satisfaction from their limited income, will use their dollars to buy those things which are wanted most. The households will reveal their preferences to the firms through their expenditure pattern.

As for the firms, if they wish to maximize profits, they will find it in their own interest to offer the consumer those goods and services which

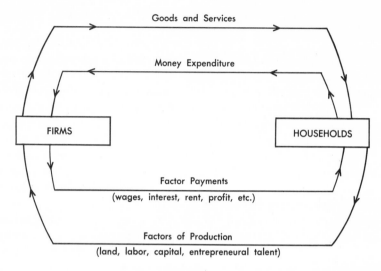

Goods and Services

Money Expenditure

FIRMS

HOUSEHOLDS

Factor Payments
(wages, interest, rent, profit, etc.)

Factors of Production
(land, labor, capital, entrepreneural talent)

FIGURE 1

he wants. This is because the households will reward those firms which provide the desired goods with a stream of expenditures and punish those which produce unwanted goods by withholding their dollars.

The successful firms, in turn, are in a financial position to hire the required resources at large and also to bid them away from the firms whose products fall into disfavor among consumers. Similarly, the owners of resources, in pursuit of the highest possible income, will be drawn towards the production of those goods which consumers are favoring with their expenditures.

Thus, even though there is no single director of a market economy and even though there is, instead, decentralized decision making, resources do get allocated according to the pattern of consumer wants as evidenced by consumer expenditures. This follows from the assumption that economic units will pursue their own self-interests.

From this, it seems clear that the market system is a fairly efficient and low-cost, in terms of resources used for administrative purposes, means of communicating information regarding consumer wants to the firms and to the resource owners. Additionally, coordination and control of resources in accordance with consumer wants wane in significance, because the resource owners will find it in their own interests to allocate the factors to those undertakings where they are most desired.

It must be noted, however, that it *cannot* be concluded that a market system necessarily produces that allocation of resources which maximizes consumer satisfaction. There are a number of reasons for this qualification; among them:

1. The market system allocates resources in response to money expenditure, whereas a maximum of consumer welfare implies an allocation of resources to the most intense wants. Yet, those citizens with the most intense wants may lack the incomes necessary to give effective expression to their wants. All that can be said is that free market choices produce the highest level of consumer satisfaction that is consistent with a *given* distribution of income.

2. Implicit in the model of resource allocation outlined here is the assumption of an intense competition in all markets. In the world today, the degree of competition that exists in many markets may be inadequate to produce optimum results.

3. Resource owners may lack knowledge of opportunities for higher earnings that are available to them for moving into lines of work where their outputs are valued more highly. Alternatively, resource owners may choose to remain in lower paid jobs for noneconomic reasons, such as desires to maintain family ties when job changes involve geographic moves.

One must not allow these reservations to obscure the primary conclusion that a market economy permits rational allocation of resources without the necessity of one unit possessing all knowledge and giving direction to all other units. Each economic unit must only pursue its own self-interest. This is because the units will find it in their self-interests to do what they would be ordered to do in a centrally directed economy within the present distribution of income. To repeat, consumer expenditures will communicate consumer preferences to the firms. In turn, the factors of production will respond to the signals of firms and move into those lines of production where they are most desired. There will be order, not chaos, in the allocation of resources.

Perhaps surprisingly, the competitive market system compares very favorably with the centrally directed economy, on the basis of resource allocation in accordance with consumer wants. The market system communicates an immense quantity of information to those who need it quickly and without the necessity of using large quantities of resources for information collection, coordination, and control.

The Role of Market Prices in the Allocation of Resources

Although the discussion of resource allocation to this point has been in terms of the effects of flows of spending, prices also play a critical role in the allocative process.

Perhaps the nature of this role can best be explained by an illustration. Consider a market economy in which resources are allocated among various uses such that there is no other allocation which will result in greater consumer satisfaction, given the distribution of income. Now, consider two individual markets in particular: the market for Schmaltz and the market for Blatz, two beverages. Initially, some quantity of resources is being allocated to the production of Schmaltz and some quantity of resources is being used to produce Blatz. This is in accordance with consumer wants.

Suddenly the situation changes. Large numbers of beverage drinkers suddenly · realize that Schmaltz is essentially a watery, tasteless brew, whereas Blatz, as the name suggests, is robust and full-bodied. Intuition correctly indicates that as a consequence of this change in taste and the resulting shift in consumer expenditure, the price of Blatz will rise and the price of Schmaltz will fall.

As the shift in consumer tastes occurs very quickly, immediate increases in production of Blatz will not be possible. There will need to be some way of rationing the available stocks. A substantial increase in the price of Blatz rations the brew to the highest bidder, just as the original price of Blatz rationed the available quantity among the then fewer Blatz drinkers.

Over a longer period of time, the higher Blatz price and the lower Schmaltz price will affect the producers' decisions regarding the appropriate output. Not only will the expectation of higher profits induce the Blatz firms to try to increase their outputs, but their increased revenue will enable them to attract the necessary quantity of inputs by offering to pay higher wages, rent, interest, etc.

Some of these resources may be obtained from the Schmaltz industry, where output is being reduced and input requirements are falling.

Some Schmaltz producers may even change to the production of Blatz. After comparing the price of inputs and the selling price of Blatz, other firms may also become interested in producing Blatz. The resulting shift in resource allocation is obviously consistent with the change in consumer tastes. In fact, it is just the type of shift that would have been ordered by a very efficient director of this economy if it were centrally directed.

In addition, the changed prices of Blatz and Schmaltz will signal all affected economic units of the change that has taken place in the relative scarcities of Blatz and Schmaltz. For instance, those who are indifferent to the taste of their beverage and who drink only for the sheer joy of swallowing, will be induced to drink Schmaltz. This will be a desirable development, since this will leave more Blatz to those who appreciate the difference.

To generalize from the above observations, prices assist in the allocative process by performing the functions of rationing the available goods, providing an incentive to producers, and serving as indices of relative scarcity.

Summary

In the course of this discussion, an attempt has been made to reconcile the decentralized decision making of a market economy with the rational allocation of resources. What is essentially involved in resource allocation is the communication of a vast amount of information to the decision makers, whether one or millions. The market economy is comparatively successful in allocating resources because the system is a good communication device employing financial flows and prices as the primary information carriers.

Questions for Thought and Discussion

1. Are there any tasks for which a centrally directed economy might be better suited than a market economy?
2. Would there be prices if there were no economic problem? Why?
3. Since the household is both the consumer and the resource owner, why is there a problem of communication between consumers and resource owners?

4. Changes in consumption patterns, as in the Schmaltz-Blatz example, require a reallocation of resources. Can you think of any real-world examples of such changes in consumption patterns? Were the resources released by the declining industry absorbed without difficulty by other industries? How do you account for this?

THE HARMONY OF SELF INTEREST

AND THE PUBLIC GOOD

Adam Smith

Every individual is continually exerting himself to find out the most advantageous employment for whatever capital he can command. It is his own advantage, indeed, and not that of the society, which he has in view. But the study of his own advantage naturally, or rather necessarily leads him to prefer that employment which is most advantageous to the society.

. . . .

. . . As every individual, therefore, endeavours as much as he can both to employ his capital in the support of domestic industry, and so to direct that industry that its produce may be of the greatest value; every individual necessarily labours to render the annual revenue of the society as great as he can. He generally, indeed, neither intends to promote the public interest, nor knows how much he is promoting it. He intends only his own security; and by directing that industry in such a manner as its produce may be of the greatest value, he intends only his own gain, and he is in this, as in many other cases, led by an invisible hand to promote an end which was no part of his intention. Nor is it always the worse for the society that it was no part of it. By pursuing his own interest he frequently promotes that of the society more effectually than when he really intends to promote it. I have never known much good done by those who affected to trade for the public good. It is an affectation, indeed, not very common among merchants, and very few words need be employed in dissuading them from it.

Adam Smith, *The Wealth of Nations* (1776).

What is the species of domestic industry which his capital can employ, and of which the produce is likely to be of the greatest value, every individual, it is evident, can, in his local situation, judge much better than any statesman or lawgiver can do for him. The statesman, who should attempt to direct private people in what manner they ought to employ their capitals, would not only load himself with a most unnecessary attention, but assume an authority which could safely be trusted, not only to no single person, but to no council or senate whatever, and which would nowhere be so dangerous as in the hands of a man who had folly and presumption enough to fancy himself fit to exercise it.

To give the monopoly of the home-market to the produce of domestic industry, in any particular art or manufacture, is in some measure to direct private people in what manner they ought to employ their capitals, and must, in almost all cases, be either a useless or hurtful regulation. If the produce of domestic can be brought there as cheap as that of foreign industry, the regulation is evidently useless. If it cannot, it must generally be hurtful. It is the maxim of every prudent master of a family, never to attempt to make at home what it will cost him more to make than to buy. The taylor does not attempt to make his own shoes, but buys them of the shoemaker. The shoemaker does not attempt to make his own clothes, but employs a taylor. The farmer attempts to make neither the one nor the other, but employs those different artificers. All of them find it for their interest to employ their whole industry in a way in which they have some advantage over their neighbours, and to purchase with a part of its produce, or what is the same thing, with the price of a part of it, whatever else they have occasion for.

What is prudence in the conduct of every private family, can scarce be folly in that of a great kingdom. If a foreign country can supply us with a commodity cheaper than we ourselves can make it, better buy it of them with some part of the produce of our own industry, employed in a way in which we have some advantage. The general industry of the country, being always in proportion to the capital which employs it, will not thereby be diminished, no more than that of the above-mentioned artificers; but only left to find out the way in which it can be employed with the greatest advantage. It is certainly not employed to the greatest advantage when it is thus directed towards an object which it can buy cheaper than it can make. The value of its annual produce is certainly more or less diminished, when it is thus turned away from producing commodities evidently of more value than the commodity which it is directed to produce. According to the supposition, that commodity could be purchased from foreign countries cheaper than it could be made at home. It could, therefore, have been purchased with a part only of the commodities, or, what is the same thing, with a part only of the price of the commodities, which the industry employed by an equal capital would have produced at home, had it been left to follow its natural course. The industry of the country, therefore, is thus turned away from a more, to a less advantageous employment, and the exchangeable value of its annual produce, instead of being increased, according to the intention of the lawgiver, must necessarily be diminished by every such regulation.

By means of such regulations, indeed, a particular manufacture may sometimes be acquired sooner than it could have been otherwise, and after a certain time may be made at home as cheap or cheaper than in the foreign country. But though the industry of the society may be thus carried with advantage into a particular channel sooner than it could have been otherwise, it will by no means follow that the sum total, either of its industry, or of its revenue, can ever be augmented by any such regulation. The industry of the society can augment only in proportion to what can be gradually saved out of its revenue. But the immediate effect of every such regulation is to diminish its revenue, and what diminishes its revenue is certainly not very likely to augment its capital faster than it would have been augmented of its own accord, had both capital and industry been left to find out their natural employments.

Though for want of such regulations the society should never acquire the proposed manufacture, it would not, upon that account, necessarily be the poorer in any one period of its duration. In every period of its duration its whole capital and industry might still have been employed, though upon different objects, in the manner that was most advantageous at the time. In every period its revenue might have been the greatest which its capital could afford, and both capital and revenue might have been augmented with the greatest possible rapidity.

The natural advantages which one country has over another in producing particular commodities are sometimes so great, that it is acknowledged by all the world to be in vain to struggle with them. By means of glasses, hotbeds, and hotwalls, very good grapes can be raised in Scotland, and very good wine can be made of them at about thirty times the expense for which at least equally good can be brought from foreign countries. Would it be a reasonable law to prohibit the importation of all foreign wines, merely to encourage the making of claret and burgundy in

Scotland? But if there would be a manifest absurdity in turning towards any employment, thirty times more of the capital and industry of the country, than would be necessary to purchase from foreign countries an equal quantity of the commodities wanted, there must be an absurdity, though not altogether so glaring, yet exactly of the same kind, in turning towards such employment a thirtieth, or even a three hundredth part more of either. Whether the advantage which one country has over another, be natural or acquired, is in this respect of no consequence. As long as the one country has those advantages, and the other wants them, it will always be more advantageous for the latter, rather to buy of the former than to make. It is an acquired advantage only, which one artificer has over his neighbour, who exercises another trade; and yet they both find it more advantageous to buy of one another, than to make what does not belong to their particular trades.

. . . . . .

Questions for Thought and Discussion

1. What role does self-interest play in a market economy, according to Smith?
2. What relationship does Smith see between the public good and individual self-interest? Do you agree?
3. Is a nation's welfare promoted or hindered by international trade? Why?

THE PRICE MECHANISM

Ogden O. Allsbrook and Edward H. Rastatter

The mechanism by which the prices of goods and services are determined is the very cornerstone of economics. The market price of an object reflects simultaneously the amount consumers are willing to pay and sellers feel they must receive for a given quantity of the object. The two forces involved are, respectively, *demand* and *supply*.

The Concept of Demand

The demand for a good can be defined as the various quantities of the good which people would purchase at alternative prices, if all other things do not change. "Good" can also mean a service such as an appliance repair, and implies no moral judgment about the commodity or service in question. "Other things" assumed not to change are such things as (1) people's tastes and preferences, (2) people's incomes, and (3) the prices of related goods. The relationship between price and quantity of the good in question is such that at lower prices more will be purchased and at higher prices less will be purchased, during a given period of time. Let us now illustrate this "law of demand" for a specific good, and then show how the "other things" affect its demand.

An Illustration of Demand

Suppose the good in question is okra. It can be assumed that the quantity of okra purchased or demanded will increase as the price is allowed

---

The authors are, respectively, Assistant Professor of Economics at the University of Georgia and Economist in the Office of the Assistant Secretary of Defense for Systems Analysis.

to fall for three reasons: First, the individual consumer can *afford* to buy more okra if the price falls without cutting down on purchases of other goods; second, the consumer will want to buy more okra and *substitute* it for other goods he usually buys (such as beans), because okra has become relatively cheaper; and third, at a sufficiently low price, some consumers will overcome their dislike for okra and begin to purchase it. Thus, as the price of a good falls, the quantity demanded will tend to increase as new consumers begin to demand some of it and old consumers demand more of it.

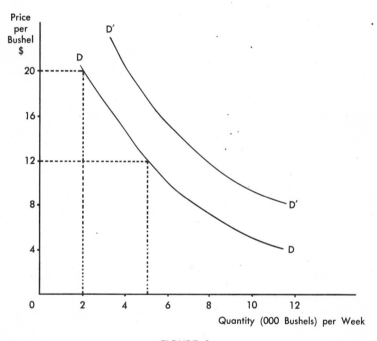

FIGURE 1

A simple device for illustrating the law of demand is the demand curve, shown in Figure 1. The vertical axis measures the price per unit, while the horizontal axis measures the quantity of the good demanded during a given period of time (per week, per month, etc.). The curve DD clearly illustrates the inverse relationship between price per unit and quantity demanded per unit of time. If the price of okra is $20 per bushel,

2,000 bushels per week will be demanded, but if the price is $12, the quantity demanded is 5,000 bushels per week.

Changes in "Other Things"

It was noted that other things were assumed not to change when describing the demand for a commodity. Suppose, however, that these other things are permitted to change. In Figure 1, DD is the original demand curve for okra. But DD assumes that consumer tastes and incomes and the prices of related goods do not change. The demand curve for okra might shift to D'D' if any of these other things changed. For example, if a concerted advertising campaign by okra growers were to change consumer tastes, consumers might be induced to buy more okra at each and every possible price, such that, had the market price been $12 per bushel, 8,000 bushels per week would be demanded, whereas only 5,000 bushels per week were demanded prior to the advertising campaign. Likewise, if consumer incomes suddenly increased, consumers would be able to afford more okra at each possible price. In addition, suppose the price of green beans (a close substitute for okra) were to increase or the price of black-eyed peas (often served with okra) were to decrease; the demand curve for okra would shift up and to the right, as from DD to D'D'. Conversely, the curve would tend to shift from D'D' to DD if other things changed in the opposite direction, such as an advertising campaign for beans, a fall in consumer incomes, a fall in the price of beans or a rise in the price of black-eyed peas.

Changes in Demand and Quantity Demanded

This illustrates a simple point that should not be confused: changes in the *price* of a good affect only the *quantity demanded* of the good (movements along the given demand curve), while changes in all *other things* affect the demand curve itself and, hence, change the quantity demanded at each and every price (a shift in the demand curve).

Elasticity of Demand

One of the most important characteristics of demand is the extent of its elasticity, or the degree of response of quantity demanded to changes in price. Elasticity of demand is defined as the percentage increase in

59

quantity demanded divided by the percentage fall in price. A simple means for diagnosing elasticity of demand is to observe the total money expenditures for the good as its price changes. If expenditures rise as price falls or if expenditures fall as price rises, demand is said to be elastic. Conversely, if expenditures fall as price falls or rise as price rises, demand is inelastic. This is illustrated in Figure 2, which repeats curve DD from Figure 1 and shows a table with readings from the curve DD. By observing the column marked "Expenditure" in Figure 2, it can be seen that

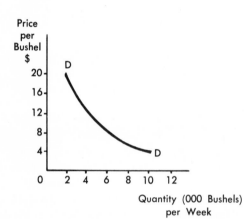

Price	Quantity	Expenditure
$20	2	$40
16	3	48
12	5	60
8	7	56
4	10	40

FIGURE 2

demand for okra is elastic (expenditures increase) when price is in the range of $12 to $20 per bushel, but inelastic (expenditures decrease) for all prices below $12 per bushel. In general, it is the case that demand is more elastic at higher prices than at lower prices.

There are three things that influence the elasticity of demand for commodities—the range of substitutes for the commodity, the proportion of consumers' income spent on the commodity, and time.

The wider the range of substitutes for a given commodity, the more elastic will be the demand for it, and conversely, the fewer the substitutes, the less elastic its demand. Actually, it depends partly on how closely one specifies the commodity. Thus, the demand for food in general is inelastic, since there are no substitutes for it; but the demand for okra is relatively elastic, since there are a myriad of substitutes. Further, the demand for salt is inelastic, since it is a necessity and has no substitutes; but the demand for a certain brand of salt is more elastic, since there are many brands of comparable quality. Thus, if the price of salt rises, consumer expenditures for salt will rise, but if a single producer of salt tries to raise the price of his salt, his revenues will fall as consumers substitute other brands.

Demand for commodities on which consumers spend a relatively small proportion of their incomes will be inelastic. Salt again falls into this category, as does tobacco, gasoline, and liquor. On the other hand, the demand for commodities that require a relatively high proportion of a consumer's income will be elastic. An example in this category is automobiles. Again, however, the relative elasticity depends on how closely one specifies the commodity. For example, the demand for automobiles may be elastic, but the demand for a certain make will be relatively more elastic.

A third factor in determining elasticity of demand is time. That is, the longer one allows for observing the reaction of quantity demanded to a change in price, the more elastic will demand appear. Immediately after a rise in the price of bread, for example, people will begin demanding smaller quantities of bread (by making sandwiches twice as thick and eating only half as many), but it takes a certain length of time for consumers to rearrange their eating habits toward more salads and only an occasional sandwich.

A Wider View of Demand

The previous sections used fairly specific examples to expose the concepts of demand and elasticity, but it should be noted at this point that the concept of demand is far wider, but a great deal less precise, than what the examples showed. For one thing, economists and statisticians have had notably poor luck in drawing real-life demand curves. While in many cases they have been able to compute elasticities of demand, success has rarely (if ever) gone farther than that. For this reason, the demand curve is best viewed as a simple pedagogical device for illustrating the relationship between price and quantity demanded.

Viewed in this light, the demand curve is simply a curve which shows the *maximum* quantity of a commodity that consumers would be willing to purchase at alternative prices. With reference to Figure 3, the area under curve DD shows that consumers would pay no more (but would certainly be willing to pay less) than the curve shows for each of the various quantities. Likewise, consumers would buy less if they could not get as much as they want at the various prices, but they could not be persuaded to buy more at each price.

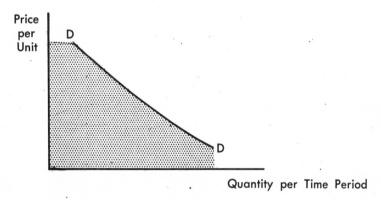

FIGURE 3

The Concept of Supply

The supply of a good or service is defined as the various quantities of that item which sellers will place for sale on the market at all possible alternative prices, other things remaining equal.

An Illustration of Supply

Just as demand is the relationship between prices and quantities per unit of time that buyers are willing to buy, supply is that relationship between prices and quantities per unit of time that sellers are willing to sell. While demand produces a negative relationship between these characteristics, supply usually produces a positive relationship, indicating that as the price of an item increases, sellers are induced to place more of the good on the market and more sellers may enter the market. A supply schedule which describes this relationship is shown below. From this schedule of alternative prices and quantities, the accompanying supply curve is constructed as seen below in Figure 4.

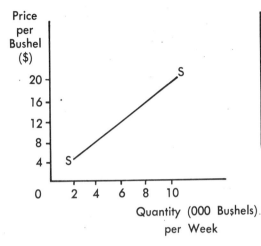

Price	Quantity
$20	10
16	8
12	6
8	4
4	2

FIGURE 4

Changes in "Other Things"

Remember that this relationship exists as long as the "other things" remain equal. By this we mean that (1) prices of closely related goods do not change, since an increase in bean prices will attract farmers to plant more beans and less okra on their available land; (2) technology remains constant, since a change in the efficiency of producing okra, perhaps through application of hydroponics to increase crop yield, will allow the farmer to produce a larger amount with the same expenditure of resources as before; and (3) other circumstances, such as weather vagaries or strikes, remain constant to guarantee the integrity of our given supply schedule and supply curve.

If, however, any of these "other things" should change, we would have a new set of possible supply quantities at alternative prices, indicating a new supply curve.

This is the distinction between the supply and the quantity supplied. When only price changes, the quantity supplied will adjust. But when something like technology changes, the supply will change, indicating a new set of alternative prices and quantities and a new supply curve.

Bear in mind this fact about any supply curve: At a given price, producers are willing to produce any quantity up to the supply curve, but will not produce any quantity beyond that. It is quite possible that they will produce some lesser quantity. This is indicated by the supply curve

63

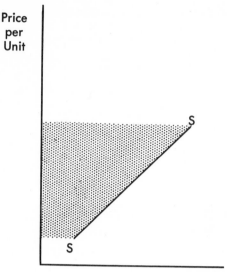

Price per Unit

S

S

Quantity per Time Period

FIGURE 5

dividing areas into regions of feasibility (shaded area) and infeasibility (unshaded area), as seen in Figure 5.

Elasticity of Supply

Just as the relationship between price and quantity demanded can be measured through a formula for elasticity, the same can be done for supply. The formula for supply elasticity is similar to that for demand—measuring the percentage change in quantity supplied to a percentage change in price. If supply is elastic over the observed range, a small change in price will produce a larger change in the quantity supplied. And if supply is inelastic, a small change in price will produce a smaller change in the quantity supplied or no change at all.

Where elasticity of demand has a shorthand method for determining elasticity by observing the total revenue, elasticity of supply has a shorthand method of surveying elasticity. If the supply curve is a straight line (linear) and, if extended, will intersect the origin of the graph, the supply curve has uniform, or unit, elasticity throughout its range. Its elasticity describes equal percentage increases in the quantity supplied to changes in price. But if the linear supply curve intersects the price axis of the graph, elasticity is greater than "one" and supply is elastic to price changes throughout all ranges. If, on the other hand, the linear supply curve intersects the quantity axis, elasticity is less than "one" and supply is inelastic to price changes throughout all ranges. For curving supply curves, the elasticity must be measured at each point in question, since it will change over the range of the curve.

Market Price Determination

As stated earlier, market prices are determined by the interactions of supply and demand. Figure 6 repeats the demand curve in Frame A and the supply curve in Frame B and superimposes them in Frame C. This overlay illustrates that the feasible areas (shaded area) are further restricted and defined when supply and demand are considered jointly. It also shows that the market price must be P_0, and the quantity supplied and demanded must be Q_0.

Figure 7 shows why this is so. Suppose sellers wanted to supply Q_1 of the commodity expecting to charge a price of P_1. Consumers would be willing to purchase that quantity only at the lower price P_2; but at the higher price that sellers are asking, they would demand only Q_2. Thus, sellers would be forced to lower their asking price or be left with unsold goods. As the asking price falls, consumers would demand greater quantities. Only at a price of P_0 would sellers be able to sell their entire offering.

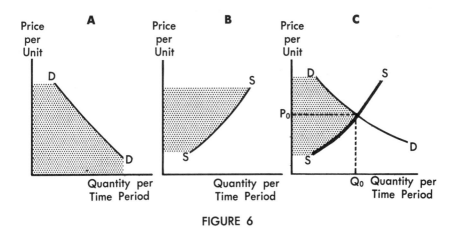

FIGURE 6

65

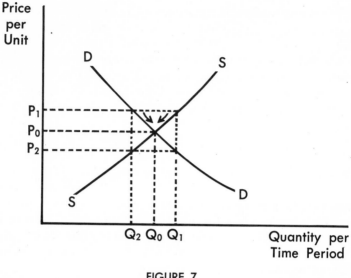

FIGURE 7

Likewise, Figure 8 shows that if for some reason price was only P_2, consumers would demand Q_1 and sellers would be willing to supply only Q_2. In other words, there would be a shortage of goods. In this case, consumers would vie with each other (by offering to pay a higher price) for the chance to buy the limited amount available. In doing so, they would

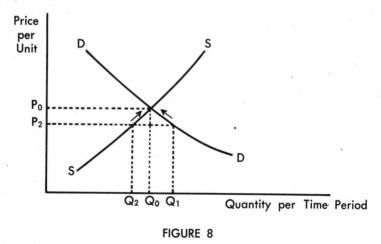

FIGURE 8

force the price up; and as the price increased, sellers would be willing to supply more. Only at a price of P_0 would both consumers and sellers be satisfied.

This tendency toward a market-clearing price is a direct result of the desires of sellers and buyers to maximize their individual satisfaction. Thus, in Figure 7 above, the initial problem is that sellers are frustrated because they have large quantities of goods not being sold; at the same time, buyers are frustrated because, while they would like to buy the quantity offered by the sellers, they aren't willing to pay as much as the sellers are asking. Sellers don't like to see their merchandise spoil (fruits) or go out of fashion (brand-new 1968 cars in 1969), so they lower the price until they reach the level of inventory they desire. Likewise in Figure 8, the initial problem is too low a price for sellers and an insufficient quantity for buyers. Buyers are frustrated because, while the price is attractively low, there isn't enough of the good to go around (like twenty customers in the butcher shop trying to buy the last filet mignon offered at 60¢ per pound). Many buyers will be willing to pay more than the current asking price and will offer to do so. Sellers are generally willing to accept a higher price if they can get away with it, and the price eventually rises.

Again it should be emphasized that these supply curves and demand curves are best viewed as pedagogical devices for illustrating the concepts of supply, demand, and price determination. Though one may never see a real-life supply curve or demand curve, the concepts they illustrate are irrefutable. That is, greater quantities will be demanded at lower prices, more will be supplied at higher prices, and during a given time period there is only one price which will satisfy the desires of both buyers and sellers. While the time required to settle on this market-clearing price will vary among goods (shorter time for perishable fruit than for autos), the market price must eventually end up at that point.

OUR ECONOMIC HERITAGE

J. Van Wagstaff

The beginning student of economics rarely gets an opportunity to relate currently accepted economic principles with the historical development of these principles unless he chooses to major in this particular field of study. Today, we accept certain economic principles—the law of diminishing returns, the laws of supply and demand, the concept of elasticity, laws governing the distribution of income, etc.—almost without question, since they are proven economic axioms that have stood the test of time. This article will attempt to expose the student to certain evolutionary aspects of economics. The purpose is twofold. First, in order to fully appreciate the current state of economic theory, we need to trace its development from the very beginning of recorded history. Secondly, we study man's problem-solving techniques in the past in order to provide some insight into today's problems and perhaps those that will face us in the future. George Santayana, the philosopher-poet-historian, once observed that the person who ignores history is condemned to repeat it.

Economics is relatively young as a separate discipline, and most writers place the beginning of economics at the publication date of Adam Smith's *The Wealth of Nations* in 1776. Smith's work was certainly the first definitive study of economic practices and principles. It was far superior to any publication that had appeared before the mid-eighteenth century, so this book provided many scholars with a convenient starting date for a study of economic theory. Many economists maintain that economic principles are derived from observed economic practices, and, of course, economic practices are as old as man (primitive man had to allocate scarce resources to fulfill his needs—the basis of economics of today).

The author is Associate Professor of Economics at Wake Forest University.

It follows, then, that if we are to render a meaningful presentation of the development of economic thought, we need to examine contributions, however small or seemingly insignificant, made before the time of Adam Smith. If we are diligent in our search, we shall discover that there are no economic revolutions as such; economics is a dynamic evolutionary discipline, one which defies a point of origin.

Obviously, a complete history of economic thought cannot be presented within the limits of a single article. Only a simplified, brief survey of some of the more important personalities or schools of thought will be offered in the hope that the reader will be stimulated to further reading and exploration. Most of the writers in the early stages of economic development are not famous exclusively for their contributions to the study of economics. They come from all walks of life—philosophy, religion, politics, and business. However, for the purpose of this chapter, we are going to extract from the profusion of literature a few examples of early economic thought which should be of interest to the novice economist.

The Biblical Period

It may seem strange that we begin our study by returning to one of the earliest records of the history of man, the Old Testament. A certain amount of skepticism may be warranted. The Bible has endured numerous translations, perhaps weakening the accuracy of the original data. Furthermore, the reader is required to perform a certain amount of interpretation, which may in itself compound such errors. Nonetheless, it is evident that the biblical people did engage in certain economic practices which established precedents for some of our contemporary legal and economic institutions. By examining the economics of this period, we can appreciate the universality of the economic problem and man's desire to understand it—and thereby acquire insights into our own economic institutions.

Agriculture

Before man actually became "civilized," he was one step removed from an animal. He was a parasite who literally lived off the land. He gathered his economic necessities from nature rather than engaging in any form of production, and his society consisted of a wandering, nomadic tribe. Gradually, man learned that he could exercise some control over his environment, and perhaps extend his life expectancy, by growing his own foodstuffs. In time, then, the tribes ceased their wanderings and began to form permanent settlements dependent upon agriculture. As man exploited the fruits of the soil by raising crops, herds, and flocks, the ownership of land became more and more important. It was the most valuable form of property.

In order to protect one's interest in land, the institution of property rights evolved. Laws and customs governing the acquisition and sale of land were developed, as well as the principle of primogeniture. These laws were designed to keep the ownership of land within the family and thus prevent the loss of the group's source of economic strength.

The geographical area inhabited by the biblical tribes progressed at a much faster pace than did other parts of the Old World. Much of this progress can be traced to favorable agricultural conditions. The land in the river valleys and oases was very fertile and was rejuvenated periodically when the rivers overflowed their banks. Furthermore, this region had unproductive seasons, which necessitated an excess of production over consumption during the growing period. The resulting surplus was stored to provide sustenance during the unproductive season. Once surpluses were created, then possibilities for trade and exchange materialized. The surplus generated by one individual or group could then be exchanged for the surpluses produced by others. Thus, a higher degree of specialization and division of labor followed from these trading opportunities. Commerce was further stimulated by the rivers which provided easy access to other settlements.

Industry

The discovery of iron ore and the development of iron metallurgy hastened the economic development of the region. Iron ore was relatively abundant; and iron tools and weapons, superior to bronze and copper in many ways, became available to the poorer working classes of society. Various agricultural implements, now made of iron, increased the productivity of the farmers, who were then capable of demanding more specialized goods and services from craftsmen. The industrial sector responded by developing greater skills and higher levels of specialization. Some of the population began to devote their full energies to such occupations as masons, smiths, carpenters, potters, weavers, etc. Machines were

71

gradually developed which increased the efficiency of construction, milling, and irrigation. In short, the development of these new tools and innovations encouraged a greater division of labor and a higher state of economic interdependency, the benefits of which could be realized only through trade.

Trade and Commerce

Trade was first accomplished by means of barter, the direct exchange of one good or service for another. A barter system, of course, is very inefficient, and many different forms of money, usually of gold or silver content, were introduced to facilitate exchange. The Persians are generally recognized as the first nationality to introduce stamped coinage, and this practice was soon duplicated by the Greeks, Romans, and Syrians. The Hebrews, because of their history of oppression, were relatively late in adopting their own monetary system. As coins of different origins and denominations found their way into the Hebrew economy, the need for moneychangers arose. The exchangers would charge a fee for trading one form of currency for another, and there is some evidence that they served as a link between savers and investors. A parable in the New Testament relates an episode in which a servant was berated for burying his talent instead of giving it to a moneychanger who would then loan the money at interest. Thus, some of the functions of our contemporary banking institutions were performed by these early financiers.

At this point, the reader may hastily conclude that we can find origins of a market economy in the earliest stages of man's economic development. To a certain extent, this observation is correct. However, we must qualify any such conclusion with a warning that many of these early practices were quantitatively insignificant. That is, most trade and exchange occurred on a localized basis until the Greeks and Romans appeared. Then trade routes were extended throughout the Mediterranean Sea basin. And finally, we must bear in mind that the economy was primarily agricultural in nature, and the capacity of this primitive agriculture to support a significant nonagricultural population was limited. Nonetheless, we do find precedents for modern economic practices in the distant past. Private property, division of labor, trade and commerce, and money and exchange are only a few characteristics of capitalism that found expression in the Biblical period.

The Greek Philosophers

Economic practices in the regions that became the basis for the civilizations of ancient Greece and Rome followed the same process of development as described in the Biblical period. Life evolved from nomadic tribes to the establishment of the city-state, around which grew the concept of the ideal political unit as conceived by the philosophers. It is in this general field of political theory, the composition of the ideal state and the functions and duties of its citizens, that we find some contributions of economic importance. Upon observing the formation and interaction of certain market forces, the philosophers addressed themselves to an analysis of market characteristics and functions.

For example, Plato recognized that the division of labor is a vital part of the productive process. In the *Republic*, where Plato discusses the formation of the ideal state, he observes that men have diverse native abilities, and better work will be done and a surplus created if each man has only one occupation. In addition to all types of craftsmen, Plato notes that the state would require importers and exporters, retail-traders, a market place, and money for purposes of exchange.

Plato did not systematically analyze the determination of market value or price, although he did make some offhand remarks about this topic. He harbored a strong prejudice against craftsmen and shopkeepers because of their ability to charge customers more than the "true value" of the goods sold. He does not explain what he means by the term "true value," but states that the merchants themselves know what it is. A liberal interpretation of Plato's discourse would imply a cost of production theory of value. In other words, the true value of a product is determined by the total costs of supplying that product to the customer. We can assume that the costs of production would include a normal profit. However, Plato was fearful that some monopolistic producers would make economic profits, or charge a price in excess of the product's "true value."

Aristotle, the brilliant student of Plato, was more prolific and analytical in his treatment of economic questions. He wrote discerningly on many subjects, improving upon the existing treatment of economics, politics, philosophy, and ethics to the extent that his influence was felt throughout subsequent economic development, especially in the Middle Ages. Unfortunately, we shall be forced to limit our discussion to a representative sample of his work.

In discussing the art of making money, Aristotle attempts to explain the derivation of value, or why a good commands a certain price in the market. This analysis leads Aristotle to conclude that an article may possess value in use and value in exchange. Goods satisfy wants directly when we use them, or indirectly when we exchange them for other commodities. The important point here is not the distinction made between value in use and value in exchange, but the realization that value is derived from the want-satisfying ability of the good. Actually, value in exchange is derived from value in use. If a commodity is not useful to a second party in a transaction, then there can be no value in exchange, because a rational person will not acquire a good that is useless to him. No exchange will take place. To summarize, a shoe may create utility or satisfaction when we wear it, or we may exchange the shoe for another article that will give us pleasure. Therefore, we demand shoes, and we are willing to pay a price for them because we expect to derive utility from their use or exchange.

Aristotle shifts our attention from the supply side of the market to a consideration of demand. He makes value subjective, depending upon the utility or usefulness of the product. Plato, on the other hand, viewed value as being determined by objective costs of production. Neither, of course, developed a complete theory of value; but taken collectively, the Greek philosophers gave us a preliminary analysis of the determinants of supply and demand which interact in the market place to establish prices of goods and services.

The Middle Ages

Most historians regard the Middle Ages as the period extending from the fall of Rome (A.D. 476) to about A.D. 1500. The first 500 years were generally known as the Dark Ages, with very little development of any kind except perhaps in the field of religion. The growth of Christianity as such does not concern us here. However, the church's role in economic development and thought in the Middle Ages is important. The church exerted tremendous influence upon every aspect of medieval life, either through direct ownership of vast economic resources or through regulation and control of trade and commerce. Most of these regulations were products of canon law as interpreted by the church philosophers, or scholastics. In analyzing economic progress in this period, we return to the three major areas of economic activity and conclude with some observations pertaining to scholastic thought.

Agriculture

By the time Western Europe had emerged from the Dark Ages, it had reverted to a purely agricultural economy, with independent land-holders playing a dominant role. Over the years, the more aggressive individuals, aided by political and military power, accumulated large tracts of land and subjugated numbers of people. These small rulers, along with their subordinates, evolved into an institutional structure called feudalism, where every person had an assigned status in society.

The landowners assumed all duties of the state and correspondingly enjoyed some of its privileges. These lords established rules and regulations, administered justice within the boundaries of the estate or manor, and provided some public goods and services to the members of the estate. For example, the lord of the domain protected its members from external invasion, allowed the serfs to use the estate's brewery, mill, and facilities, and provided internal order. The rulers charged rent (usually payments in kind) for the use of the land, collected fees for the use of the public enterprises, and levied fines and other penalties upon violators of the laws and customs of the manor.

The other inhabitants of the estate were categorized into several classes, depending upon their degree of servitude to the landlord. The freemen were the most independent of the cultivators of the soil. They were tenant farmers who worked the land and paid a fixed rent to the landowner and, in some cases, rendered military service. The serfs, on the other hand, were not allowed to leave the manor; they and their descendents were tied to the soil. In return for the privilege of working enough land for their own subsistence, the serfs normally worked a certain number of days each week for the ruler, on a portion of the estate reserved exclusively for maintenance of the lord and his staff. Another landless class was known as cotters, and these individuals cultivated a relatively small plot of land—too small, in fact, to provide themselves with basic sustenance. The cotter was forced to supplement his income by working for the landlord or some prosperous freeman as an agricultural worker; or perhaps he had the opportunity to work as a miller, baker, blacksmith, weaver, or brewer. Slaves, as a component of the work force, diminished in importance during the Middle Ages.

Crop rotation was commonly practiced to allow the soil to recover some of its reproductive capacity. The available land was divided into two or three large fields which, in turn, were subdivided into small strips. The peasants were then assigned strips in each of the large fields but would cultivate land in only two of them, perhaps planting a spring crop in one and a fall crop in the other. Thus, the third field was allowed to remain fallow. This practice retarded soil exhaustion and thus prolonged the productive capacity of the estate, although it also meant that one-third of the land was unproductive at any time.

Industry

The growth of industry is usually complemented by expansion of agricultural production, development of stable political structures, and improvements in trade and commerce. History records that there is seldom any unilateral progress in any one sector of the economy. In the initial stages of industrial development in the Middle Ages, some specialization of labor occurred on the relatively self-sufficient estate, as we have previously noted. Craftsmen in the villages catered to local demands, and trade was conducted primarily on the retail level. As the years passed, some of the more ambitious craftsmen and merchants expanded the scope of their businesses, obtained raw materials from distant sources, sold their goods in foreign markets, and reorganized their means of production to achieve advantages of further specialization.

The "putting out" system became an integral part of this reorganization. At first, the workers themselves owned the necessary tools of production and performed all the tasks involved in completing the final product. The evolution of industrial technique saw the subdivision of a single craft into several distinct processes. For example, in the textile industry, a merchant would purchase wool from an importer, put it out to be washed by individuals specializing in that particular process, take the wool to other specialists who would spin the wool into yarn, then to weavers who produced cloth. Finally, after shrinking and dyeing, the finished product might be sold at the wholesale level to another merchant who would, in turn, sell it at retail. Several specialized trades were created in the production process, and this roundabout means of production required larger amounts of capital investment and more sophisticated management.

The capitalist soon discovered that he could save time and energy by bringing these specialists together under one roof rather than moving the work in process from one dwelling to another. Small factories appeared, and the ownership of the tools of production became divorced from the use of the tools. In other words, the capitalist now provided the building as well as the tools required to produce a certain product. This movement toward a factory system was abetted by the use of the water wheel, which supplied power to fulling mills, feed mills, and iron works. As a necessary requisite for the establishment of the factory system, progressively larger amounts of capital investment were needed, more than could be provided by a single individual. Thus, production and commerce began to be centered in large corporate bodies or trading companies.

Trade and Commerce

Quantitatively speaking, the largest amount of trade during the Middle Ages was conducted at the retail level and was transacted in the local market place. In the early years of this period, little long-distance trade occurred, although peddlers did ply their wares from house to house and village to village. They sold needles, toys, utensils, and other household items which could be carried on their backs or by packhorse.

As the towns and cities became more politically stable and powerful, they afforded some degree of protection along the trade routes. An increased volume of trade accompanied the growth of the towns, and traveling merchants and other middlemen increased in numbers to meet the growing demand for specialized goods produced in other countries. These merchants traveled with their goods, either by ship or by caravan, from one distant city to another. Some of these merchants formed guilds which protected their members from one another as well as from outsiders. Unfair competitive methods were strictly forbidden in transactions between the guild's members; and, in some instances, the guild acted as a collective unit, exercising monopolistic privileges.

One of the most important developments in the field of commerce was the rise of the sedentary merchant. Instead of traveling with his goods, the merchant found that he could spread his risks and save valuable time by establishing a commercial house or trading company and settling down in some city. Trade would then be effected through agents, partners, or employees, who would specialize in buying, selling, and transporting the goods. Trading ventures became more ambitious and, of course, increased in volume. Events which led to the rise of the sedentary merchant included the evolution of the permanent partnership and the development of insurance, the bill of exchange, and double-entry bookkeeping.

Medieval Thought

Scholasticism, which began early in the twelfth century, is important in discussing the theoretical issues of the times. This school of thought attempts to merge Christian doctrine with Aristotle's philosophy and apply the resulting principles of ethics to economic practices of the period.

St. Thomas Aquinas is the best known of the Scholastics. He supported Aristotle's views toward private property, the accumulation of wealth, and trade. However, his theory of value rested upon a code of ethics rather than utility. According to Aquinas, the market price of a good should be commensurate with the "just price," and the just price exists when goods are exchanged at equal values. The price must satisfy both parties, and neither should take advantage of the other. A vague cost of production theory of value is implicit in this concept of just price. If it costs just as much to produce good A as it does to produce good B, then one unit of A should be exchanged for one unit of B; or, in other words, they should command the same market price. The demand side of the market is ignored. Regardless of the want-satisfying ability of the good or the willingness of the buyer to pay a high price for the good, the just price would be established in relation to the costs involved in supplying the article. Selling goods and services at prices higher than the costs of production would lead to an unnatural accumulation of wealth, which was condemned by the church.

As a corollary to the just price dogma, church authorities condemned the practice of usury (the taking of interest on a loan). The position of the church was that the people who borrow money do so because they are poor, have suffered some economic misfortune, or otherwise find themselves in dire economic straits. Again, it was immoral to take advantage of someone under these circumstances.

The concept of the just wage was also derived from the theory of just price. Labor was the major component of the costs of production; and the worker, in selling his labor or the fruits of his labor to other craftsmen or manufacturers, was said to be justified in asking a wage sufficient to enable the worker to maintain his station in life. In other words, the worker's cost of production was equal to the money needed for him to exist at his accustomed standard of living.

In general, the prevailing attitude of this period was one of *status quo*. The economic norm was one of stability and order, rather than expansion and progress. The economic system was characterized by rigidity and regulation, and economic policy and thought rested upon the assumption that individuals could not extend their level of prosperity without impinging on the standard of life of others.

Mercantilism

The new system of merchant capitalism, or mercantilism, slowly triumphed over the self-sufficient, highly regulated feudal system. The towns and villages of the Middle Ages grew into large trading centers, which, in turn, formed the nuclei for the formation of the national state. Trade and commerce flourished, aided by the discovery of gold in the New World and the development of a money economy. The teachings of the Scholastics gave way to economic necessity, and the rewards of trade and commerce provided the basis for the growth of strong nation-states. These states faced intense competition from their rivals in expanding foreign markets, acquiring new colonies, and seeking new sources of precious metals. Mercantilism, as a body of thought, was developed to promote the rise of nationalism, and the merchant capitalist became the key figure in this period of military acquisition and economic expansion.

There were many individuals from several countries who made contributions to the school of thought which supported these nationalistic practices; however, we shall be forced to consider these personalities as representing a unified school of thought, even though complete agreement among them would have been rare, indeed.

In general, the mercantilists were nationalists dedicated to policies which would increase their country's economic wealth (usually at the expense of another nation), and wealth was measured in terms of the quantities of gold and silver possessed by the country and its citizens. All economic and political activity had a common goal—the acquisition of precious metals.

Several methods were used to obtain bullion. The most direct approach, of course, was to develop and exploit the gold-bearing lands in the colonies in the New World. Spain was very successful in bleeding wealth from her colonies and obtained an initial advantage over her rivals. Some of the other countries were forced to use a more indirect approach. For example, they thought that if they could maintain a favorable balance of trade with Spain, or any other nation for that matter, gold would naturally flow into the country. A surplus of exports over imports was, therefore, necessary if payments were to be received in gold bullion, and every step was taken to insure that this favorable balance occurred. However, a basic fact of international trade is that all countries cannot simultaneously enjoy a surplus of exports. Consequently, it was concluded that one nation could acquire wealth only at the expense of its competitors. Thus, a "beggar my neighbor" policy became the byword of the day.

A strong central government was needed to organize and control the resources of the community in an effort to achieve these nationalistic goals. For example, the export of manufactured goods was encouraged and, in some cases, subsidized by the government. The importation of competing goods was restricted by tariffs. Companies engaged in foreign trade were often granted monopoly privileges which increased their economic power abroad, and they were protected and aided in their endeavors by strong navies and merchant fleets.

Colonies were developed for the sole purpose of exploitation by the mother country. Colonial manufacturing was restricted or completely forbidden, and certain colonial products had to be sold only to the mother country. In general, the colonies furnished a supply of essential raw materials and a market for manufactured goods.

The inhabitants of the colonies were not the only people subjected to complete domination by the central government. The mercantilists encouraged the growth of a large domestic population that would work for low wages, and the general attitude toward the poorer classes was one of suppression and exploitation. Bounties were paid to skilled immigrants; child labor was encouraged; and severe penalties were levied upon ablebodied vagrants, beggars, and thieves. The mercantilists' goal was wealth for the nation, but very few people were able to share in this wealth.

One of the most advanced writers in this period, whose work actually bridges the gap between mercantilist doctrine and the physiocrats (who believed the land and its products to be the only true wealth), was Richard Cantillon (1680-1734). The reason for treating Cantillon separately is that his *Essai sur la nature du commerce en général* (written in the 1720's but not published until 1755) represents the most analytical, unified exposition of economic principles published before *The Wealth of Nations*.

As an example of the quality of Cantillon's work, he developed a theory of market value as contrasted to the cost of production value theory of his predecessors. The supply cost, or intrinsic value, of a good is the measure of the quantity of land and labor entering into its production. But Cantillon noted that many commodities which have intrinsic values were not necessarily sold in the market according to that value—that market value would also depend upon "the humors and fancies of men and on their consumption." In other words, the state of consumer demand for a commodity, interacting in the market place with the costs of supplying that commodity, will eventually determine the price at which exchange takes place between the buyer and seller.

Cantillon also gave an excellent account of the specie-flow mechanism, which refutes the mercantilist notion that a nation can permanently maintain a favorable balance of trade. He believed that an export surplus could not be sustained indefinitely. Eventually, certain adjustments in the economy would eliminate any trade surplus. He invoked the quantity theory of money (the price level depends upon the quantity of money in circulation) to show how prices would react throughout the economy in such a way as to prevent a long-run surplus or deficit in the balance of trade. A nation which sells more goods to other countries than it buys from those states will normally receive specie. As money flows into the country, merchants prosper and increase their expenditures, which increases the demand for goods and services of other workers. Unless business has the capacity to expand in the face of this additional demand, domestic prices will rise; spending on foreign goods will increase; and goods produced at home, now selling at higher prices, will find it difficult to compete in the world market. The subsequent increase in imports and decrease in exports will then cause specie to flow out of the country, thereby eliminating the initial trade surplus.

Another outstanding observation made by Cantillon was that enterprise, or entrepreneurship, should take its place, along with land, labor, and capital, as the fourth factor of production. Businessmen invest these other resources in some venture in the expectation that they will make a profit. There is, of course, no guarantee that these expectations will materialize. Profit, then, becomes the reward for risk-taking, a vital prerequisite for the functioning of a capitalistic economy.

Unfortunately, Cantillon had very little influence upon his contemporaries, since his book was not published until about 20 years after his death, and even then it did not receive much response. In retrospect, however, his contributions to economic thought, which deserve considerably more attention than given here, place him in the vanguard of pre-Smith economists.

The Physiocrats

The physiocrats were members of the first recognized school of economic thought. They comprised a school in the sense that most of their literature followed a similar theme, and their economic analysis was used as a means to justify common political ends. The influence of the school was short-lived. The beginning of the physiocratic school is usually dated at 1756, when Quesnay published one of his first articles, and the conclusion is usually dated with the dismissal of Turgot as France's finance minister and the publication of Adam Smith's *The Wealth of Nations* in 1776.

As suggested above, physiocracy was politically motivated. The prevailing mercantilistic policies had resulted in corruption of government, severe regulation of business, oppression of the working class, and in general, economic stagnation. In reacting to these conditions, the physiocrats advocated restoration of competitive forces by reducing government restrictions (laissez-faire) and abolishing government-sanctioned monopolies and guilds. Consumption of luxury goods would be discouraged, and the wealthy landowners would bear the burden of a single tax.

The theoretical foundation of this policy rested upon Quesnay's famous *Tableau Economique*, in which he analyzed the circular flow of goods and services between three major occupational classes—farmers, landowners, and manufacturers or artisans. The keystone of this economic model was the farmer, who was the sole producer of a surplus. Nature, of course, was the real provider; and the farmer, in cooperation with nature, produced more than he consumed. However, this surplus was paid to the landowner in the form of rent. It followed, then, that the landowner should bear the burden of taxation. The artisans simply convert one form of matter into another. They do not create any surplus; therefore, by physiocratic definition, they are unproductive, or sterile. All classes essentially live off the production of the land.

Regardless of faulty reasoning and inaccurate assumptions, the *Economic Table* represents the first systematic analysis of aggregate economic variables. The flow of wealth, as illustrated by Quesnay, opened up an entirely new field of study, which is known today as national income analysis, or macroeconomics. The table also emphasizes economic interdependency. All sectors of the economy are so closely related to one another that any change in one sector will induce repercussions throughout the entire economic system.

Adam Smith

It would be impossible to do justice to the "father of political economy" in a survey of this nature; and, indeed, no attempt will be made to do so. Rather, our purpose has been to show that the study of economics did not suddenly begin with the appearance of Adam Smith—that Smith, Ricardo, Marshall, Keynes, and all of us who call ourselves economists owe a great debt to a multitude of individual contributors who have continually sought to analyze and understand the economic universe. Smith, like all economists, was the beneficiary of what had gone on before him.

Smith, for example, begins the development of his value theory with a discussion of exchange value and use value, which reminds us of Aristotle's work. He then proceeds to show how "market price," at any given moment, is determined by supply and demand; but market price, in a longer period of time, will tend to fluctuate around the "natural price," which is determined by the cost of production. There is no evidence that Smith was aware of Cantillon's publication, but one could safely say that the value theory enunciated by Smith was an extension of Cantillon's previous analysis. An entire section of *The Wealth of Nations* is devoted to an attack on mercantilist theory and policy, a position which formed the basis of physiocracy. The physiocrats were admired by Smith, and he adopted their prescription of laissez-faire, competition, and free trade to cure the ills of the economic system. We may conclude that if Smith is considered the father of political economy, others who came before him deserve a place in the family tree.

Questions for Thought and Discussion

1. What economic contributions were made by Plato, Aristotle, Cantillon, and the physiocrats?
2. What relationships would you expect between economic thought and economic history?
3. What is mercantilism, and how does it differ from the economics of the physiocrats?

Section III

INTERNATIONAL TRADE AND EXCHANGE

GAINS FROM TRADE: THE CLASSICAL CASE

E. Ray Canterbery

Why does trade take place? On the surface, the answer appears obvious. Trade must have mutual advantages for nations; otherwise, countries would not have traded among themselves for the past four hundred or so years. Although one could embrace the philosophy of Thomas Hobbes' *Leviathan* that nothing man does ever makes much sense, the burden of proof appears to be on those who argue that trade gains are meager. Though there are exceptions, the classical economic justification for trade still appears a good one. Its rudiments are presented herein without much qualification; this is simply a reproduction of the basic arguments. However, we can note a quick caveat. While natural relative advantages in trade (such as climate) are immutable, the importance of natural advantages in the production process may be declining.

The bases for international trade are specialization and mutual economic advantage. This is easy to understand at a personal level—when there are no tariffs and quotas—but slightly more difficult to visualize on a world level. First, let us take the case of intracommunity trade, exchange among persons in the same community. We normally do not cut our own hair. We seldom mow our own lawns. Professors do not grade their own papers. People usually do not build their own houses. For those who try, the story of two of the three little pigs is sufficient to cause the do-it-yourselfer to ponder, at least, the possibility of seeing a specialist (of some sort).

We pay others to provide for us services and products for several reasons. Some tasks we are not able to perform. Males are not adept at housekeeping; they either marry a specialist (woman), hire a house-

The author is Assistant Professor of Economics at the University of Maryland.

keeper, or both. Some tasks are performed better by others. Persons trained as automobile mechanics usually are more skilled in repairing automobiles than is a college professor. The "opportunity costs" of doing certain kinds of work may exceed the outside cost. This is the economist's way of saying that the income foregone by a person in order to use hours to accomplish a particular task may exceed the expense of hiring someone else to do it for him. The lawyer may be able to type 70 words a minute, but he may forego a fee of $100 for every hour of typing. This is his opportunity cost. If he is sufficiently intelligent to earn $100 an hour, he will also hire a secretary to do his typing at $2 per hour.

Intra-national trade, exchange of goods and services among differing economic regions, also is common. We eat oranges from Florida, potatoes from Idaho, steak from Kansas, and barbecued steak from Texas. The causes of this regional specialization are differing native and acquired endowments of resources in various regions. Potential factor inputs—including natural resources, capital, labor and managerial skills—vary widely in a large country. The climate in Miami makes it a tourist haven for people living in northern Michigan. There is iron ore in Pennsylvania but not in Arkansas. There are large quantities of water in Minnesota but not in Arizona. These differences in endowments cause the costs of producing certain products to be greater in some areas than in others. Business enterprises tend to produce products that are least costly to manufacture in their particular locale. As a result, then, of divergent costs of inputs, a region can experience a comparative cost advantage in the production of certain products.

There are examples. Have you ever heard of Michigan wine? Grapes can be raised in hothouses in Michigan at a very high cost. But why not import cheaper wine from California, where the climate facilitates natural growth at much lower costs? Did you ever wonder why the American steel industry developed at the north end of the Great Lakes, while the automobile industry developed at the south end? Both iron and coal ore are of heavy density and can be transported only at high cost. On the north side, however, coal and iron ores are in close proximity. They can be brought together at relatively low cost for steel production. Water is the cheapest vehicle of transportation. Meanwhile, back in Detroit, there is a labor force comprised of skilled immigrants. Hence, heavy steel is shipped inexpensively to the south side (or sometimes around the lakes) where skilled labor fashions it into automobiles.

If differing availability and quality of potential factors of production induce intra-national specialization, this is an even greater justification for specialization among countries where the possibilities for diversity are even more immense. Conditions in certain countries altogether prevent the production of certain products. The climates of Italy and Brazil are conducive to raising, at low costs, grapes for wine and coffee beans for coffee, respectively. While the United States has iron, coal, and oil, Bolivia has copper and tin. The labor supply of India is great in quantity while that of Switzerland is great in skills. The industrialized nations have a substantial quantity of good quality machines and tools (capital) while the developing nations have low quantities of low quality capital.

The United States specializes in producing capital goods. Great Britain specializes in producing woolens. Turkey specializes in producing and selling tobacco. India produces a large quantity of hemp. Australians raise sheep and export raw wool. Producers in various nations tend to specialize in the production of those goods that can be produced at lowest costs, given their endowment of the factors of production. International trade is made imperative by specialization and specialization makes international trade possible. Specialization lowers production costs while limiting the availability of domestic goods to consumers. Low costs, however, enable such producers to sell abroad, filling the consumer gap left by specialization in foreign nations.

The advantage of specialization, while necessary, is not a sufficient reason for engaging in international trade. Beyond this, nations must be shown that there are mutual gains from trade. There are several ways of demonstrating this. One method is to use production functions, production-possibility curves, and consumer indifferences maps. Such an approach has the advantage of explicitly including demand alongside supply. But lurking behind even today's most sophisticated explanations of why trade occurs, is the comparative advantage notion of the theoretician-stockbroker David Ricardo. The Ricardian case sufficiently states, for the beginning student, the gains from trade. The model herein will incorporate some modern adaptations.

Let us assume there are two nations and as many products. The products are wine and machine tools; the nations are Italy and the United States. We also assume that all productive factor costs (inputs) are combined under one called "labor"; wages are identical in the two nations or else accurately reflect labor's contribution to each product unit; technology is constant; all resources are fully employed; the cost of foreign currency is one unit of domestic currency; there are no transportation costs or else they cancel out; there is international factor immobility and internal factor mobility; perfect competition prevails in the domestic economies; and there are no tariff barriers to trade. In such a model, advantages are given; they are not attained.

Total output of each product in each nation is measured in the number of units produced by one man in one day (one man-day's labor), given the state of technology, availability of resources, and so forth. By assumption, one Italian in one day can produce either 12 kegs of wine or 3 machine tools. An American can produce in one day either 3 kegs of wine or 12 machine tools. National output, of course, would equal one man-day's output times the total man-day's employed.

OUTPUT

(Based on One Man-Day's Labor)

	Wine (Kegs)		Machine Tools (Nos.)
Italy	12	or	3
U.S.	3	or	12
TOTAL OUTPUT	15		15

Behind the potential output of each nation, of course, are the costs and supplies of the factors of production. Italy can produce wine with less manpower (i.e., more cheaply) than can the United States. This reflects climate and tradition more than, say, the size of the Italian feet that crushes the grapes. The United States can produce capital goods more cheaply, probably a consequence of her endowment of natural resources plus a highly skilled labor force. Adam Smith would say that the United States has an absolute advantage in the production of machine tools, while Italy has an absolute advantage in winemaking.

Suppose each nation divides her man-day's labor equally between the two products. Assuming there is no trade,

OUTPUT

(Based on One Man-Day's Labor)

	Wine (Kegs)		Machine Tools (Nos.)
Italy	6	and	1½
U.S.	1½	and	6
TOTAL OUTPUT	7½		7½

The world experiences no net gain in output, but the people in each nation enjoy a greater variety of products. The Italians can now buy a few machine tools along with their kegs of wine. Complete specialization clearly would require trade and, at the same time, make trade advantageous. Under complete specialization, Italy would put all her resources into producing what she produces at lowest cost. Wine production would soar to 12 kegs per man-day in Italy, while machine-tool output would rise to 12 machine tools in the United States. Each nation might export three units of her favorite product to the other. Total world output would rise to 12 machine tools plus 12 kegs of wine per man-day, leaving some of each for consumption in both nations.

Can a nation gain from trade even though she does not have an absolute advantage in producing anything? Economist David Ricardo thought so in the early nineteenth century. There is a gain for such a nation if she specializes in the production of that commodity that she produces at lowest cost. Invoking the identical assumptions, but traveling down the Mediterranean shore to Greece, we have:

OUTPUT

(Based on One Man-Day's Labor)

	Wine (Kegs)		Machine Tools (Nos.)
U.S.	3	or	12
Greece	1	or	2

The United States has an absolute advantage in both cases shown in the last table, but a comparative advantage in machine tools. An American worker can, given the state of the art, manufacture six machine tools for every one produced by a Greek. Moreover, an American can squeeze out three kegs of wine to a Greek's one. Efficient in producing both products, the United States is relatively more efficient in manufacturing machine tools. The comparative advantage for Greece is in wine production; a Greek can produce one keg of wine while the American is producing three, but only one machine tool while the American is manufacturing six.

The concept of opportunity cost proves why total output is augmented under comparative advantage. Social opportunity cost is the value of other goods given up in order to produce one unit of a particular good. (This also is the domestic cost of the commodity produced.) The opportunity cost of one unit of each good (before trade) are:

91

OPPORTUNITY COSTS

	One Keg of Wine	
	Greece	U.S.
Machine Tools	2	4

	One Machine Tool	
	Greece	U.S.
Wine	½ keg	¼ keg

The Greeks give up fewer machine tools than do the Americans to generate a keg of wine, while the Americans give up less wine than the Greeks in manufacturing a machine tool. It is possible, then, to specialize and trade. (As a technical footnote, we see that the opportunity costs for the machine tools are the reciprocals of those for wine.)

The United States will trade machine tools for wine, *if* she can obtain a keg of wine for less than her domestic opportunity cost of producing a keg herself (i.e., four machine tools). In this way, wine would, in real terms, cost the United States less abroad than at home. Such a bargain can be struck, for the Greeks can put together a keg of wine for as little as two machine tools. If Greece can obtain a machine tool for less than her domestic opportunity cost of manufacturing one herself (i.e., one-half keg of wine), she will trade. This exchange also is well within the realm of possibility. The United States' machine tool cost can be as low as one-quarter kegs of wine. This bargaining relation places the limits of trade between 4MT:1W and 2MT:1W.

These ratios indicate the volume of exports required to obtain a given amount of imports. "Terms of Trade" for the United States might end up at the midpoint, so that $Xus/Mus = 3/1$. Now, the mutual gains from trade can be estimated. First, we calculate the labor cost for each unit of either product.

UNITARY LABOR COSTS

	Cost, 1 MT	Cost, 1 Keg W
U.S.	1/12 man-day	⅓ man-day
Greece	½ man-day	1 man-day

Assuming the United States must export three machine tools for every keg of wine, the domestic costs in each nation of duplicating this ratio of output can be specified. From this, the labor "saved" per exchange can be estimated.

LABOR GAINS AT 3:1 "TERMS OF TRADE"

	Quantity	Domestic Costs	Labor Saved
U.S.			
Wine Imports	1	⅓ man-day	1/12 man-day
M.T. Exports	3	¼ man-day	
Greece			
M.T. Imports	3	1½ man-day	½ man-day
Wine Exports	1	1 man-day	

It is clear that both the United States and Greece gained from specialization and trade, even though the United States began with an absolute advantage in the production of everything. Indeed, in this particular case, the country with the greatest original disadvantage enjoyed the greater gain in terms of labor "saved" from trade. Americans and Greeks alike now savor the benefits of a greater variety of products as well. The gain is not only in production but also potential consumption. By importing capital goods at a lower real cost, Greece may be able to industrialize faster.

So goes the classical case for trade. If trade is beneficial between New Mexico and New York, why not between the United States and Italy? David Ricardo demonstrated that even a nation inefficient in producing everything may have a comparative advantage in producing something. If so, that nation could, theoretically, gain from trade. The model, of course, is oversimplified. There are no tariffs between New York and New Mexico, and New Mexico can invoke no territorial claims upon New York so as to dictate the "terms of trade." But the classical justification is pretty solid, and the burden is upon its detractors to show in what "special" cases international trade is not beneficial. While comparative costs in developing nations are increasingly man-made (by technology), the comparative cost doctrine nonetheless, remains the most fundamental factor in trade.

Questions for Thought and Discussion

1. Why do nations choose to trade? Explain the possible advantages for a particular nation, and discuss the mutual gains for several nations.

2. Are there cases in which international trade does not yield net benefits to nations? If so, specify and discuss what these cases might be, and indicate the alternatives to a nation that chooses not to trade.

3. Give a numerical example of absolute versus comparative advantages in trade.

PETITION OF THE CANDLEMAKERS

Frédéric Bastiat

Frédéric Bastiat (1801-1850) was a French economist who is best known for his satire on the economic issues of his day. The "Petition of the Candlemakers" was written shortly after France raised its import duties in the 1840's. In it, Bastiat ridicules all the conventional arguments of those who seek tariff protection.

Petition from the Manufacturers of Candles, Wax Lights, Lamps, Chandeliers, Reflectors, Snuffers, Extinguishers; and from the Producers of Tallow, Oil, Resin, Alcohol, and Generally of Everything Used for Lights.

. . . We are subjected to the intolerable competition of a foreign rival, who enjoys, it would seem, such superior facilities for the production of light that he is enabled to *inundate* our *national market* at so exceedingly reduced a price, that, the moment he makes his appearance, he draws off all custom from us, and thus an important branch of French industry . . . is suddenly reduced to a state of complete stagnation. This rival, who is no other than the sun, carries on so bitter a war against us, that we have every reason to believe that he has been excited to this course by our perfidious neighbor England. . . . In this belief we are confirmed by the fact that in all his transactions with that proud island, he is much more moderate and careful than with us.

Our petition is, that it would please your honorable body to pass a law whereby shall be directed the shutting up of windows, dormers, skylights, shutters, curtains, . . . in a word, all openings, holes, chinks, and

---

From *Economic Sophisms* (New York: 1882).

fissures through which the light of the sun is used to penetrate into our dwellings. . . .

First, if by shutting out as much as possible all access to natural light, you thus create the necessity for artificial light, is there in France an industrial pursuit which will not, through some connection with this important object, be benefitted by it?

If more tallow be consumed, there will arise a necessity for an increase of cattle and sheep. Thus artificial meadows must be in greater demand; and meat, wool, leather, and above all, manure, this basis of agricultural riches, must become more abundant.

If more oil be consumed, it will cause an increase in the cultivation of the olive tree. This plant, luxuriant and exhausting to the soil, will come in good time to profit by the increased fertility which the raising of cattle will have communicated to our fields.

Our heaths will become covered with resinous trees. Numerous swarms of bees will gather upon our mountains the perfumed treasures which are now cast upon the winds, useless as the blossoms from which they emanate. There is, in short, no branch of agriculture which would not be greatly developed. . . .

Navigation would equally profit. Thousands of vessels would soon be employed in the whale fisheries, and hence would arise a navy capable of sustaining the honor of France. . . . But what words can express the magnificence which Paris will then exhibit! Cast an eye upon the future and behold the gildings, the bronzes, the magnificent crystal chandeliers, lamps, reflectors, and candelabra, which will glitter in the spacious stores, compared with which the splendor of the present day will appear trifling and insignificant.

There is none, not even the poor manufacturer of resin in the midst of his pine forest, nor the miserable miner in his dark dwelling, but who would enjoy an increase of salary and of comforts.

Gentlemen, if you will be pleased to reflect, you cannot fail to be convinced that there is perhaps not one Frenchman, from the opulent stockholder of Anzin down to the poorest vendor of matches, who is not interested in the success of our petition. . . .

Questions for Thought and Discussion

1. If you were the French National Assembly, would you grant the candlemakers' petition? Why?

2. Who is benefitted by a protective tariff? Who is injured by a protective tariff?
3. If you were a low-cost producer of some commodity in world markets, would you want a domestic tariff on that commodity? Why?

A FABLE OF TRADE AND TECHNOLOGY

James C. Ingram

During the middle decades of the twentieth century, an adventurous entrepreneur bought a thousand acres of the Great Dismal Swamp in coastal North Carolina. After draining the land and building a road and rail spur, the mysterious entrepreneur, Mr. X., built a 12-ft. electrified fence around his entire property, posted guards at the gates, and allowed no one to enter except his own trusted employees. He advertised for workers, offering $3.00 per hour, and hired 5000 workers, all sworn to secrecy.

Mr. X announced that he had made several scientific discoveries and inventions which enabled him to transform coal, wheat, tobacco, petroleum, machinery, and other products into a variety of finished products, including textiles, cameras, watches, chemicals, and TV sets. Within a few months, vast quantities of materials were pouring into Mr. X's guarded compound from all parts of the country, and a flood of low-price industrial and consumer goods began to pour *out of* Mr. X's gates and into the nation's markets, where housewives and industrialists eagerly bought them at prices 20 to 30% below the competition. Mr. X's company, Consolidated Alchemy, Inc. (CAI), reported large profits, and was soon listed on the New York Stock Exchange where it became the growth stock of the century—a favorite of institutional investors.

Meantime, the nation hailed Mr. X as a genius and benefactor of mankind, a man whose inventions greatly increased the productivity of labor and improved the standard of living of the masses. He was favorably compared to Eli Whitney and Thomas Edison.

It is true that grumbles were heard in some quarters. Several manufacturers of TV sets tried to prevent their dealers from stocking or serv-

By permission of the publisher. (New York: John Wiley & Sons, Inc., 1966, pp. 43-45.)

icing CAI sets; textile manufacturers tried to persuade Congress to establish production quotas for each firm based on average output in the previous 50 years; a labor union picketed stores carrying CAI merchandise; and three New England legislatures passed laws requiring that stores display "Buy New England" posters. None of these activities had much effect, however. Buyers could not resist the low CAI prices, and many communities were prospering because of their rapidly increasing sales to Consolidated Alchemy. The Houses of Congress resounded with speeches calling upon the people to accept the necessity for economic adjustment and urging the benefits of technical change.

As for coastal North Carolina, it was booming as never before. Schools, houses, and roads were constructed; the Great Dismal Swamp was drained and used for truck gardens, its extraordinarily fertile land was selling for $3000 per acre; employment expanded, and average wages rose to $4.00 per hour.

Then, one Sunday morning, a small boy, vacationing with his family at a nearby seaside resort, tried out his new skin-diving equipment, penetrated Mr. X's underwater screen, and observed that Consolidated Alchemy's "factories" were nothing but warehouses and that its "secret technical process" was nothing but trade. Mr. X was, in fact, a hoax; his firm was nothing but a giant import-export business. He bought vast quantities of materials from United States producers, loaded them under cover of night onto a fleet of ships, and carried them off to foreign markets where he exchanged them for the variety of goods that he sold throughout the United States at such low prices.

When the boy told what he had seen, a wire service picked up the story, and within 24 hours Mr. X was denounced as a fraud, his operation was shut down, his thousands of high-paid workers were thrown out of work, and his company was bankrupt. Several Congressmen declared that the American standard of living had been protected from a serious threat of competition from cheap foreign labor, and urged higher appropriations for research in industrial technology.

Questions for Thought and Discussion

1. Should low-cost foreign imports be allowed to come into domestic markets where the effect will be to damage domestic producers?

2. How can a developed country with a high standard of living and high wages compete in international trade against countries with cheap labor?

IN'S AND OUT'S OF INTERNATIONAL TRADE

An Introduction to International Economics

John Adams

International trade is an everyday fact of life. Americans pilot multi-hued VW's full of gasoline distilled from Venezuelan crude oil, sip Scotch whisky sitting on stylish Danish settees, and keep their ears plugged with Japanese radios blasting the latest English tunes. Daddy may well work on the production lines or in the offices of a U.S. company with large overseas operations, such as General Electric, IBM, or Chas. Pfizer. Thus, consumption habits, job opportunities, and company sales, in America as elsewhere, reflect the participation in international commerce of the nation's people.

It is tempting to conclude from these examples that international trade yields a larger variety of things to delight the consumer, creates additional employment for the working force, and increases the prosperity of the nation and its enterprises. Unfortunately, the blessings of international trade are inevitably accompanied by unpleasant effects. Exports to foreign markets do create jobs in the United States by enabling a firm to expand its production and hire more workers. But, at the same time, cheap foreign goods imported into the American economy force production cutbacks, bankruptcies, and unemployment. The American clothing and steel industries are contemporary examples of sectors of the economy which feel themselves pinched by the ability of foreigners to provide similar goods to the American consumer at lower costs. Other countries encounter the identical problem: exports are desirable, but trade with the

The author is Assistant Professor of Economics at the University of Maryland.

United States depresses levels of production and employment in home industries operating in direct competition with the Americans.

The first lesson to be learned is that the international exchange of goods always involves a mixture of gains and losses. Exports represent a loss in the amount of goods available for home consumption, while imports flow into the economy and contribute to raising the real standard of living. But although exports raise employment and sales, imports compete with the products of U.S. firms and reduce these same two variables. Any intelligent assessment of the benefits of trade must balance the positive and negative effects of such trade. The value of the product losses should be compared with the value of the product gains, employment increases must be set off against the number thrown out of work, and larger export sales should be contrasted with sales declines in the import-damaged industries. Also of interest is the connection between trade and the long-term growth of the economy.

On the surface, toting up the consequence of international trade would appear to be an elementary undertaking. In practice, however, there are almost an infinite number of "suppose's" to worry about. Suppose an industry about to be damaged by imports has an effective lobby in Washington which can affect the votes of elected representatives and switch the sentiments of civil servants toward tariffs and other protective devices. Such an industry may pull the levers of political power and ensure that its jobs and its sales are preserved, regardless of the impact additional trade would have on national employment and revenues. Suppose the goods to be imported are primarily defense products, such as guns, tanks, and aircraft. Should a nation maintain no defense industries of its own and depend for its supplies on potentially hostile neighbors? Suppose the nation discovers that its role in international trade seems to be that of supplying one crop only, say cocoa beans, to world markets. Any look at the future suggests that chocolate milk shakes may go out of style, foul weather might upset crop production, or Dow Chemical may come up with a soybean substitute for chocolate. In light of these contingencies, what nation would want to risk its future welfare on a single export commodity?

International economics is the science of unraveling the mysteries surrounding the in's and out's of international commerce. It is dedicated to analyzing the conditions under which trade is desirable for a nation. International trade theory revolves around three basic questions: (1) What motivates trade between nations? (2) What fundamental characteristics of an economy determine the products to be traded? (3) What are the short- and long-term effects of trade on the economies of the participating nations? There are no firm, perfect answers to these questions, and they mostly serve to guide discussion of the benefits of trade. The history of international economic relations is of no less importance than theory in answering these questions, so some evidence from the past follows.

Two Patterns of Trade

A pattern of trade is a generalization about the content of a nation's trade (*what* is traded) and the direction of that trade (*with whom* the what is traded). In order to become seriously analytical, it is necessary to make a simple distinction between two types of trade. This complication is unfortunately necessary because both theory and history indicate that there are discernible differences in the motives for and consequences of trade, depending on which of two patterns of trade is under discussion. Table 1 displays in schematic form the two basic trade arrangements.

TABLE 1

WORLD TRADE PATTERNS

I. Colonial Trade Pattern		
Advanced Nation	M ◄——————— raw materials ——————— X X ——————— manufactured goods ——————► M	Backward Colony or Under-developed Nation
II. Industrial Trade Pattern		
Advanced Nation I	M ◄——— manufactured goods ——————— X X ——————— manufactured goods ——————► M	Advanced Nation II

In the colonial pattern (pattern I), an advanced nation imports raw materials and primary commodities (cotton, oil, ores, rubber, coffee) from one of her backward colonies. The industrial country processes or consumes these and, in return, ships finished goods of its own manufacture back to the colony. The colonial pattern, which dominated nineteenth-century trade relations on a worldwide basis, thus involves two distinct trading roles, each sustained by economic and political forces. The economically advanced country serves as an industrial center, pulling in raw

105

materials from its empire and, in turn, spewing forth the modern products of an arising capitalist state. After 1820, for instance, raw cotton from India was turned into finished textiles in England and sent back, only to destroy the livelihood of the native textile weavers. The modern heri- tage of the colonial pattern is the commerce which is conducted between developed countries and the now independent underdeveloped states.

The industrial pattern (pattern II), which has come to be the prevailing type of twentieth-century trade, involves trade in industrial goods between two nations at more or less equivalent stages of economic sophistication. In this scheme, machine tools exchange for television sets, aircraft for precision microscopes, or even Cadillacs for Jaguars. The industrial trade pattern has increasingly dominated world trade because the rate of expansion of trade in manufactured goods has outpaced that of raw materials. The North Atlantic has now become a pond of frenetic activity in trade between the United States, Canada, and the developed nations of Europe. The ascendance of the industrial pattern, vis-à-vis the colonial, has generated many difficulties for the nonindustrialized underdeveloped areas.

Motives for Trading and Not Trading

There are two sorts of motives for trade: economic and political. Economic motives may be summarized in two concepts: availability and cheapness. In a nutshell, what these two ideas signify is that a nation will buy where it can as cheaply as it can, and, on the selling side, a nation will offer what it can at the lowest possible cost. To elaborate, if a nation (or more realistically, a firm or agent) seeks to buy a good, it looks first for the possible suppliers—those capable of making the good available on any basis. If a U.S. firm, for example, needs iron ore, it will approach those countries with deposits—India and Sweden would be two possibilities. International shopping is analogous to searching for a desired commodity in any local store. Shoes are found in shoe stores, not hardware stores or hi-fi centers.

Although availability is a logical necessity for trade to occur, it is not a sufficient motivation in and of itself. To the sheer ability to mine, grow, or manufacture must be added the principle of cheapness. Without this additional economic rule, it would be impossible to determine who wants to import what from whom. Nations, like careful housewives, tend to buy where things are obtainable most cheaply. Much international trade is, therefore, a result of direct price comparisons in the international market place. If wool sells for $1.10 per pound delivered from New Zealand to New York and $1.25 delivered from Argentina, a buyer will make his deal for New Zealand wool. Similar decisions, reached after much "comparison shopping," explain most of the content and direction of world trade flows.

Although availability and cheapness together account for much that happens in the world's markets, political guidelines set up by various national governments, separately and in concert, are of equivalent significance. National and international political decisions design the framework of rules within which the game of international trade is played. Restrained by this political atmosphere, availability and cheapness are unleashed to operate as prime movers of trade.

One of the chief powers reserved by a nation-state is the control of commerce over its borders. Today all countries in the world exercise this right in varying degrees. Tariffs, pure food acts, arms controls, quotas, and outright prohibitions on trade are some of the more common tools of governments to control trade. In addition to these universal privileges, many nations attempt to use their political influence to manipulate their trade interests in other countries. Large, powerful countries are particularly well situated to advance their economic interests abroad through reliance on their political and military strength. Both the normal right of nation-states to control their trade and the ability of governments to advance economic interests through political intervention are the principal political guides underlying the colonial and industrial trade patterns.

Major industrial powers, such as Great Britain, France, the United States, and the Soviet Union have a natural interest in obtaining adequate, secure, and stable sources of raw materials for their industries. At the same time, large-scale firms in such economies are capable of producing vast quantities of goods, some of which can be disposed of in market outlets overseas. Consequently, a relatively small number of large companies have vested interests in developing overseas sources of supplies of locally unobtainable inputs and in securing markets for finished goods.[1]

The economic interests of these firms lie in maintaining access to the minerals, raw materials and, subsequently, product markets in the relatively backward parts of the world. They seek concessions, agreements,

---

[1] Two hundred corporations control two-thirds of the United States' industrial assets.

and treaties with the governments of the countries from which they obtain supplies and in which they sell their output. Much of this negotiation is of the sort which cannot be carried on between firm and government. This means that the national governments of the industrial states must intervene, an action which indicates the influence at home of the industrial giant.

It is inevitable that the economic aims of the major firms of the industrial states are intertwined with the political interests of their national governments. Trade concessions contracted between backward states and industrial powers during the period of colonization in the eighteenth and nineteenth centuries ordinarily culminated in the outright seizure of all political authority by the outside powers. Even in contemporary times, home governments are frequently drawn (or leap) into diplomatic maneuvers and military forays designed to help their industries strengthen overseas operations. In days not so far past, India, Africa, and China were bones of contention between many European and American firms and governments. Today, the oil of the Middle East lubricates an endless assortment of political and military stratagems.

The intimate relationship between international politics and world trade has never been more clearly discernible than in the great colonialist-imperialist period of the nineteenth and early twentieth centuries. There had been some penetration of the non-European parts of the globe before the English Industrial Revolution of 1780-1820, particularly of the relatively empty New World. But the wholesale carving up of Asia and Africa followed directly on the emergence of industrial forces which created simultaneous needs for materials and markets. The Industrial Revolution also provided the military technology which proved vital to the conquest of the desired areas. It is no rare coincidence that the major industrial state, Great Britain, was the paramount empire-builder and led all others in the masses of people and lands drawn under her political, military, and economic hegemony. By 1914, England, France, Germany, Holland, Belgium, Portugal and, on a minor scale, the United States had divided the world into colonies, tributary states, and spheres of economic and political influence.

The evolution of politically defined trading areas during the colonial period in no way invalidates the economic principles of availability and cheapness. Within the vast European empires, there were still active searches for the available and least-cost sources of supply. And, it was not particularly rare for colonies or mother countries to look outside their own trading sphere if a desired good was unavailable inside or if its cost was vastly higher than that which prevailed in another area. But almost without fail, colonies traded predominantly with their European overlord state.

As former colonies have become free, the common finding has been that it is easier to sever political ties than economic ones. Most under-developed countries still serve as raw material suppliers to the developed countries and as market places for the products of industrialized nations. Economic connections with the major world corporations are still in place. The remnants of colonial trade patterns are readily apparent, and it is not always easy or desirable to sweep them away and try to go it alone with no dependence on the world economy. A leap into the arms of the Soviet Bloc often results in the substitution of one set of dependency relations for another, with no amelioration of internal economic conditions.

In commercial relations among the developed nations (pattern II of Table 1), the economic principles of availability and cheapness come to the fore. Opportunities for political ascendancy and military enforcement of trade patterns are much fewer between states of roughly equal power, and there are sound economic gains from orderly trading in the community of advanced states. The lowest price is ordinarily the guiding force behind trade flows of the second class. Firms eager to expand their sales and profits, aggressive commercial entrepreneurs, and widely available trade information account for the stimulation of trade.

Even in the highly commercial environment of world industrial trade, political factors are of background consequence. They intrude in two forms: (1) tariffs, simply defined as any administratively imposed addition to the market price of an imported good, and (2) direct restrictions imposed by law on the direction or content of trade.

Imperial spheres of influence have been superseded in the main by these at-the-borders techniques of control.[2] But the net effect of such national controls on the level, composition, and direction of world trade today is probably at least as great as the grand schemes of the last cen-

---

[2] Although the imperial pattern dominated the nineteenth century, it is not an extinct phenomenon in the middle of the twentieth century. Portugal, for one, has major territorial possessions. And most underdeveloped countries have not broken out of the trade connections of the bygone era. By the same token, while the dominant techniques of control are more direct and apply at home rather than in far-flung dominions, tariffs and direct controls also existed in force in the earlier period.

tury. By raising the price of an import in the home market, tariffs run directly contrary to the rule of cheapness. An addition in price following the imposition of a tariff often diverts purchases from a low-cost foreign source to a home industry which otherwise would be struggling to survive.

Direct restrictions on trade are of major influence in many forms. In June, 1967, a temporary embargo was placed on arms shipments to the Middle East. Rhodesia bears world-supported trade sanctions on exports and imports placed there after her seizure of independence from England under terms which deprived the majority of the population of representation in the government. United States' citizens may not purchase anything coming from the People's Republic of China, nor can sales be made there. Trade with all socialist countries is heavily restricted, although trade between the United States, Russia, and Eastern Europe is expanding rapidly in recognition of joint advantages. Mutual agreements prevent Japanese textile manufacturers from shipping more than a fixed quota of finished goods to the United States.

Tariffs and direct regulations are the outcomes of decisions made through the political process. They are concrete manifestations of a country's belief that the national interest is best served by administrative (in contrast with market) controls over what is to be traded with whom. There are a number of possibly valid reasons for preferring administratively-controlled trade to cheapness-guided trade. Consider just three:

1. Defense considerations traditionally have been recognized as among the most plausible. The enemy, or potential enemy, is not to be traded with; domestic industries important to defense and essential raw materials should be protected. (Counterargument: Perhaps if we traded with them, neither of us would be so hostile. Networks of economic and political dependence tend to go together.)

2. It is acceptable to protect an industry, such as agriculture or steel in the United States, which is of sentimental and political importance. Any dying industry will plead most emotionally in legislative councils for its survival when it is being displaced by cheaper, more efficient foreign sources of supply. (Counterarguments: It does not pay to maintain a stable of aged dinosaurs. Moribund industries are a drag on economic growth and can only damage the long-term ability of the nation to compete in international commerce.) The major thing to be considered in applying tariffs

or direct protection is that there is ordinarily an economic cost involved. If the nation is willing and able to afford economic costs, then of course it should go ahead. The real danger is that powerful special-interest groups will secure tariff-protected sanctuaries from competition and thus damage the larger national interest in obtaining the most goods at the lowest cost.

3. Perhaps the most legitimate of all reasons for protection from foreign competition arises when a country wants to create a particular new industry. It stands to reason that foreign firms with which the newcomer will contend for sales will not be overjoyed at the prospect of a modern competitor joining their ranks. If the domestic market is not protected by tariffs or direct measures, foreign firms will dump cut-rate goods into the country and sabotage the effort to raise the new firm. Protection is therefore usually needed to shelter the "infant industry," as it is usually called, until it is firmly established and can compete on an equal, or perhaps superior, footing with the old-line firms. Underdeveloped countries, who lag desperately behind in industrialization, are especially prone to utilize protective devices to foster new enterprises.

If carefully applied, there is no sound route for disagreement with the infant industry argument. Unhappily, a number of protected infant industries look suspiciously like ancient gnomes resting in the cradle of privilege. Even if an infant is an infant and does plan to grow up, a direct cash subsidy from the government can sustain the enterprise in its formative years. And with the subsidy, the people and the administration have an exact figure for the national cost burden of maintaining the firm. The protected, inefficient firm and its cronies in power are not, of course, eager to have such a cost figure general knowledge. A tariff is so much more discreet.

In summary, the rules of availability and cheapness have operated to shape both the colonial and industrial patterns of trade. Empire building, defense interests, and the desire to develop an industrial base are among the political considerations which also motivate, restrict, and guide trade.

The Economic Basis for Trade

In order to penetrate further into understanding the circumstances under which trade occurs, it is necessary to take political constraints as given[3] and focus attention on the economic principles of availability and cheapness. In the colonial pattern, availability and cheapness depend on technology, resources, and the distribution of labor and capital in the world. The level of technological advance is of primary importance in determining the division of the world into advanced and backward portions. This can be called briefly the "relative state of development" concept. Economies at different levels of technological development specialize in different kinds of products for trade.

The needs of the developed states for materials and markets followed their nineteenth-century rush into industry. The backward regions of the world did not participate in the technological advance that has become a way of life in Europe and the United States. Colonies with favorable climates, large amounts of unskilled labor, and underutilized land were ideal gardens for requisite supplies. Mining and agricultural activities do not demand levels of technological advance beyond the easy reach of the peasant farmer or the native laborer. Territories favored with natural supplies of petroleum, gold, copper, iron, and the other necessities of the European economy are especially likely to enjoy a short-run export boom. But peasant agriculture, mining, and plantations do not appear to generate technological advance with the same quickness and regularity as manufacturing. This means that colonies find themselves trapped into specializing in lines of commerce which are not conducive to their further development and trade.

The relative state of development concept explains how the colonial pattern was the consequence of a polarization of the world's economies into industrial and raw materials producers. The developed countries were suited to the mass production of cheap industrial goods. While these nations had cost advantages in finished goods, their colonies turned out low-cost industrial inputs. The rules of availability and cheapness thus acted, in compliance with the politically set outlines of the colonial empires, to direct trade flows between the colonies and the imperial states.

In the industrial pattern of trade, technological advantage also ap-

---

[3] The phrases "taken as given," "given X, Y, and Z," or "hold constant" are economists' jargon for "ignoring." The effects of deliberately limiting the field of inquiry are (1) to simplify the world so that economists (and their public) can reason and learn about it in manageable terms and (2) to fail to consider some of the more important elements of the situation being analyzed. If the gains from (1) exceed the losses from (2), then the science increases in sophistication; if not, economics becomes irrelevant sophistry.

pears as a primary determinant of availability and price advantage. The difference in this case is that technological variations are more subtle than the gross discrepancy between advanced and backward states. Nations tend to make and trade goods which are unavailable elsewhere, or cheaper goods, on the basis of innovations and cost reductions associated with technological supremacies in highly specialized lines of commerce. The United States, for example, is superior in producing large cars, Europe in building smaller cars. The United States is able to sell to Europe ordinary commercial aircraft such as the Boeing 707, only to have to purchase the next generation of supersonic commercial planes from a British-French consortium. Technological progress now seems safely built into the American and European economies. Expenditures on research and development of new ideas, products, and processes undoubtedly will continue to grow. Technological advances will thus continue to propel trade forward for nations of the dynamic industrial pattern.[4]

The Effects of Trade

The weighing of gains and losses from trade depends on an evaluation of the effects of trade on the trading countries. It is generally true that consumers will get more goods at lower prices. Another immediate, or short-run, impact of trade on the economy is to stimulate production and employment in the export industries and depress them on the import-competing side. Because export industries are presumed to be comparatively more efficient, the net production and employment effects are positive for the economy as a whole. Trade thus increasingly leads to specialization among the world's nations, as labor and production become increasingly centered on a few export industries and other nations are depended upon for a broader range of imports. The result is that each nation specializes in those areas in which it has a technological or resource advantage.

There also exist long-run effects on economic development as a result of trade. These must not be ignored in setting out a full accounting of the impact of trade on an economy. The major variables underlying

---

[4] On the connection between technology and trade, see: W. Gruber, D. Mehta, and R. Vernon, "The R&D Factor in International Trade and International Investment of United States Industries," and D. B. Keesing, "The Impact of Research and Development on United States Trade," both in the *Journal of Political Economy*, February, 1967.

113

economic development are the advance of technology, the spread of knowledge, and the enhancement of the skills of the population. Whether or not trade is conducive to improvement in these variables depends on which pattern of trade is operating. Historical experience and theory suggest strongly that one partner in the colonial pattern, the colony or underdeveloped area, does not experience long-term economic benefits from trade, although the industrial country does. In the industrial pattern, both partners apparently enjoy development gains as a consequence of their participation in trade.

Table 2 summarizes the probable net effects of trade under each of the trading patterns. In the short term, trade is beneficial to all parties. There is a movement of labor out of relatively inefficient industries into more productive export industries. Even in the colony or underdeveloped country there is likely to be a net gain in employment and productivity. The backward, isolated colony gains further from being brought into contact with the world economy. The increased use of money earned from selling crops or working in the mines and on the plantations increases the freedom of action of the peasants and laborers and may also be accompanied by a small, temporary rise in the real standard of living.

As the sole minus entry of Table 2 indicates, the picture of the long-run effects of trade differs sharply between the industrial economy and the colonial economy. Advanced countries, in either the colonial or industrial arrangement, benefit from the spread of knowledge and the improved skills of the labor force which follow from trade and specialization. Concentration on a few areas of advantage also stimulates further techni-

TABLE 2

PROBABLE NET EFFECTS OF TRADE

I. Colonial Pattern		
	Short Term	Long Term or Developmental
A. Advanced Country	+	+
B. Colony/Underdeveloped Country	+	—

II. Industrial Pattern		
	Short Term	Long Term or Developmental
A. Advanced Country I	+	+
B. Advanced Country II	+	+

cal advances. All in all, international trade makes its contribution to the general upward spiral of development typical of Europe and the English-speaking countries.

In the colonial economies of the nineteenth century and the under-developed countries of the mid-twentieth, long-term economic develop-ment has simply not occurred. The level of living in Asia and Africa, in particular, is probably no better for the average man than it was at the time of the European conquests two centuries ago. This is odd, because the first rush of commerce between Europe and the remote areas of the world was a clear stimulus to economic activity. The nineteenth century, in which the colonial pattern held sway, was truly a golden age of trade. Spurred by improvements in ocean transport, railways, and port facilities which reduced the cost of shipping, colonies and imperial countries ex-changed unprecedented amounts of goods. Tea, rubber, and coffee plan-tations were carved out in the colonies; mining and drilling operations were begun; and the peasant, who suddenly discovered that his rice, wheat, or cotton was in great demand, expanded his acreage, output, and income.

In the perspective of several generations, the happy prospects gen-erated by the first wave of colonial development were not realized. The expansion of plantations, mining, and peasant agriculture did not really require any new techniques, skills, or knowledge. A strong back was vir-tually all that was needed. Europeans occupied posts demanding special talent and were not inclined to establish educational systems which would train natives to replace them. Where workers were scarce, immigration from India or China provided cheap labor for the plantations and mines, depressing local wages. Population expanded rapidly in underdeveloped areas following the introduction of Western standards of public health and medical care. These population increases spread over the available lands and made it impossible further to expand output for export. In gen-eral, colonial governments were the creatures of the mother country and did little or nothing to aid the development of the local economies. As a consequence of all these circumstances, the colonies found themselves "locked into" the production of raw materials, a kind of economic spe-cialization which followed from their contact with the European econ-omy. Development effects of trade—particularly in the area of dynamic technology—were sadly lacking.

Underdeveloped countries who are still trapped into the colonial pattern of trade find even today that international trade does not bring benefits to them. Often, their rich mineral and petroleum resources are being rapidly depleted without creating any lasting replacement industries. Because of specialization in only two or three products, exports of the underdeveloped countries are particularly susceptible to weather, price changes, and business cycles. Such fluctuations are likely to upset the growth of the whole economy and make planning for future development more difficult.

Policies and Prospects

In advanced countries, most economists and policy makers are aware of the manner in which trade operates to create generally beneficial short- and long-term gains from trade. As a consequence, the removal of needless, politically inspired restrictions on trade has continued since World War II. There has been a series of international conferences which have succeeded in reducing tariffs and eliminating direct barriers to trade. It is entirely likely that trade will become even freer in the future, particularly between the disintegrating Soviet Bloc and the so-called Free World.

In the "Third World," as the French like to call the underdeveloped areas, economists and politicians also recognize the situation they have inherited.[5] They do not believe that free trade, following the old colonial pattern, will assist their efforts to develop. There is therefore great emphasis on the administrative control of trade. Indeed, not only do the spokesmen of these nonindustrial regions feel that they should protect their own new industries from unrestricted foreign competition, but they have recently urged that the developed countries grant their products preferential entry. This would mean that these goods, especially industrial products beginning to be produced in the currently backward areas, would have created for them special price advantages over home goods and those imported from other industrial areas. This would mark a kind of reverse colonialism in which political decisions override once more the economic rules of availability and cheapness. While it is not at all apparent that this policy would be the wisest course to take to solve the trade and development difficulties of the underdeveloped countries, the fact

---

[5] It is unfortunate that a number of economists and policy advisers in the developed countries misapply the lessons of their own experience to the underdeveloped areas. They fail to distinguish the beneficial impact of trade on their economies from the disappointing long-term effects of trade on development of a backward area.

that it is seriously presented indicates these countries' despair at being left to flounder in the backwaters of international commerce.

Questions for Thought and Discussion

1. There are two sorts of motives for trade—economic and political. What separate factors explain and lie behind these two different motives? Are the two motives related?
2. We know that trade is generally advantageous. Under what conditions might trade be disadvantageous for a developed country? For an underdeveloped country?
3. What is the importance of the "relative state of development" concept? Discuss the importance of technology in determining what nations will trade.

Section IV

MONEY AND MONETARY POLICY

MONETARY ANALYSIS IN ECONOMIC HISTORY

Thomas Mayor

The fundamental basis of all societies, past or present, is the production and distribution of those items which make life both possible and
enjoyable. Money and monetary institutions derive their importance,
their very reason for being, from the crucial role they play in this economic process. Without a smoothly functioning monetary system, the
efficient operation of economic life and all that it supports in all societies,
except perhaps for the highly primitive or the highly sophisticated,
would be extremely difficult.

If that is indeed the case, curiosity might lead us to pose the following queries: (1) What sorts of historical events does money affect? (2) In
what way and to what extent are they affected? (3) What explanations
or theories do we have to account for the influence that money is thought
to exert on these historical events? Unfortunately, the answers are not
simple. On the contrary, they are often quite complex and frequently
controversial, even today when economists know more than ever about
the functioning of an economy.

Nevertheless, modern scholars generally agree that money can have
important effects on a broad range of human activities. In precapitalist
or underdeveloped societies, the introduction of money and monetary
transactions is often thought to be a significant catalyst for promoting
economic and social change. Some historians go so far as to stress, perhaps over-stress, the causal role played by money in the early development of capitalism in Europe and the attendant rise is market-oriented
production. Some specialists in economic development emphasize the

The author is Assistant Professor of Economics at the University of Maryland.

importance of money in the economic progress of the underdeveloped portions of the modern world.

In addition, money and monetary disorders are thought to affect the overall stability of the economy. For example, inflation, which is simply a general all-around increase in the prices of goods and services, is ordinarily associated with substantial increases in the quantity of money. Such was the case in Europe during the sixteenth century, in the southern states during the Civil War, in Germany during the period between the two world wars, and in China in the 1940's. Deflation, depression, and unemployment may also be the result of monetary disorders. In fact, some economists have argued that the great depression of the 1930's and the enormous social repercussions of that depression—fascism and world war—could have been avoided or at least substantially mitigated by a stronger set of monetary institutions and a policy which would have avoided the drastic decline in the quantity of money which occurred in the early phases of the crisis.

In order to see more clearly the connection between money and such historical events, let us examine, in turn, the meaning of money, the role of money in society, and some of the more important theories which help to explain how that role is played.

What Is Money?

Money can be, and has been, a variety of things. At one time or another societies have monetized such unlikely items as tortoise shells, woodpecker scalps, porpoise teeth, boar tusks, and, to be sure, wampum. But when societies reach a certain level of economic development money ordinarily assumes a more familiar form. In the civilized ancient world as well as in medieval Europe, money was usually synonymous with precious metals, gold and silver in particular. The relative popularity and widespread use of these metals is understandable. They are virtually indestructible, easily transported, of constant and determinable quality, and limited in supply—attributes particularly appropriate for a monetary commodity.

In the past century or two, the economically advanced countries have gradually switched from a money based on precious metals to a money based on credit. In the United States, for example, money is usually defined as currency in circulation (paper money and coins) and checking accounts, which are sometimes called demand deposits. Neither type of money has a significant nonmonetary value, although some coins do possess a high, albeit declining, content of expensive metals. Actually, if the governments of the world were to release their gold stocks and refrain from subsequent purchases (in the United States the government buys and sells gold at $35 an ounce), the value of gold would decline precipitously. It is quite literally true that gold derives its value from money rather than vice versa, as is sometimes thought.

While the definition of money can not be completely clear-cut, money has customarily been thought of as anything which is generally used as a means of payment. Currency and demand deposits meet this test. What about savings accounts, which are often called time deposits? Since they do not meet the test, most economists do not consider them to be money. But some do.

What Are the Functions of Money?

In order to analyze the connection between money and historical events, we need to know more than simply what money is. Specifically, we need to know, among other things, how money functions in an economy, what role it plays, and how this role may vary with different types of societies and different historical periods.

It is, of course, possible to conduct the important business of an economy without the use of money. But think how difficult it would be in any other than the most primitive of economies. Without money, for example, a shoemaker who wished to purchase a loaf of bread would have to find a baker who simultaneously wished to purchase a pair of shoes or, failing that, some third party who was willing to accept shoes in exchange for some product desired by the baker. And think how much more difficult the situation would be if, as we know to be the case, a pair of shoes ordinarily exchanges for many loaves of bread. Is the baker to accept a tenth of a shoe in exchange for a loaf of bread? Or is the shoemaker to accept 120 loaves of bread when he only wants one? Moreover, the shoemaker's difficulty would not end here, for without the use of money he could not conveniently measure his costs, revenues, or profits. Furthermore, if he wished to sell his shoes on credit or to purchase raw materials on credit, how would payment be arranged? Individuals could conceivably agree on payment in terms of some specific commodity (shoes, for example), but this would be fraught with difficulties. What if one of the persons involved did not want repayment in shoes? Also, how would the quality of the repaid commodity be controlled? Similar difficulties arise if the shoemaker wished to save. Is he to save by accumulating shoes? Certainly that would not be a desirable way of doing so.

Fortunately, money is able to eliminate these problems by performing four functions, each of which counteracts one of the specific shortcomings of barter encountered by our hypothetical shoemaker. In these functions, money serves as (1) a unit of account, (2) a means of exchange, (3) a standard of deferred payment, and (4) a store of value.

Once a society develops even a modest amount of specialization and exchange, the temptation to invent money is virtually irresistible. But what sort of commodity will serve as money? Obviously, only one which avoids most, if not all, of the problems which plagued our shoemaker. In order to do this, the commodity must have a low or nonexistent cost of storage and transportation and have a relatively stable and determinable value. But it is not necessary for the commodity to be officially dubbed "money" by the authorities, for even without a government to establish and to regulate a monetary system, some commodity —the one which demonstrates most strongly these desired attributes— will likely emerge as money. An attempt to destroy money in an advanced economy is bound to fail, for even if the normal monetary commodity is destroyed, some other commodity will take its place. Cigarettes became just such a commodity when the German monetary system collapsed after World War II.

How Does Money Affect the Economy?

In outlining the specific functions of money, we noted that, once a certain stage of development has been reached, a money-using economy is likely to be more "efficient" (that is, able to produce more goods and services) than a barter economy. But this is not the only way in which money affects the overall workings of an economy. As we shall see, money can have an impact on such items as the general level of prices, the amount of employment, and the stability of business activities. To assess this impact, we need to examine some fundamentals of monetary theory.

The Quantity Theory

The quantity theory is one of the oldest and most successful monetary theories. Although in recent times it has been significantly modified, it

124

is still highly regarded and can be quite useful in historical analysis if judiciously employed.

The theory, simply stated, assumes that in a given economy the quantity of money, let us call it M, is a constant fraction, k, of the total value of annual production, PQ, where Q is a measure of "real" production and P is the average price of a unit of production. Symbolically,

$$M = kPQ$$

How do we rationalize this theory? One approach, popularized by the American economist Irving Fisher, is to suppose that (1) people hold money solely for transaction purposes (i.e., to use as a medium of exchange) and that (2) the amount of money they must hold for such purposes is proportional to the volume· of transactions. It then follows that if PQ is equal to the volume of transactions (or proportional, which is more likely), PQ will also be proportional to the stock of money, as is suggested by the equation $M = kPQ$.

If we continue to follow this interpretation, the reciprocal of k may be thought of as the "income velocity of money" because it measures the number of times the money supply "changes hands" during the year $(1/k = PQ/M)$. According to Fisher, this velocity is largely determined by time lags between receipts and expenditures. People do not wish to hold money for its own sake. They prefer to spend it on commodities or to lend it at interest to someone who does. Thus, people hold money balances but only in order to meet their bills during periods in which they have insufficient receipts.

How does the quantity theory work? Let us suppose, for example, that the supply of money rises. If the economy is initially producing at its capacity with all resources fully employed, then Q cannot increase. And according to the quantity theory, the general price level, represented by P, will have to rise proportionally because, at the initial level of PQ, people find that they have larger cash balances than they require, inducing them to spend their extra cash, bidding up prices in the process.

On the other hand, if the quantity of money should fall, the theory suggests that people will reduce their spending in an attempt to increase their cash balances. They will be content only when PQ has fallen far enough for the new stock of money to be sufficient for transaction purposes. At that point, the value of production will just equal the amount of spending which is forthcoming. Looked at from another still simpler (though not necessarily more· correct) viewpoint, when the stock of money falls, spending must fall, because money circulates at a fixed velocity. This is, of course, very close to Fisher's conception of the quantity theory.

Modern Monetary Theory

While the quantity theory may be a useful first approximation, it has undergone considerable revision and refinement in recent times, especially since the important work of John Maynard Keynes which appeared in the late 1930's. The revisions are predicated on two grounds, the first theoretical and the second empirical. Let us briefly examine each in turn.

Theoretically, the quantity theory seems to rest on the assumption that the "means of exchange" function of money is paramount. People are assumed to hold money because it is the generally recognized means of making payments. But what if we consider the implications of the "store of value" function? If people hold money as a means of storing wealth, the quantity of money they demand may be quite variable, for they may attempt to convert wealth into money whenever business conditions seem unfavorable, or, when conditions seem good, the demand for money may fall. In addition, modern theory presumes that when the expected rate of return on business investments or bonds rises (falls) people would demand less (more) money, since these other alternative ways of holding wealth would become increasingly attractive. Because of these considerations, modern theory frequently assumes that the demand for money depends partly on transactions requirements and partly on store of value requirements.

The empirical evidence also casts doubt on the quantity theory. The velocity of money fluctuates greatly in the short-run, and there is evidence that velocity is affected by changes in the yields of alternative ways of holding wealth.

How Can Monetary Theory Be Applied to Historical Analysis?

Building upon the very elementary analysis of the preceding sections, let us consider two recurrent problems in economic history, both of which are related to the way in which money affects economic phenomena.

Inflation and Growth

One of the important issues in economic history is the impact that inflation has on economic progress. The issue was raised by Earl Hamilton in the late 1920's when he attempted to explain the economic growth of sixteenth and seventeenth century England as the result of a large increase in the supply of money, occasioned by the influx of precious metals from the New World. Hamilton's argument is that the rise in prices caused a redistribution of income in favor of capitalists. Since capitalists of this period probably saved a relatively large part of their income, the argument implies that an increase in the supply of money stimulated capital accumulation and economic growth.

As is often the case, this historical issue is not without its contemporary meaning. Today, for example, specialists in the problems of underdeveloped countries still debate the effects of inflation. Many local experts, particularly in Latin America, argue that inflation is a necessary, and perhaps beneficial, accompaniment of economic growth. On the other side of the argument are aligned many experts in the developed countries as well as the official policy of the influential International Monetary Fund.

Without becoming too embroiled in this debate, let us examine Hamilton's thesis a bit more closely. According to the quantity theory, an increase in the supply of money (whether or not it comes about through the discovery of new sources of precious metals) will raise the price level provided that real output does not grow as fast. Thus, if real output during the sixteenth and seventeenth centuries was growing at approximately 2 per cent per year, the supply of money would have to have risen at something greater than 2 per cent (assuming a constant income velocity of money) in order to have caused a general increase in prices. This does not appear to be unreasonable.

We now come to the second aspect of the thesis. Did an increase in the quantity of money, and the resulting inflation, cause a redistribution of income in favor of capitalists? Thus far, we have developed no theory to handle this question. Traditional economics, of which the quantity theory is a part, teaches that changes in the quantity of money affect the price level and nothing else. The distribution of income in capitalist economies is thought to be determined exclusively by such nonmonetary factors as the supplies of capital and labor, the technical

127

knowledge of society, and the institutional arrangements which determine the relative bargaining power of various groups.

Is there any reason to challenge this traditional view? Perhaps there is, at least on two grounds. First, the evidence on business cycles in advanced capitalist economies suggests that profits are very sensitive to the stage of the cycle. On the upswing, profits rise relative to wages; and on the downswing, the reverse takes place. Very often, an increase in the quantity of money will trigger an upswing of the cycle (if output is less than full capacity, an increase in the quantity of money may cause spending to rise and consequently real output) and indirectly an increase in the share of national income accruing to capitalists. The evidence for this behavior is unmistakeable. But could this explain the probable rise in capital's share of income in the sixteenth and seventeenth centuries? The answer is "probably not." Experience with various types of modern economies tells us that these monetary-induced shifts in income distribution do not persist over long periods of time.

A second possibility is that the increased supplies of money initially went to capitalists, perhaps through their earnings in foreign trade, and that they were able to bid resources away from other groups in that economy. However, this explanation appears inadequate for anything other than a once-and-for-all change in the distribution of income, whereas the evidence points to a gradual shift in income distribution over a relatively long period of time.

What are we left with? Our analysis does indeed point to the crucial role played by money in inflationary situations. But if we are looking for an explanation of substantial long-run changes in the distribution of income, our search should not concentrate on purely monetary phenomena. More important may be the many "real" forces which operate on the distribution of income. Population changes and changes in institutional arrangements which favored the entrepreneurial class are possible candidates for investigation.

Economic Stability

A second problem which we may examine involves the cyclical fluctuations which occur in economic activity. Apparently these fluctuations or business cycles, as they are frequently called, owe their origin to the establishment of capitalist institutions, for as these institutions developed and matured so did the inherent tendency toward cyclical instability. The fact that the business cycle has been relatively mild in the post-World War II period does not imply a reversal of the tendency. On the contrary, the relative stability in the recent period, largely brought about by an expanded and increasingly active role of the federal government, is a reflection of the failure of laissez-faire institutions to cope with the problem of instability and the accompanying fluctuations in employment. To be sure, in precapitalist societies, fluctuations in economic activity take place. But most of these disturbances are due to changes in weather conditions, wars, disruptions of trade routes, and similar circumstances. Business cycles as a regular characteristic of the economy are notably absent or at least very weak.

How can we explain the relationship between instability and the development of capitalism, assuming that it exists? Let us begin by considering a hypothetical barter economy where money is not used and production is conducted by individual peasants and artisans for a local market. Is a depression or the problem of "general overproduction" likely to occur? The answer is clearly "no." If a member of this mythical society wishes to obtain some given commodity in the market place, he simply produces some other commodity which can be exchanged for the one he desires. In this case, "Say's Law" prevails, i.e., "supply creates its own demand," because no one produces unless he also intends to spend.

Let us now complicate the analysis by introducing money into our hypothetical economy so that peasants and artisans take their goods to market and exchange them for money rather than goods. They may keep or spend the money as they see fit. Does Say's Law also hold under these new conditions? Evidently not, for an increase in the supply of goods does not necessarily evoke a corresponding increase in demand. Suppose, as an illustration, that each producer plans to exchange his goods only for money. Quite obviously, no goods will be sold as long as these plans are maintained, since there will be no buyers. Thus, the possibility of a "glut" on the market or "general overproduction" does exist in a monetary economy.

There are, however, several reasons to suppose that any such "overproduction" will be slight in this simple type of economy. To begin with, production is primarily directed toward consumption so that a substantial desire for more money as a store of value is not terribly likely. Moreover, there is little risk in production, since producers do not have to contend with the problems of capitalist entrepreneurs—the preservation of capital, the payment of debts, the avoidance of bankruptcy, and similar factors. And since there is little risk, the demand for money as a safe store of value is likely to be less volatile. Finally, there is reason to suspect that prices would be relatively flexible in such an economy for many of the same reasons. This implies that any glut on the market would be short-lived because falling prices would induce some holder of money to purchase goods.

However, when an economy develops basically capitalist institutions, the problem of overproduction becomes more serious. The very history of capitalism, at least until recent times, is a succession of booms and busts. Each panic was accompanied by an apparent scarcity of money and a general inability of entrepreneurs to convert their unsold goods into money. By all outward appearances, therefore, money played an important role in the cycle, so much so that many reformers concentrated their attention on monetary matters. American populists, for example, favored a policy of making money abundant through various "easy money" schemes. In England, reformers such as Robert Owen went so far as to advocate the complete abolition of money. Largely overlooked in these debates was the fact that it is the institutional arrangements of society which dictate the properties of money, rather than something intrinsic in money itself.

In short, the increasing specialization of production which is so important to economic progress requires the use of money. But once the use of money takes place in a market economy there is no guarantee that there will always be sufficient demand to purchase all of the goods and services that people wish to produce. This is especially true when capitalist institutions are developed.

Let us make one final comment. Certainly money is important. However, money alone is not the key to an understanding of all economic events. What happens in an economy is still very largely the result of nonmonetary factors.

Questions for Thought and Discussion

1. How is the current development of credit cards likely to affect the demand for money? Could credit card arrangements be considered as money?
2. Distinguish between the microeconomic and macroeconomic functions of money.

3. Which function of money suggests that the demand for money may depend upon the rate of interest? Why?
4. What sort of problems can an economy encounter if its money is mismanaged? Explain how these problems may arise and how they can be cured.

THE ECONOMICS OF CENTRAL BANKING

Ogden O. Allsbrook

Introduction

One of the most important institutions in a market economy is the central bank. A central bank's activities influence many sectors of the economy in a general manner. In the United States, the Federal Reserve System is the central bank. This bank establishes the policy required to manage the money supply, including credit, and directs the economy toward certain basic macroeconomic objectives.

The Federal Reserve System seeks to achieve various economic objectives through monetary and credit policy. The general objectives of monetary policy are maintenance of the international value of our currency, preservation of a reasonable degree of stability in domestic prices, the achievement and maintenance of full employment and output, and the creation of an economic climate whereby employment, output, and real income will grow.

Each of these objectives is important, but all are not equally important. The reason for this lies in the pattern of change generic to an industrial economy. At one moment, for example, there may be difficulty in our balance of payments with foreign nations. Here is where the first objective can be most important. In addition, a changing political environment can produce a reordering of the priority of economic objectives. One political party may generally emphasize price stability while another opts for rapid economic growth with inflation. The choice of objectives is, to some extent, a rational economic choice. But when

The author is an Assistant Professor of Economics at the University of Georgia.

133

a conflict in objectives occurs, such that one objective may be pursued only at the expense of another objective, any decision must be based on some normative or subjective criterion.

It is these objectives to which all questions of monetary policy must finally be addressed. As the reader becomes aware of the characteristics, background, and operations of the Federal Reserve System, we hope that he will be better equipped to evaluate the propriety of the objectives served by monetary policy.

Characteristics

A central bank has certain characteristics which differentiate it from ordinary commercial banks and enable it to perform in a regulatory capacity. One primary characteristic setting the central bank apart from other banks in a nation is the difference in motivation. A central bank acts as an intermediary in regulating the economic activity of a nation through its member commercial banks. It acts without concern for its own profit. A commercial member bank acts as any other business seeking to realize profit through its banking activities. Commercial banks are owned and operated as corporations, and corporations have an obligation to seek to make profits for their shareholders. The central bank in this country is owned by its member banks and may or may not realize profit. Profit is only incidental to the operations of the Federal Reserve System, and is not a primary motive in its regulation of the "owners".

The second major difference between the Federal Reserve Bank and commercial banks is the type of customer served. The member banks accept the general public as their customers, providing services such as checking accounts, savings accounts, loans and other financial services, and even correspondent services for other commercial banks. The central bank and its branches in each of the 12 Federal Reserve districts accept only member banks (and nonmember banks under certain conditions), mutual savings banks, trust companies, and industrial banks as customers; in addition, the Federal Reserve System acts as the fiscal agent for the United States Government.

A third important distinction between the central bank and commercial banks is almost purely physical. In this country the power to issue the bulk of "money" known as currency is held by the Federal Reserve System, with the U.S. Treasury issuing the remainder of our cash money supply, largely coinage. The bills circulating among us today are almost entirely "Federal Reserve Notes." The paper currency issued by the U.S. Treasury is quantitatively not very important. The currency money (recognized bills and coin) is insignificant when compared to the "money" created through the commercial banks under the regulation of the Federal Reserve System. The enormous bulk of the total U.S. money supply is in the form of demand deposits lying in commercial banks and representing, to the commercial banks, liabilities, since they are promises to pay cash (currency or coin) upon demand. This distinction is most important and deserves further elaboration.

Commercial banks obtained these liabilities, or demand deposits, when people entrusted their money to them for safekeeping. What is done with these deposits? This is explained by what has come to be called the "goldsmith's principle." If people deposit their money earnings and savings with banks and adopt the bank as a clearinghouse for the settlement of debts through a checking system of payment, it is clear that much of the money which circulates is no longer demanded in currency or coin but is merely transferred, accounting-wise, to other checking accounts or banks. These transfers of funds by check become deposits in another party's account and the next party, in turn, may repeat the procedure. As the practice has developed, enough trust has been placed in this system to permit banks to realize that a safe margin of cash to have on hand against the occurrence of a demand for cash averages about 20 per cent or less of total deposits.

This application of the "goldsmith's principle" to commercial banking is sanctioned by the Federal Reserve System and is known as "fractional reserve" banking. The Fed may, at its discretion, alter the margin of cash required to be held on hand by its member banks. In addition, the Federal Reserve may establish different reserve requirements for different areas which do not have the same requirements for cash on hand due to geographical, institutional, or cultural reasons. In recent years, alteration of the reserve requirements to meet changing business or economic conditions has fallen into disuse as a tool of monetary policy.

The application of the goldsmith's principle, first observed in the days when goldsmiths acted as quasi-bankers to merchants and patrons alike, is a common principle in the relationship between both the individual and his commercial bank and the commercial bank and the central bank. The germ of the notion is that the individual anticipates an average daily cash requirement of not more than 20 per cent of his monetary assets. This is his "required" cash estimate. The commercial bank anticipates an average daily cash requirement of not more than 20 per cent of the "cash" (deposits) entrusted to it by depositors. This is the "required reserve" necessary to maintain operability of a bank.

Periodically, violations of the goldsmith's principle occur, such as at Christmas time when greater than normal use for each is found due to the abnormally large number of relatively small items purchased. When these deviations from "normal" behavior occur, they present a crisis to an individual or a bank unprepared for the event. To the individual at the cash register with insufficient cash to cover his purchases, the alternatives are a check to cover his purchases, a credit account to charge purchases, or returning the excess purchases to the shelves. To the banker at his window, faced with an abnormally large demand for cash by his depositors, the alternatives are a check written on his account at the Federal Reserve Bank, a "loan" negotiated with the Fed or a correspondent bank, or the rejection of claims for cash made on his bank by patrons because the bank was caught with "insufficient funds." The last alternative of the banker would force him to close his doors and, generally, has been a force in triggering "runs" on banks.

It is a primary goal of the Federal Reserve System to avert crises which could develop from deviations from the goldsmith's principle. Theoretically, these deviations might occur at any time, but generally can be predicted for certain periods based on historical observation of seasonal variations and categorically-typed events.

In overcoming irregular demands for cash on banks, the central bank must become, in effect, a "bankers' bank." In acting to provide funds for commercial banks in cases of need, the Fed may become a lender-of-last-resort if other sources, notably correspondent banks, prove inadequate in providing relief to a distressed bank. When the Fed acts to relieve a bank suffering large cash drains, it normally makes a loan to the particular bank and charges for this service at the current *discount rate*, which is the interest rate charged to commercial banks for borrowing at the central bank. Member banks generally receive priority and specifically receive a lower discount rate than nonmember banks. Another means by which commercial banks may gain cash is to sell to the Fed "commercial paper" (loans) which they hold. When the commercial bank sells the "paper" to the Fed, the latter "buys" by crediting the account of the member bank, thereby giving that bank excess reserves which may be drawn upon as required.

As a banker's bank, the Federal Reserve Bank is not only in a position to make loans to commercial banks when necessary, but also to act as a final clearinghouse for transactions among banks by drawing on the balance of one bank to pay another bank. In the everyday business of banking, the latter operation is extremely significant. Commercial banks must be able to meet exigencies such as heavy payments to depositors of other banks. To do this, the bank must control assets which can be rediscounted or pledged. This ability to convert assets readily to currency through the Fed is more generally known as "liquidity."

The primary responsibility of the central bank is to provide sufficient liquidity to support the real factors of economic activity. These real factors, such as available natural resources, technological conditions, productivity, stocks of capital, and the rest, are necessary to achieve any level of economic output. The output potential, however, can go unachieved without a money supply adequate to encourage the utilization of the factors of production with greater efficiency. The real economic factors are necessary for achieving any level of output but are insufficient to guarantee the achievement of the maximum output attainable. The real factors and monetary factors are complementary rather than substitutes for each other. Both are necessary conditions for an economy before any measure of economic growth can be realized and sustained. Neither is sufficient to bring about growth alone. An inadequate monetary policy can seriously retard growth, but an efficiently operating monetary policy is not in itself sufficient to produce real economic growth. The realization that money is command over resources rather than a resource per se is a big step toward correct analysis.

Insuring that the economy has sufficient liquidity at the right time and place can be aided or impeded, depending on whether the "unit" or "branch" banking system has developed under the central bank. With a unit banking system as in England and the United States, the central bank is a bankers' bank and unavailable for banking services to the general public. In England, however, the central bank is even more aloof from its customers, utilizing bill brokers to act as intermediaries between central and commercial banks. With a branch banking system, such as France and Belgium possess, the central bank is divided into a system of branch offices throughout the nation which serve individuals directly. In this case, the central bank functions as an agent to dispense banking services to the general public. There are some very beneficial aspects to this system from the viewpoint of a central banker. Generally, a branch banking system will aid in the flow of funds (liquidity) between areas. There is consequently easier access to liquidity on the part of the immediate customer. Under the unit banking system, commercial banks must first rely on correspondent banks to help overcome the divisional character of banking outlets to the general public. They may also seek funds from the central bank located at a distance, but the smoothness of fund transfers is obviously lacking when compared with the branch banking system.

Although the Federal Reserve System is broadly classified as a unit banking system, it has banks in each of twelve districts into which the country is divided; these district banks operate in a manner consistent with overall policy and speed in implementing this policy throughout the United States. To a large extent, then, there are at least some aspects of decentralization in the Federal Reserve System which compare with a branch banking system, if only physically. And even within districts, large distances are further abridged by having branches allocated to cities on the basis of markets and distance from the main district Federal Reserve Bank.

The current structure and institutions of the Federal Reserve System have evolved from the skeletons of earlier attempts to create a central bank and formally began with the passage of the Federal Reserve Act creating the Federal Reserve System in 1913. While earlier banking institutions never fully attained the scope of activity of the current system, attempts were made through the First Bank of the United States (1791-1811), the Second Bank of the United States (1816-1836), and the Independent Treasury System of the United States Treasury (1846-1920) to organize a means of developing strong central banking practices in the United States. It is quite possible that the Federal Reserve System would have met with the same lack of success as earlier systems had it been made a political scapegoat under the hand of an ineffectual central banker. The choice of Benjamin Strong as the first manager of the Federal Reserve System was probably the most significant development in shaping the policies of the Fed effectively within the permissive enacting legislation. It was with a firm view of what a central bank should be that Governor Strong guided the Federal Reserve System in the formative years of 1913 through 1928.

While the Federal Reserve Act became the foundation for our current central banking system, it is interesting to recall the alternative proposal for a central bank at that time, the Aldrich Plan. The Aldrich Plan called for a single central bank in Washington with branches in each of

15 districts. The Aldrich Plan differed from the Federal Reserve Act primarily in placing less autonomy with its district banks. This would have created a central bank without particular attention being given to remedying the existing problems of reserve concentration in New York and the cumbersome clearing and collection facilities for handling checks.

The Federal Reserve Act, as well as the alternative Aldrich Plan, grew directly out of the 1907 financial crisis in which the Independent Treasury System and the national banks foundered, resorting to the suspension of gold payments, cessation of banking operations, and resulting in the failure of hundreds of banks. This monumental crisis verified the suspicions of financial experts that the basic problem in the country's monetary arrangements was the lack of responsiveness of the money supply to the needs of the public. Inelasticity of the money supply was the fundamental defect that the creation of the Federal Reserve System was intended to reform.

The need to overcome the inelastic qualities of the money supply has been a recurrent theme in monetary history. Thus, the principal objective in constructing a Federal Reserve System was to guarantee an elastic money supply, one which is capable of expanding to meet the needs of an expanding real sector and is regulated to overcome the tendency toward unwarranted expansion and consequent inflation. The importance of an elastic money supply cannot be overstated. Without the responsibility for insuring the supply of money and credit just sufficient to balance aggregate supply and demand, little rationale for a truly central bank would exist.

In acting as guarantors of an elastic money supply, central banks must have a full range of powers, or tools, with which implementation of expansionary or restrictive policies may be pursued. In general, certain tools have evolved as major elements in shaping monetary policy while others have fallen into relative disuse. In order to catalog completely the authority with which the Federal Reserve System acts, a complete list of the policy tools available to the Fed will be discussed.

One of the most important tools of Federal Reserve policy is the ability to buy and sell Treasury obligations in the open market. It is today, in fact, the most powerful tool of monetary policy available by which the volume of commercial bank primary reserves is controlled and, therefore, the total money supply is regulated.

While the Federal Reserve Act enables Reserve banks to buy and sell several kinds of market instruments, only the purchase and sale of

U.S. Treasury obligations and bankers' acceptances have been significant in the history of the Federal Reserve. In fact, most transactions today involve only Treasury obligations. There are four classes of these "governments," ranging from short-term to long-term. Treasury bills and certificates of indebtedness are short-term, Treasury notes are intermediate-term, and Treasury bonds are long-term obligations. The availability of this Federal "debt" in such large quantities means that commercial banks are able to step into the open market and augment their secondary reserve portfolios as desired.

The Federal Reserve Banks buy and sell these Treasury obligations through the Federal Open Market Committee, which utilizes the Reserve banks as its agent in dealing with recognized dealers and dealer-banks. Once the Open Market Committee has directed the Reserve bank to buy or sell securities, the mechanical process of creating or destroying reserves of commercial banks follows. If a Reserve bank is directed to buy $500,000 of "governments" from recognized dealers, for example, it issues cashiers' checks on itself to cover the purchase. The security dealers involved then deposit the checks drawn on the Reserve bank in their commercial bank accounts. The commercial banks receiving these checks for deposit send them to the Reserve banks for payment, and the Reserve banks then credit the accounts of the commercial banks. This process, thus, has caused "money" to flow from the vaults of the Fed to the commercial banks, increasing the commercial banks' reserves. The commercial banks now find that they have surplus reserves and are thereby in a position to expand their loans or investments by the value of the surplus. The increase in money supply has thus been discharged into the economy. If, instead of recognized dealers selling securities to the Fed, the Fed buys securities from the large metropolitan commercial banks known as dealer-banks, the Fed then directly credits the reserve account of these banks for the value of the securities. In both cases, the aggregate effect on the total banking system as a whole is the same.

If the Federal Reserve System pursues a "restrictive" monetary policy through open market operations, it will attempt to reduce the supply of money in circulation by selling Treasury obligations. When the Fed sells these government securities, its buyers, who may be the securities dealers or dealer-banks, will make payment and thus find their liquidity position reduced. In the case of the dealers, their cashiers' checks are offered in payment to the Fed and allow the Fed to collect the funds from the commercial banks to credit to the Federal Reserve. This effectively withdraws money from circulation. In the case of the dealer-banks, the Fed merely debits the reserve accounts of these banks to cover their purchases of the Federal Open Market Committee's offering of securities for sale. Open market operations are generally considered to be superior to other tools of the Fed in regulating the money supply, both in direction and strength.

A second important tool of Federal Reserve policy is the ability to set and alter discount rates. The discount rate, as discussed earlier in regard to "bankers' banks," is the rate charged commercial banks for loans from the Federal Reserve Bank. The purpose of this operation is to prevent commercial banks from becoming insolvent when they find cash drains larger than anticipated. The discount mechanism permits the Fed to secure liquidity for any commercial bank which lacks sufficient primary reserves to meet the demands of business during a given period. Excessive use of the discount mechanism by a particular bank is discouraged by close supervision of banks' requests for loans.

A third tool of Federal Reserve policy is control over the reserve requirements of commercial banks. This tool is little employed because of the drastic nature of credit response to changing reserve requirements. Reserve requirements are analogous to the "goldsmith's principle" discussed earlier. Reserves are held to guarantee the ability of banks to meet demands for cash. For member banks of the Federal Reserve System, the reserves required to be held against their liabilities may be increased or decreased by the Fed. If reserve requirements are raised, a larger volume of reserves must be held by the member banks to "cover" their liabilities, demand deposits. If a member bank had reserves in excess of the legal minimum before reserve requirements were raised, its excess reserves have now been reduced or eliminated. If a member bank had just sufficient reserves before the requirements were raised, it now has insufficient reserves and must recall loans, sell current investments, or borrow funds (from a correspondent bank or the Fed) in order to regain its legally required reserve position. Conversely, if reserve requirements are lowered, a smaller volume of reserves now becomes sufficient to cover current liabilities of member banks. If, before the reduction in reserve requirements, a member bank had insufficient reserves and was faced with the task of restoring adequate reserves, the change in reserve requirements could automatically restore their reserve position to the proper legal minimum. If a member bank previously had excess reserves with which they might consider making further loans or buying more securities, they now have even more excess reserves after the reduction in reserve requirements.

141

They would now be able to expand loans or investments even more. In any event, the effect of lowering reserve requirements is to expand the effective money supply; conversely, raising reserve requirements "tightens" the money supply in the economy.

The computation of primary reserves can also affect the state of reserves of a member bank. Demand deposits, upon which legal required reserves of member banks are computed, include all demand liabilities less the total of certain assets which the member banks may collect upon demand. Currently, member banks must add all deposits of individuals, corporations, partnerships, and governmental units which are payable either on demand, within 30 days, or upon notice of less than 30 days, all the similar deposits of other banking institutions (domestic and foreign), certified checks and cashiers' checks outstanding, and letters of credit and travelers' checks which were sold for cash. From this total, a member bank is allowed to subtract the sum of deposits with other banks (incorporated) other than Reserve banks (subject to immediate withdrawal), cash items in the collection process, and cash items on hand which will be presented (for payment) or forwarded (for collection) within one day. It is the net of this computation which determines the base upon which the amount of reserves required by law is calculated. Currently, reserve requirements for demand deposits are 16.5 per cent for member banks in cities where Reserve banks are located and 12 per cent for member banks elsewhere. The reserve requirement for time deposits is 4 per cent for member banks everywhere.

Exactly what types of assets may be defined as reserves will also affect the state of reserves of a member bank. Currently, reserves held by the Federal Reserve Bank for the member bank and all cash held in vault may be included as reserves of the member bank. Member banks are not allowed to include as reserves deposits with one or more correspondent banks. State banks which are not members of the Federal Reserve System, however, are generally permitted to include these deposit balances with correspondent banks in satisfying legal reserve requirements. For a member bank, these interbank deposits serve rather as convenient accounts by which services of banks in other cities are obtained through the maintenance of sizeable balances, otherwise without charge.

Other important powers held by the Federal Reserve System generally are used in connection with the three major tools just discussed. That is, the actual implementation of certain operations is carried out through the institutional procedures of the Federal Reserve System, and these operations are designed to reinforce, where appropriate, the planned policies of the monetary authorities. Among these powers are the issuance of currency with full legal tender power and the rationing of loans in various direct ways. Other powers, or operations, include the responsibilities involved in acting as the chief fiscal agent of the United States government. Among these responsibilities are the holding of Treasury deposit balances, the cashing, clearing, and collection of checks drawn on or deposited to these balances (domestically and abroad), assistance in the sale of federal debt instruments and consequent exchanges and payment of interest and principal, and the purchase of securities for the Treasury's own special accounts. Additionally, the Reserve bank in New York is responsible for the operations of the Exchange Stabilization Fund. This Fund was established in 1934 to enable the Treasury to control the value of the U.S. dollar in international exchange. The Reserve banks also provide services to departments of the federal government, foreign governments, foreign central banks, and international financial institutions (such as the International Monetary Fund). The Federal Reserve System likewise acts as agent in supplying the nation with money created by the U.S. Treasury. Finally, although this listing is in no way exhaustive, the Fed's services in the administration of check clearing and collection for commercial banks are also noteworthy. As should now be clear, banking is big business and the regulation of banking through the Federal Reserve System is necessarily complex.

In using its powers to guarantee an elastic supply of money, the Federal Reserve System holds certain objectives paramount, as mentioned earlier. These are the objectives of economic policy which are charged to the Fed to implement insofar as the System's powers over monetary policy permit. We have seen that there are four objectives of major importance in determining the Federal Reserve's courses of action; to repeat, they are maintenance of reasonable stability of domestic prices, the preservation of the international value of domestic currency, the achievement and maintenance of full employment and national output, and the creation of a climate whereby employment, output, and real income grow.

Achievement of the four major objectives of economic policy, and consequently monetary policy, requires delicate consideration of the alternative courses of action. Because the application of one Federal Reserve power may correct an existing problem but create another, the use of monetary policy demands discretion in the solution of current problems. If lower interest rates and more liberal credit conditions are employed by the Fed to underwrite expansion in the money supply, the probable goal of the Fed is greater employment of economic resources and greater national output. But, in attempting to achieve the maximum potential from the economy at any given period, the danger of too rapid an expansion of credit and consequent inflation tempers the Fed's decisions. The goals of increased employment and output may conflict with the maintenance of stable domestic prices. The art of regulating the money supply has often been likened to walking a "razor's edge," indicating the difficult problems of judgment involved in applying monetary policy.

The considerations noted are essential to the policy maker. All too often, however, experience since World War II has reflected an obvious priority of goals without the balance accompanying an even-handed consideration of all goals. As evidence of the emphasis placed on high levels of employment and output, we need look only to the steady, though slow, increase in prices and subsequent erosion of a once favorable balance of payments situation. While it is not true that our recently worsening balance of payments results exclusively from emphasis on economic growth, the primacy of growth has certainly been an exacerbating factor.

To return to the example just cited, an increase in the price structure of an economy brought on by inflationary monetary policy can impair the successful pursuit of fully balanced growth. Before the abandonment of gold convertibility, when currency could be redeemed in gold at a fixed rate, the flexibility (elasticity) of the money supply was limited to the flexibility of the gold stock. Now, after the abandonment of gold convertibility, when currency can domestically be redeemed only for central bank notes and currency flows abroad can be controlled by restrictions on trade or payments; or by lowering exchange rates, the flexibility of the money supply is limited to the power and will of the Federal Reserve System and its governors, operating, as they do on the basis of the act which created the System, independently of the executive branch of the federal government. Previously, inflationary (and deflationary) safeguards were more automatic and impersonal in regulating certain excesses of economic activity. Under the gold standard domestic inflation would result in gold flows out of the country and thereby reduce the domestic monetary base. Today's safeguards against excessive inflation or deflation ·depend on action by the authorities rather than automatic "rules" under which the response of the monetary system would theoretically be self-initiating as critical circumstances developed.

The implementation of monetary policy through "rules" rather than the present "authority" remains a vision. Similar in principle to such automatic fiscal devices as the proposed negative income tax, monetary rules would provide an automatic response to other changes in the economic system, such as a lack of sufficient liquidity with the nonbanking public. With such rules, a rapid and timely response would replace a slower process of judgment and decision-making. Another characteristic of rules would be the certainty of action by monetary authorities which other sectors of the economy could rely on. An extension of the "rules" approach is the automatic growth in the money supply at a fixed annual rate of 3 per cent. This expansionary rule would reflect a timed and certain policy designed to accommodate anticipated real growth of the national economy. Such policies are designed to reduce the uncertainty of the future and, in the process, relieve one major cause of economic fluctuations. When plans for the future can be made on the bais of greater knowledge and information, there will be less chance for unexpected deviations from plans to occur. The assurance of continuity in growth of the money stock should qualify as genuine information about the future.

Under present arrangements, conflict among the objectives of economic policy is not extraordinary. It is unlikely that even with fixed monetary rules rather than discretionary authority guiding monetary policy could there be complete resolution of the conflicting objectives. Whichever system offers the better prospect for stability and economic growth should be embraced. At the present time, it must be clear that certain actions by the Federal Reserve System will improve some situations and worsen others. The choice of which goals are attained and which are bypassed now depends in large part on the judgment of the Fed in discerning the relative importance of the goals of the moment.

Questions for Thought and Discussion

1. What do you consider the weakest tool of control possessed by the Federal Reserve System. Would a reorganization of the powers of the Fed alter its ability to implement policy more effectively?

2. It has been argued that "elasticity" of the money supply is the most important objective of general monetary policy. Would it be fair to use "liquidity" as a synonym for "elasticity" in this context?

3. What case can be made for a fixed growth rule being applied to the monetary system in place of current arrangements? What arguments can be advanced in opposition to the fixed growth rule? Based on a summary of the arguments, which position appears to offer the better prospect for stability and responsiveness in the monetary system to an expanding economic environment?

4. Consider what you have read here, although far from complete, as history—a record of events until now. Given the developments leading to the current structure of banking in the United States, what appears to be the future of these institutions? Will the "checkless society", for example, based on automated debits and credits to individual accounts initiated at time of commercial transaction, alter the system only by degree or by more fundamental change. What is the likelihood that other more general proposals will come to be influencing factors on banking activity?

ECONOMIC IDEOLOGY AND CENTRAL BANKING

Thomas M. Havrilesky

Introduction

All nations in the Atlantic Community have institutions called central banks. All central banks examine and supervise commercial banks (institutions which make loans to business enterprises and offer checking account services). Central banks also serve as a depository for government checking accounts and help clear checks being transferred between commercial banks. In the modern world the most important function of the central bank is the regulation of the flow of bank credit and money.

Today, we tend to take central banks for granted. Yet, in most European countries, central banking only began in the late eighteenth century. Rather than view the purposes of central banking as an institutional absolute in economic life, one should critically examine the rationale for the behavior of central bankers.

The criteria by which money and credit are regulated (the "objectives" of monetary policy) have changed considerably since the emergence of the modern industrial state in the Western world. This change reflects, in part, an important evolution of Western economic ideology. At the outset of the Industrial Revolution and for many years afterward the flavor of political and economic thinking was strongly procepitalist. In contrast, the modern, activist, democratic welfare state has come to recognize the demands of diverse non-business interests.

This change in economic ideology is reflected in the changing objectives of central bank policy. Today, the most important criterion of

The author is Assistant Professor of Economics at the University of Maryland.

monetary management is the discretionary control of the business cycle and the payment's balance in the public interest. Surprisingly, a few decades ago such activity was seldom thought either proper or necessary. Instead, money was regulated so that it might soley and automatically serve the demands of the international and domestic business community with little regard to the business cycle. Before this monetary evolution can be more deeply explored, the basic concepts of money, credit, and central banking must be reviewed.

Some Basic Concepts

The economist's concept of money rests upon its modern use as a means of payment and a store of value. As a means of payment, money enables people to concentrate their productive efforts in fields where they are best prepared by aptitude, interests, or the advantages of privileged birth. By facilitating the exchange process, money allows individuals to specialize.

As a store of value, money is usually a safe means of holding wealth in a form which can be easily exchanged for earning assets such as stocks or bonds. It also is a relatively riskless way of being prepared for future contingencies such as accidents or illness.

Thus, money is important for the smooth operation of a modern economy, and its volume would seem to influence a nation's ability to produce goods and services. Practically all the money people use reaches them through banks either because it is borrowed from a bank or is held as a checking account at a bank. The ability of commercial banks to make loans and allow people to hold checking accounts is legally limited by the size of the bank's reserve deposit with the central bank.

As discussed in the work of Ogden Allsbrook in this book, the central bank can directly influence commercial bank reserves primarily by buying and selling government bonds with checks that are eventually deposited in commercial banks. As these checks are claims against the central bank, these purchases or sales directly affect the size of commercial bank reserve claims on the central bank.

By affecting commercial bank reserves, the central bank can directly affect the amount of bank borrowing and the amount of checking accounts in an economy. As seen in the article by Thomas Mayor in this book, this directly affects spending and total income in an economy. If there is too little borrowing and too little money supplied, a serious decline in spending could cause depression and unemployment. As the modern laborer, unlike his preindustrial counterpart, is not self-sufficient, unemployment is immensely harmful in today's Western economies.

Conversely, when there is too much money and credit, excessive spending by consumers and businessmen on a volume of goods and services limited by the capacity of the economy may cause price inflation. A rapid price inflation may harm individuals living on incomes which are not frequently raised to keep abreast of rising prices.

Changing Objectives of Monetary Policy

It is only in the last few decades that central banks have begun to take action to prevent heavy unemployment and rapid price inflation. This metamorphosis derives from the changing ideology of Western, and particularly American, economic life.

Until the nearly lethal Great Depression the free market mechanism was thought to forestall and/or correct the problems of unemployment and inflation. Corrective action by the central bank was therefore unnecessary.

In the most simple terms too much or too little purchasing power in the economy was believed to be self-correcting through the rise or fall of prices. For instance, if workers and goods were in surplus, wages and price were thought to be so flexible downward that the excesses would be absorbed at lower prices and wages.

The sobering development of the Great Depression of 1929-1941 demonstrated that these beliefs were hopelessly outmoded in a hyperorganized society where the monopoly power of unions and business firms eliminated much downward wage-price flexibility.

Before the Great Depression central bankers, as most of society, clung to the belief that the unfettered price mechanism would militate against dangerous swings in the business cycle. The central bank did not feel it necessary to provide additional reserves (and hence encourage credit and money supply expansion) during depression and to restrict reserve growth (and discourage credit and money supply expansion) during inflation. Instead, the amount of reserves was automatically regulated by international gold flows and the domestic demands of the business community. These criteria for bank reserve determination are implicit in the operational application of what economists call the (Classical) Gold Standard and the Commercial Loan Theory of Banking. As both satisfied the ideological prerequisite of minimal interference with the market, they delighted those members of the business community who already had inordinate market power, such as manufacturers and financiers, and immensely discomfited those groups, such as the nineteenth century farmer, which had little market power.

The (Classical) Gold Standard

During the nineteenth century most Western nations used gold or some other precious metal to balance their international accounts. The use of gold automatically was supposed to correct the market phenomena which caused an imbalance in international transactions. Importantly, this was achieved without considerable direct central bank interference with the supply of commercial bank reserves. In fact, the central bank, if it existed, merely assured the smooth functioning of the gold standard mechanism.

For example, if more British goods and services were purchased in the United States than American goods were sold in Great Britain (ostensibly because British goods were cheaper), the American banks, in order to settle the accounts, would have to ship gold to British banks. As gold was used as bank reserves, the British supply of money and credit would rise and the American supply of money and credit would fall. Since this directly affected spending, the British price level would tend to rise and the American price level would tend to fall. Such an equilibrating movement in the price levels of either country would tend to automatically correct the cause of the trade imbalance, because British goods and services *in toto* would no longer be "cheaper" than American goods and services. While the corrective mechanism could also work through interest rates as well as the level of income in either country, this paradigm essentially depicts the operation of an idealized gold standard.

This system was greatly favored by large manufacturers because it facilitated international trade and by commercial bankers because of its obvious automaticity and stability. The self interest of these parties was redounded in their support of *laissez faire* ideology. Control of a bank's gold reserves by blind market forces (over which large businesses exerted a dominant influence) was preferable to control by government or central banks (over which large businesses could conceivably have less influence).

On the other hand, the automatic gold standard was viewed with displeasure by other economic groups for two reasons. First, it encour-

150

aged, rather than quickly corrected, domestic price changes. Second, because the world's discovery of new gold was not growing as quickly in the nineteenth century as the world's trade, gold reserves and hence the money supply did not increase rapidly enough to prevent a secular (long-run) decline in the price level. In other words, as more and more goods and services were being exchanged with a relatively fixed money supply, the overall prices of goods and services had to decline. Unstable price levels and secular price deflation especially displeased the farmer-debtor class. They were forced to repay loans with dollars which could buy more goods and services for their banker-creditors than the dollars they originally borrowed from them.

In the late nineteenth century United States, this disaffection gave rise to the antideflation, easy-money political parties, *viz.* the Greenback, Silver, and Populist parties, as well as the rise of the easy-money wing of the Democratic party under William Jennings Bryan. In Europe, related controversies pitted a distrust of conscious, central bank control against the desire for "easy" (that is, *more*) money. The argument against easy money on either side of the Atlantic was supported by reference to historical episodes such as the French and American Revolutions when excessive supplying of currencies by government resulted in ruinous inflations.

Only after the technological development of the checking account and the discovery of Alaskan gold fields was money supply expansion sufficient to halt the deflationary process in advanced Western nations.

Nonetheless, the *laissez faire*, Gold Standard rationale for central banking prevailed well into the twentieth century. In fact, it was only after the debacle of 1929-1941 that the central banker's disregard of the domestic consequences of inflation and unemployment became indefensible.

The Commercial Loan Theory of Banking

Bank reserves were not only influenced by gold flows but also could be affected by the commercial bank's borrowing reserves from the central bank. In the United States after the Federal Reserve Act of 1913, the dominant role of the central bank was to extend loans to commercial banks who, in turn, were extending loans to businesses to meet their commercial needs. As the recurring nineteenth century financial panics demonstrated a nation was courting disaster if it could not meet these needs by instituting a central bank which could readily supply reserves. In the pre-Federal Reserve era, commercial banks were often forced to sell their financial (paper) assets and meet the loan and currency demands of businessmen and farmers. This, in turn, would precipitate a general price decline in financial assets, such as stocks and bonds, which often brought a brutal halt to business activity.

Therefore, to insure adequate response to the needs of business within an acceptable *laissez faire* framework, the Federal Reserve was empowered by Congress to accept loan paper, which the businessman proffered the commercial bank, as the basis for its reserve loan to the commercial bank. In this way, if business loan demands increased, commercial banks could always obtain sufficient reserves by borrowing from the central bank, the Federal Reserve System. Conversely, if the needs of business decreased, the banks could repay their earlier borrowing with superfluous reserves.

Thus, the volume of reserves and therefore the money supply and bank credit varied directly with the tempo of economic activity; as the pace of the economy quickened, bank credit and the money supply expanded, and as activity declined, they shrunk. There was little thought given to preventing excessive business borrowing.

To the modern reader who perhaps views the *laissez faire* ideology as a rather quaint moralism, the central bank's bolstering, rather than suppressing, business cycle fluctuations seems absurdly reckless. Yet, to the faithful believer in the self-adjusting nature of the unhindered market mechanism, *not* catering to the needs of business was unthinkable. Occasional pleas to dampen the wild swings of the business cycle through more strict control of commercial bank borrowing from the Federal Reserve System were labeled irresponsible meddling. Indeed, the Commercial Loan Theory of Banking was a consistent adjunct to the wonderful world of *laissez faire* philosophy.

Concluding Comments

Modern economic man has some difficulty empathizing with the abounding faith of his pre-1929 counterpart in the Invisible Hand. Any alternative code would have been, of course, a heretical breach of faith, especially when it involved the stolid world of money and finance. The central bank could scarcely then be imagined without its twin bastions of the Gold Standard and the Commercial Loan Theory. Yet these once sacrosanc pillars of our economic system have surely crumbled.

Today the objective of central banking is clearly to control the business cycle and (since 1958-1959) to ease the balance-of-payment's deficit. If we are to learn by experience, any objective criteria for the regulation of bank credit and the money supply should be viewed with skepticism. Hopefully, in economic life, as in other scientific pursuits, absolutism has retreated.

With continued technological progress and the changing configuration of economic institutions so likely in the openly critical and progressive Western world, today's most hallowed precepts should be expected to become tomorrow's hollow platitudes.

Questions for Thought and Discussion

1. What was the attitude of the classical economists toward the business cycle? Why?
2. Describe the automatic self-adjusting process of the classical gold standard.
3. Was countercyclical monetary policy a purpose of the early Federal Reserve System?

Section V

COMPETITION, MONOPOLY AND MARKET STRUCTURE

COMPETITION AND MONOPOLY

IN ECONOMIC ANALYSIS

John W. Snow and John V. Donovan

Competition is one of the most important concepts in economic analysis; but its usage is not always unambiguous. As an aid to understanding what economists mean by the term "competition," it may be helpful to set forth the different senses in which the term may be used. The concept of competition has three distinct aspects: (1) as behavioral activity or as a process; (2) as a notion pertaining to market structure; (3) as a prescriptive norm for the evaluation of public policy alternatives.

Competition as behavioral activity is a direct response to the economic problem—the fact of scarcity. Scarcity requires men and societies to decide what to produce, how to produce, and how to distribute the output. Since all societies are confronted by the economic problem, it follows that there will be rivalry among alternative techniques and alternative forms of social organization; and it is in this sense that competition serves an organizing behavior function.

The task of a social system is to define what form competition shall take. Some societies in world history have been organized around principles of status or caste in which birth determines social role and tradition or social custom may be used to fix the details of the standard of living for everyone. Other societies have been organized along autocratic or military lines in which the structure of social decision is predetermined. There are, of course, other ways in which a society may order or organize social activity.

The solution to the economic problem based on free exchange and private property is characteristic of modern economic society in western

John V. Donovan is Assistant Professor of Economics at the University of New Hampshire.

nations. This form of economic organization, called capitalism, did not emerge abruptly from the ashes of feudalism. Rather, its development was a gradual process marked by the creation of new legal, political, and social institutions which mirrored the increasing monetization and commercialization of society in seventeenth and eighteenth century Europe.

Mercantilism was the nexus between feudalism and capitalism. Mercantilist thinkers emphasized the importance of commerce and industry, and the role of the state in promoting economic development and national wealth. A primary objective of the state was the maintenance of a favorable balance of trade, serving to increase the supply of money and precious metals. The state assumed considerable power over the direction of economic activity and established a complex system of subsidies, tariffs, and regulations. Merchants turned to the state for monopoly privileges and received them. The British East India Company, whose monopoly on the importation of tea into the American colonies was an important factor in the pre-Revolutionary economic disagreements between Britain and the colonies, is a representative example.

It is against this background of extensive state manipulation of the economy that the publication of Adam Smith's *The Wealth of Nations* (1776) has importance. This book, the first major work of modern economic thought, places the activity of exchange at the core of a market society. Smith provides a grand philosophical assault on the policies of mercantilism and exalts the ideals of economic and political liberalism. The market, according to Smith, achieves its highest efficiency when free exchange is permitted. There must be no restrictions on the right to buy or sell in the market place. The mercantilist rigidities of social organization, in Smith's view, must be overturned.

In a free exchange, both parties must benefit, for otherwise there would be no exchange. Exchange activity is in fact a combination of cooperation and competition—cooperation in organizing the exchange and competition in defining the limits, the terms, of the exchange. The final exchange ratio results from the process of bargaining and mutual adjustment on the part of both buyer and seller, with the buyer gaining relatively more the lower the price, and the seller benefitting relatively more the higher the price.

Adam Smith clearly conceptualized the notion of exchange as competitive, behavioral activity. Smith saw competition as a force tending to equate market and "natural" price. According to Professor Stigler, Smith had five conditions of competition:

1. The rivals must act independently, not collusively.
2. The number of rivals, potential as well as present, must be sufficient to eliminate extraordinary gains.
3. The economic units must possess tolerable knowledge of the market opportunities.
4. There must be freedom [from social restraints] to act on this knowledge.
5. Sufficient time must elapse for resources to flow in the directions and quantities desired by their owners.[1]

These conditions underlie the modern notion of competition as a market structure. But it must be emphasized that Smith did not construct a notion of competition as a market structure; that was the contribution of later economists.[2] Before developing the notion of competition as a market structure, however, it would be proper to develop more fully the idea of competition as a system of social organization.

The system of mutual exchange and competitive processes provides simultaneous solutions to basic economic problems. The competitive interaction of buyers' demands, the responses of business firms and the supplies of factors of production determine the overall rate of output of business firms. Further, the interaction of buyers' demands and the attempt of business firms to maximize profits establish the types of goods and services to be produced, the quantities of each, and their relative prices. Concurrently, the competitive process also allocates the scarce supply of productive factors among their many alternative uses and establishes their relative prices.

We must now look behind the outline of this network and examine in detail the specific market structures of the economic order.

Monopoly and competition are polar points on the economist's spectrum of market structures. In economic theory, competition is the antithesis of monopoly.

The theory of competition, the economist's so-called competitive model, is a highly developed, internally consistent, powerful analytical tool. This theory is based upon four basic conditions or assumptions. These assumptions are:

1. The market has many buyers and sellers.
2. The product is homogeneous.

---

[1] George J. Stigler, *Essays in the History of Economics* (Chicago: University of Chicago Press, 1965), p. 237.
[2] Cf. P. J. McNulty, "A Note on the History of Perfect Competition," *Journal of Political Economy*, LXXV (August, 1967), 395-99.

3. Entry and exit are easy.

4. Producers and buyers have good knowledge.

Given these conditions, no individual seller will have any power over price and each firm can sell its entire output at the market prices. The industry will always tend toward an equilibrium which occurs when firms are producing at their lowest average cost. Under the competitive model, excess profits or losses will be eliminated readily by entry or exit, and price tends towards equality with the lowest average cost of production.

The essence of the competitive model is the existence of many substitutes for the product of every firm in the industry. Because of the existence of substitutes, every firm is a price taker. In the language of economics, the demand curve facing every firm is perfectly elastic. Each firm will be able to sell all it can produce at the market price. No firm acting alone can affect the industry price by any decision it makes. Price power is nonexistent. Under pure competition, the output of every firm is a negligible portion of industry output so that no firm acting alone can affect price by varying its own output.

Monopoly is the antithesis of pure competition. The pure monopoly situation in economic theory exists where there is only *one firm* selling a product with *no close substitutes* and *no threat of entry*. The firm and the industry are coterminous. The monopolist is free of competitive restrictions. The monopolist firm is the entire industry, and the price of the product is determined by the monopolist rather than by the competitive process of the market. The absence of close substitutes and the resulting power over price are the fundamental characteristics of monopoly. The essence of monopoly is price power.

The monopolist's task is to determine what price will yield the maximum profits. Because the demand curve facing the monopolist is the entire industry demand curve, the monopolist can sell a larger output, *ceteris paribus*, only by lowering price. The monopolist will try to choose that level of output (which means some determinate and corresponding level of price) from which any move would be less profitable. This position is the well known equality of marginal cost and marginal revenue.

The monopolist's determination to make maximum profits means that he seeks to maximize the difference between total revenue and total costs. This will be accomplished at that output at which marginal revenue equals marginal cost. If the monopolist were to expand output beyond this point, he would find that he adds more to costs than he adds to revenues at the margin. That is, the extra costs exceed the extra revenues and it would, therefore, be to his interest to contract output. Conversely, if the monopolist were producing at an output smaller than that at which marginal revenue equals marginal cost, he could increase his profits by expanding output, and he would continue to do so until he reached the output at which marginal revenue equals marginal costs.

At the monopolist's equilibrium output, excess profits may exist, and they can continue indefinitely because entry is restricted and the firm's equilibrium price will never correspond to the lowest average cost of production.

It is notable that monopoly and competition as used here are essentially concepts derived from market structure. Monopoly and competition are structural concepts. If we have certain structural elements or conditions, the market is said to be competitive. Where other elements are present, the market is classified as monopoly. But in neither case does the ordinary connotation of competition as rivalry have any place. Rivalry is wholly absent under pure competition, since every firm can sell all it produces at the market price. This truism led an eminent economist, Frank Knight, to stress that in pure competition there is no competition. Likewise, rivalry is ruled out under monopoly by the assumption of no close substitutes. Needless to say, neither pure competition nor pure monopoly has much correspondence to the real world. This is not to condemn the concept, since no theory or predictive model corresponds entirely to reality. The failure of the models is not that they are abstract but rather lies in their inability to tell us much about competition as a creative, vital, real-world process. A gifted economist recently emphasized this point:

> A market is not competitive by assumption or by construction. A market becomes competitive, and competitive rules come to be established, as institutions emerge to place limits on individual behavior patterns. It is this becoming process, brought about by the continuous pressure of human behavior in exchange, that is the central part of our discipline, if we have one, not the dry-rot of postulated perfection.[3]

Economists consider competition, the competitive model, preferable to the monopoly situation because it produces a better allocation of re-

---

[3] James M. Buchanan, "What Should Economists Do?" *Southern Economic Journal*, January, 1964, p. 218.

sources. In the long-run equilibrium for the competitive firm, production is at the output of minimum average costs, and firms charge that price consistent with these costs. This implies that firms are employing the best available technology at least cost. For the consumer, this condition translates into the highest volume of production and the lowest product price under existing cost conditions.

Under pure competition, consumers also benefit, because price just equals marginal costs of production. The economist's concept of cost is broader than the accountant's concept of cost. Economists use costs as an index of foregone alternatives, i.e., as opportunity costs. Thus, the opportunity cost of X measures the value of the other goods that the resources used in the production of an additional unit of X could otherwise have produced. It measures the sacrifice, from the standpoint of society, of other goods in using resources to produce more X. In pure competition, the profit-maximizing entrepreneur carries production to the point at which price (which is marginal revenue for the purely competitive firm) equals marginal cost (equals marginal revenue). This means that each good is produced to the point at which the value of the last unit is equal, at the margin, to the value of the alternative goods sacrificed by its production. To produce short of the price equals marginal cost output implies an underallocation of resources since society values additional units of the product more highly than the alternative uses to which the resources are allocated. Similarly, if output exceeds that at which price equals marginal cost, this implies an overallocation of resources in that activity, since resources would be placed in the production of a good for which society has more highly valued uses in terms of alternative goods sacrificed.

Monopoly, on the other hand, misallocates resources because price is in excess of marginal cost. The industry has too few resources for an economic optimum, and consumers are misled about the underlying scarcity of resources and are forced to pay a higher price than under competitive conditions.

The economic waste associated with monopoly can be made clear by an example. Suppose an industry exists with a sufficient number of firms that no individual firm has any power over price. Each firm will necessarily represent only a negligible portion of the industry output. Every firm will be a price-taker. The industry will be purely competitive. No firm will charge a price above the market level because no buyer will pay more than the market price. No firm will charge less than the market price because the firm can sell all its products at the going price.

Now suppose that this competitive industry was the object of a widespread merger movement that resulted in only one firm remaining. The structure of the industry has been transformed from competition to monopoly. How will market performance be affected? Assuming that no efficiencies result from this consolidation, the fundamental change will be in the nature of the demand curve facing the individual firm. What was the industry demand curve is now the firm's demand curve. Instead of facing a perfectly elastic demand curve, the firm will be facing a downward sloping demand curve. The competitive industry demand curve has not changed but the demand curve facing the firm has changed significantly.

The monopolist will find that the competitive output is too large and the competitive price too low to maximize profits for the industry. Whereas the competitive firm could sell any quantity without affecting price, the monopolist can sell a larger quantity only by accepting a lower price. Because the monopolistic demand curve is downward sloping, the addition to total revenue from selling one additional unit of product will be less than the price of the additional unit sold. That is, marginal revenue is always less than price where demand is downward sloping. The monopolist knows that to sell additional quantities he must accept a lower price for every unit sold, since the same product can not sell for different prices in the same market. Why would the monopolist ever lower prices? The answer, of course, is that the monopolist is interested in maximizing profits, not price or marginal revenue, and will therefore sell additional units as the addition to total revenue (marginal revenue) exceeds the addition to total cost (marginal cost).

The competitive industry operates at a larger level of output than would be consistent for a monopolist. For the competitive firm and industry, the output at which marginal cost equals marginal revenue, the maximum-profit output, is greater than that at which the monopolist operates. In fact, if the monopolist were to operate at the competitive output, he would add more to costs than to revenues at the margin and would not be making maximum profits. In light of this discussion on the efficiency of competition in which price equals marginal cost, the characteristics of monopoly are disturbing.

For one thing, the monopoly situation in which price exceeds marginal costs implies that the monopolist will find it more profitable to sell a smaller output and to charge a higher price than a competitive producer. The monopolist's product price is greater than marginal cost, and the monopolist is not combining productive factors in the most efficient manner. At the same time, it means that society attaches greater value to extra units of the monopolized produce than to the alternative products for which the resources would otherwise be used. By restricting output and by charging a higher price than would be obtained in a competitive situation, the monopolist misallocates resources and employs fewer resources than are justified from society's standpoint.

Our extreme hypothetical case demonstrates that, *ceteris paribus*, transforming a competitive industry into a monopoly results in a misallocation of resources, economic waste in the form of smaller output, and higher prices; and consequently less desirable economic results, a lower level of economic performance. On traditional resource allocation analysis, competition is preferable to monopoly.

Can we, therefore, take it to be a general axiom of economics that competition is superior to monopoly? Does competition always produce better economic results than monopoly? Will transforming an industry with monopoly characteristics to competition necessarily produce a more desirable economic performance?

This line of questions is beset by an inherent but little understood logical difficulty. It is appropriate to compare one situation vis-à-vis another only when genuine alternatives exist. It is inappropriate to compare noncomparables. We have just seen from the competition-to-monopoly hypothetical case that competition and monopoly may be genuine alternatives. But are monopoly and competition always genuine alternatives? Of course, the answer is no. The industry may be subject to technological difficulties or conditions that limit the number of firms which can operate efficiently in the industry to something less than the number required for price competition. Where these conditions exist, the industry is subject to economies of scale. To be efficient, the firm must have an output which is large relative to the total industry output. It is clear that if a firm reaches efficient operation at an output of 100,000 units and the total industry output is 300,000 units, the industry will not support the requisite number of efficient firms for pure competition to exist. The industry is subject to economies of scale.

Now, let us return to the question posed earlier. Is the purely competitive market structure more efficient than any other? It was suggested that the question may be subject to certain logical difficulties. The difficulty is that it is proper to compare competition with something else only where competition can exist and survive as an independent market structure. We have seen that competition can be transformed into monopoly, but it may be impossible to go the other way because of technological conditions in an industry. The market, with inexorable force, will limit the number of firms in an industry where significant economies of scale exist. Under these conditions, asking which market structure is more efficient involves a false question. Pure competition can not exist without some market intervention which will undoubtedly cause all firms to operate less efficiently. Pure competition is not a viable market structure where significant economies of scale exist.

Pure competition requires the existence of many firms. Economies of scale limit the number of firms which an industry will support. Pure competition can not exist where economies of scale are significant. An essential underlying condition of pure competition is, therefore, the absence of scale economies or, in other words, the existence of either diseconomies or constant costs at an output level which is small relative to the entire industry output. We can now go back to our merger illustration and observe that, *ceteris paribus*, monopoly will result in a smaller output and higher prices than pure competition.

Comparing competition with alternative market structures is improper unless the market process could allow a competitive market structure to exist. Otherwise, one is comparing noncomparables. If an industry will not support the requisite number of firms for pure competition, attempts to create a purely competitive structure may produce significant inefficiencies.

Comparing competition with other market structures requires a prior question: Can this industry support a larger number of firms without sacrificing efficiency? It is only where one gets an affirmative answer to this question that the comparison can properly be made. Competition can be compared with something else only where competition is a genuine, viable alternative. Monopoly may be unrelated to scale economies. Monopoly may result from horizontal integration, as in our earlier example. Here, competition is a genuine alternative, and governmental intervention to restore competition could increase the efficiency and economic performance of the industry.

Summary

In summary, the following essential points may be emphasized:
1. Competition may be understood in several ways: as behavioral activity, as a market structure, as a basis for evaluating public policy alternatives.

2. The system of mutual exchange and competitive processes is a highly efficient mechanism for the organization of production and the resolution of conflict.

3. The economist's primary test of competition is power over price, not degree of rivalry.

4. Monopoly power is the ability of a firm to control the price at which it buys or sells.

5. Under pure competition, each firm is a price-taker, exercising no power over price.

6. Competition produces a more desirable economic result than monopoly on resource allocation grounds, *ceteris paribus.*

7. Monopoly is always an alternative to competition, but the converse is not always true.

8. Economies of scale prevent pure competition from being a viable market structure.

9. Where economies of scale exist, it may be improper to compare competition with monopoly.

Questions for Thought and Discussion

1. What role does competition perform in a market economy?

2. What is the market structure of pure competition? Monopoly? What is the essential difference between the monopoly and pure competition market structure?

MONOPOLY AND COMPETITION

Adam Smith

A monopoly granted either to an individual or to a trading company has the same effect as a secret in trade or manufactures. The monopolists, by keeping the market constantly understocked, by never fully supplying the effectual demand, sell their commodities much above the natural price, and raise their emoluments, whether they consist in wages or profit, greatly above their natural rate.

The price of monopoly is upon every occasion the highest which can be got. The natural price, or the price of free competition, on the contrary, is the lowest which can be taken, not upon every occasion indeed, but for any considerable time together. The one is upon every occasion the highest which can be squeezed out of the buyers, or which, it is supposed, they will consent to give: the other is the lowest which the sellers can commonly afford to take, and at the same time continue their business.

The exclusive privileges of corporations, statutes of apprenticeship, and all those laws which restrain, in particular employments, the competition to a smaller number than might otherwise go into them, have the same tendency, though in a less degree. They are a sort of enlarged monopolies, and many frequently, for ages together, and in whole classes of employments, keep up the market price of particular commodities above the natural price, and maintain both the wages of labor and the profits of the stock employed about them somewhat above their natural rate.

. . . . . .

People of the same trade seldom meet together, even for merriment and diversion, but the conversation ends in a conspiracy against the public, or in some contrivance to raise prices. It is impossible indeed to pre-

Adam Smith, *The Wealth of Nations* (1776).

vent such meetings, by any law which either could be executed, or would be consistent with liberty and justice. But though the law cannot hinder people of the same trade from sometimes assembling together, it ought to do nothing to facilitate such assemblies; much less to render them necessary.

Questions for Thought and Discussion

1. Why would a monopolist keep his market "constantly understocked"?
2. Do you agree that the monopolist's price will be "upon every occasion the highest which can be got?" What is the monopolist's primary objective?

COMPETITION AMONG THE FEW

John W. Snow and Hartley Mellish

We have now examined the polar concepts of competition and monopoly. Pure competition and pure monopoly are primarily theoretical models useful in organizing one's thoughts and indicating the forces at work in a market, but neither is particularly relevant to modern industrial organization.

The conspicuous fact of modern economic life is industrial concentration. Modern industry is characterized by a small number of large firms controlling the output of given industries. This concentration makes pure competition an improper model of analysis and the presence of some substitutes within the industry for any firm's product makes the monopoly model inapplicable also. The most troubling current antitrust problem is determining the competitiveness of these concentrated industries. What is competition where the structural conditions of pure competition do not or can not exist? How will competitive behavior manifest itself under these conditions? What is the economics of concentrated industry? It is to these questions which antitrust students must turn for direction if policy is to have a rational foundation in economics.

Economic analysis can provide insight into the nature of competition among the few, but to do so it must depart from the structural notion of competition found in the purely competitive model. Rivalry is the essence of competition where there are few sellers. Active rivalry is the surest manifestation of competition in concentrated industries and rivalry is fostered by uncertainty.

Economists apply the term oligopoly to industries where a small number of firms account collectively for a large share of total industry

Hartley Mellish is Professor of Economics at the University of Florida.

output. Oligopoly theory attempts to explain the behavior or performance of concentrated industries as pure competitive theory explains the behavior of industries with many sellers, and monopoly theory explains the behavior of industries with one seller.

The distinguishing feature of oligopoly theory is its failure to provide an equilibrium answer to the industry's behavior. Both pure competition and monopoly provide a definite equilibrium level of prices and output toward which the industry always tends. Oligopoly has no such equilibrium. Pure competition always tends toward the equality of price and minimum average cost. Monopoly always tends toward the equality of marginal cost and marginal revenue. Oligopoly theory has no such determinant solution. Rather, we find two fundamentally conflicting forces at work, neither of which is likely to remain dominant indefinitely. The oligopoly solution will depend on which of the conflicting forces has the upper hand at any given point in time. These conflicting forces to be examined in detail in the following paragraphs are the tendency to collude on the one hand and the tendency for price competition to develop on the other.

Interdependence is the watchword of oligopoly. The distinguishing and characteristic feature of oligopoly is the recognized interdependence among the sellers. Each oligopoly firm is acutely aware that any competitive move on its part will be noticed and met by the other firms in the industry. The smaller the number of firms, the greater the competitive impact on each of an increase in the market share of any rival. Interdependence would have a maximum value where two firms of equal size producing a homogeneous product supplied the entire output for some industry. Here, if firm A cuts price sufficiently to increase its market share by 50 per cent (to 75 per cent of industry output), firm B will have its sales reduced by half. With 10 equal sized firms, a price cut sufficient to double any given firm's market share would reduce the other firms' shares by only 11.2 per cent on the average. With 100 equal sized firms, doubling of any one firm's market share would require an average loss of only one-tenth of one per cent to the other firms. The smaller the effect on rivals of any given firm's competitive move, the less intense the interdependence. The smaller the effect on others from an adjustment by one firm, the less the probability of a corresponding retaliatory reaction. It is for this reason that economists feel that larger numbers of firms produce more competitive results. In an oligopoly, each firm is acutely conscious of the competitive moves of its rivals and of their reaction to any change in their competitive policies. This interdependence makes the position of each oligopolist inherently precarious.

The market power possessed by oligopolists acting together approaches that of a monopoly. If oligopolists are able to establish a perfect cartel, the industry will have a monopoly price and monopoly output. The perfect cartel produces the same market result as a monopoly. Under a perfect cartel, the objective is to maximize industry profits and only monopoly price will achieve this objective. The problem facing the cartel is determining the price and output levels that maximize the cartel profit which, of course, is the monopoly price. The perfect cartel will therefore produce the same price-output level as a monopoly. The cartel is in effect a pure monopoly.

In studying competition among the few, economists have identified two conflicting tendencies or forces which constantly recur. The first is the tendency for oligopolists to act in unison. The perfect cartel represents the extreme and most successful expression of this tendency. Unity of action is a by-product of recognized interdependence. The economic position of any oligopolist depends upon the competitive policies of rivals. Price cutting is the most severe form of competition. Price competition must be met and retaliation in kind is a sure reaction to price chiseling by any oligopolist.

Price competition is a negative-sum game for the industry. The whole industry suffers when price competition develops. The oligopolist's desire to avoid price competition is easily understood. Price competition is dangerous and destructive from the industry point of view. It is for this reason that antiprice competitive devices, such as the basing-point system, full cost pricing, trade association price lists, market sharing, and price leaderships, are found in oligopoly market structures.

The second tendency always found in oligopoly is for price cutting to develop. This may seem enigmatic and contradictory in view of the already noted tendency for the oligopolist industry to find ways of avoiding price competition. The answer to this riddle lies in the fact that the interests of the industry and the individual firm do not always coincide. While price competition is a negative-sum game for the industry as a whole, individual firms can make short-run gains by secret price cutting. The demand curve facing the individual oligopoly firm is much more elastic than the demand curve facing the industry. The firm's demand is much more elastic than the industry demand because there are more substitutes for the firm's product than for the industry's product. The greater

171

the number of substitutes, the more elastic the condition of demand. Therefore, the oligopolist firm has a continuous incentive to cut price below the going market price. Price cutting holds out the possibility of great profits to the individual oligopolist.

The price chiseling will be clandestine, since the price cutter wishes to postpone retaliation for as long as possible. For this reason, it is essential to determine trading price as well as list price in studying oligopoly. List price alone is likely to give a distorted picture of the industry, camouflaging the true nature of competition within the industry by giving a fictitious uniformity of prices. Of course, no matter how effective the price cutter is in concealing his conduct, the other oligopolists will feel the losses and retaliation will occur eventually. Despite the threat of retaliation, the prospect of greatly increased short-run profits provides a strong temptation for the individual firm to cut price. It is this profit prospect that makes the cartel inherently precarious and unstable.

It is the ever-present incentive to chisel or shade price that undermines the cartel and makes economists feel that the cartel is less pernicious than a one-firm monopoly. While the functioning cartel is likely to produce monopoly results—high price, low output, production short of full exhaustion of a firm's economies—the fact is that cartels are unlikely to hold together without governmental support. The greater the cartel's success, the greater the danger of its collapse, for the success of a cartel sows the seeds of its own destruction. Where the cartel achieves the monopoly objective, the prospective gain to any one firm from secret price concessions can be enormous. In the case of a homogeneous product, the miscreant or deviating firm may capture a very large portion of the market before the inevitable retaliatory pricing occurs. Thus, even limited price concessions can have drastic effects upon the oligopoly. One price cutter is sufficient to cause serious losses to other oligopolists and the whole industry. Once the price concessions are discovered, all firms must reduce their prices. The cartel price is forsaken and the cartel collapses. Price cutting is the death knell of the cartel, and price cutting is an almost inevitable consequence of a cartel's success.

The cartel is, of course, the extreme case of oligopolist unity of action. Other lesser examples of the same tendency find expression in price leadership. A fundamental distinction between the cartel and price leadership is that collusion is not necessarily present in the latter. The cartel is pure collusion. Its objectives could be obtained only by maintaining close working relationships among all members, detailed agreement, and strict observance of established rules of behavior. Anything even approaching cartel would immediately violate Section I of the Sherman Act. The cartel is, therefore, of limited importance in this country, although this is not the case in Europe. Its importance for our purpose is in demonstrating the extent of market power inherent in unified oligopoly action.

In this country, antitrust law has foreclosed the cartel solution to the oligopolists' problem of interdependence, but price competition can be avoided noncollusively. Oligopolistic uncertainty can be greatly minimized by the widespread practice of coordinated pricing. Oligopoly industries often achieve this objective through price leadership. Economists have identified two distinct varieties of price leadership—dominant firm price leadership and barometric price leadership.

Dominant firm price leadership exists where the dominant firm establishes a price which all other firms accept as the industry price. The dominant firm chooses its most profitable price and allows the other firms to sell the quantities they desire at that price. The dominant firm supplies the remainder. Under dominant firm leadership, the industry has in effect a monopolist or several strong oligopolists and everybody else behaves as a purely competitive firm.

An important study of oligopoly pricing published in 1958 found evidence of dominant firm pricing in the retail grocery industry:

> . . . A & P is generally the price leader in the territory in which it operates. Where this coincides with Kroger, it is clear that Kroger is usually a follower. . . . Its [Kroger's] pricing is, as for so many operators, largely a matter of finding out what A & P charges on the most important food items and then coming very close to A & P's prices.[1]

United States Steel Company has been the historic dominant firm and acknowledged price leader of the steel industry. The testimony of Ernest Weir, President of National Steel, before the Celler Committee in June 1955 illustrates the traditional leadership position of U.S. Steel:

> Congressman McCulloch: In recent years has this uniform price [for tin plate] been the price as fixed by the United States Steel Corporation, for instance?
>
> Mr. Weir: I would say in the majority of cases, yes. But there is no necessity, except that it would be a normal, natural price.

[1] A. D. H. Kaplan, Joel B. Dirlam, and Robert F. Lanzillotti, *Pricing in Big Business: A Case Study* (Washington, D.C.: The Brookings Institution, 1958), p. 206.

> Mr. McCulloch: Does your company ever fix prices or announce prices that are lower than your competitors' by reason of your more efficient operations?
>
> Mr. Weir: Well, we have made prices that differ from our competitors' based on reasons that we thought were good reasons.
>
> Mr. McCulloch: Does that happen often?
>
> Mr. Weir: No, it doesn't.

Another illustration of dominant firm price leadership is the historic position of the American Brass Company in the beryllium alloy products industry. In hearings before the Temporary National Economic Committee (TNEC) in 1939, the President of Riverside Metal Company, Mr. Randall, gave the following testimony:

> Congressman Cox: Mr. Randall, would it be correct to say that there is a well-crystallized practice of price leadership in the industry in which you are engaged?
>
> Mr. Randall: I would say so.
>
> Mr. Cox: And what company is the price leader?
>
> Mr. Randall: I would say the American Brass Company holds that position.
>
> Mr. Cox: And your company follows the prices which are announced by American Brass?
>
> Mr. Randall: That is correct.
>
> Mr. Cox: So that when they reduce the price you have to reduce it too, is that correct?
>
> Mr. Randall: Well, we don't have to, but we do.
>
> Mr. Cox: And when they raise the price you raise the price?
>
> Mr. Randall: That is correct.
>
> . . . . . .
>
> Congressman Arnold: You exercise no individual judgment as to the price you charge for your product, then, in a situation?
>
> Mr. Randall: Well, I think that is about what it amounts to; yes sir.

From the foregoing illustrations, it is apparent that dominant firm price leadership is, in effect, monopoly pricing under which the dominant firm's price becomes the industry price. Fear of retaliation by the dominant firm is the major factor explaining the passive behavior of the rest of the industry.

The second type of leadership, barometric leadership, involves the voluntary acceptance of the price moves made by the "barometric" firm. The barometric firm conventionally is the first to announce price changes which are then accepted by the other firms in the industry. The barometric firm is not necessarily the largest or most powerful firm. Stigler tells us that "For example, International Paper was for a long period the price leader in newsprint although it produced less than one-seventh of the output and it was succeeded in this role by Great Northern, a smaller firm."[2]

A firm will be accepted as a barometric price leader only as long as the other firms regard its actions as an adequate weathervane or barometer of underlying market conditions. Barometric price leadership develops generally as a device to minimize oligopolistic uncertainty and make the industry safe from price wars. Kaplan, Dirlam, and Lanzilloti provide a general explanation of the origin of barometric price leadership.

> The development of price leadership in large-scale industry has roots in the earlier experience of violent price fluctuation and cut-throat competition, which culminated in consolidation of competitors, as in steel, copper, oil production, tin cans, and farm equipment. Such experience has generated a distinct predisposition on the part of managements to avoid price changes except through periodic, well-considered, and well-publicized alterations in recognized base prices. By relating price changes to such formalized bases as changes in direct costs or style and quality changes, the firm attempts to avoid the extreme fluctuations in return on investment that were attributed to frequent, uncontrolled disturbances of the price structure.[3]

Thus, price leadership in some form is characteristic of oligopoly, but the problem of chiseling, deviation from the pricing norm, is ever-present. Secret price concessions are more widespread under price leadership than under cartel organization. The same forces that make cartels fundamentally unstable also operate to undermine the oligopolistic practice of noncompetitive pricing through means which avoid overt collusion.

---

[2] George J. Stigler, "The Kinky Oligopoly Demand Curve and Rigid Prices," in Stigler and K. E. Boulding (eds.) *Readings in Price Theory* (Homewood, Ill.: Richard D. Irwin, Inc., 1952), p. 43.

[3] Kaplan, Dirlam, and Lanzilloti, *op. cit.*, p. 271.

Summary

1. Under oligopoly, a few firms dominate the market.
2. Oligopolists are interdependent.
3. Oligopolists seek to avoid price competition; price competition is dangerous from the industry's point of view; and practices to avoid price competition like price leadership are common.
4. Tendencies toward *collusion* and *chiseling* are always present in an oligopoly market, but oligopoly has no determinate equilibrium.
5. The uncertainty associated with price changes may lead to stickiness of prices and orderly movements of price from one level to another.
6. The cartel solution to the problem of interdependence produces a monopolist output and price for the industry.
7. Oligopoly frequently leads to higher-than-average profits—prices above the competitive level.

Questions for Thought and Discussion

1. What is an oligopoly? Why would an industry have an oligopolist market structure?
2. What is price leadership, product competition, collusion, cartel pricing? What is their relationship to oligopoly?

MERGERS, SUPERCONCENTRATION,
AND THE PUBLIC INTEREST

Harrison F. Houghton

The purpose of this essay is to explore some basic issues which arise as the American economy moves into a new era—the era of superconcentration.

What do we mean by the term "superconcentration"? What basis is there for concluding that we have reached such a status? What are the causes of superconcentration? Is it inevitable—an evolutionary development in the American scene? Is it dictated by the requirements of mass output, mass markets, and mass nuclear defense? Is it possible to restore a market economy? Or is some new form of regulation required? These are a few of the broad questions which we may consider here, and these general problems suggest a multitude of more detailed and penetrating inquiries.

As Walter Lippman has said:

> We believe that for every problem there must be a solution, and it irks us badly when we find . . . that there are problems which cannot be solved and have to be lived with.[1]

Nevertheless, it is the hope of this effort to bring into sharp focus some of the key questions—to put them into a context where solutions may be suggested.

The author is an economist with the Federal Trade Commission.

[1] *Washington Post*, February 21, 1963.

The Rise of Concentration in the American Economy

It is useful to begin with a review of recent history to see how we arrived at our present status—a highly concentrated economy with a proliferation of oligopolies in individual markets dominated by a corporate power structure centering in a few hundred giant corporations.

As that statement implies, there is a dual aspect to concentration. It may be gaged in terms of specific lines of commerce in particular geographic markets. It may be measured in terms of products or industries on regional or national bases. Or it may be measured by the position in the total economy or some relevant major segment of the economy occupied by, say, the 100 largest or the 200 largest firms.

Neither the product-market measurement nor the global largest corporation variant is wholly satisfactory in assessing the importance of concentration. More and more the large corporations are not only sitting astride a multiplicity of related product markets, and controlling significant segments in the vertical flow of products from their basic resource state to the end products sold to final consumer. But of even more significance, the giant corporation of today is a conglomerate organization with basic interests in an array of industries. Indeed, the conglomerate merger movement, which we discuss further later, is rapidly breaking down traditional industry categories.

Product Concentration

Concentration in particular product markets does not take into account, for example, the fact that General Electric may be the largest producer of lamps, and at the same time the leading manufacturer of heavy steam turbines—quite distinct products with unrelated markets. Or take United States Steel. Its position in steel rails is quite more pronounced than its share of the market in steel sheets, although it is the leading producer of both. It also happens to be the nation's largest cement manufacturer.

Market concentration data similarly have an iceberg aspect. They don't reflect the vertical structure lying beneath the surface.

A dramatic example of market concentration is the recent disclosure of General Motors' "embarrassing" position in the domestic car market. News has been made by two developments involving General Motors.

First, General Motors has passed AT&T, and is now the world's largest corporation in both sales and profits. Second, General Motors now is responsible for well over half of all the automobile sales in the American market. According to the report:

> General Motors set an alltime world record for profits of $1.46 billion in 1962. It accounted for 51.9 percent of all domestic car sales, highest percentage for any company since Ford's model T heyday in 1920-21. More recently it has taken as high as 59 percent of total sales over brief periods.[2]

And inevitably, the antitrust implications of General Motors' growing size and position were explored:

> Chairman Frederic G. Donner and President John F. Gordon held a rare, 90-minute news conference in which they expressed optimism about the future and dismissed suggestions General Motors might be running scared because of recurring reports of possible Government antitrust actions.
>
> . . . . . .
>
> Donner said he does not accept the premise of official unhappiness on the part of the Government with General Motors' size, profit position, or market share. . . .[3]

We can go down industry by industry and cite similar, if less aggravated, concentration conditions. Voluminous studies have been issued, spelling out the extent of concentration by various industries—the most recent of which were released a few years ago by the Kefauver committee.[4]

The Large Corporations

Two recent studies indicate that the position of the largest firms in our economy has risen during the post-World War II years to reach the highest level of the past half century.

The most recent study is that issued by the Senate Subcommittee on Antitrust and Monopoly. In releasing that study, Senator Kefauver re-

---

2 *Washington Post*, Feb. 19, 1963.

3 *Ibid.*

4 *Concentration Ratios in Manufacturing Industry*, 1958 report prepared by Bureau of the Census for Antitrust Subcommittee, Senate Judiciary Committee, 87th Congress, 2d Session, pt. I, April 26, 1962.

vealed that the per cent of value added accounted for the 200 largest manufacturing companies had risen from 30 per cent in 1947 to 38 per cent in 1958. The proportion accounted for by the 100 largest manufacturers had shown a similar increase—from 23 per cent to 30 per cent.

Another recent study, under the sponsorship of the Giannini Foundation and published in the *American Economic Review*,[5] revealed that the 100 largest U.S. industrial corporations—that is, the largest firms in manufacturing, mining, and distribution—accounted for just under 30 per cent of the assets of all industrial corporations in America. That was for the year 1958.

During the two decades, 1909-29, the study indicated, the concentration of assets in the 100 top industrials rose from perhaps under 18 per cent to over 25 per cent, a rise of 7 percentage points. A slight additional increase occurred during the next two decades; but since the late 1940's, the rise had been fairly sharp. Indeed, when it is recognized that each successive increase in concentration is superimposed on a previously high level, the recent gains are remarkable. Moreover, if data were available for the end of 1962, it is probable that an even further rise in concentration would be shown.

The Failure of Antitrust in the Three Great Merger Movements

Vigorous antitrust enforcement might well have forestalled the growth of concentration, except for curious court interpretations and faulty draftsmanship of antimerger legislation. The merger movement of the 1890's, it will be recalled, commenced almost immediately after the passage of the Sherman Act. The first case to reach the Supreme Court under the new act involved a major merger. The American Sugar Refining Co. had organized a merger involving firms controlling 98 per cent of the industry. Not only was monopoly power clear, but its exercise was reflected in the fact that prices were immediately advanced following the merger.

There was no question of the monopolistic purpose or intent, and competition in the industry had been completely suppressed. Nevertheless,

---

[5] Norman R. Collins and Lee E. Preston, "The Size Structure of the Largest Industrial Firms, 1909-58," *American Economic Review*, LI, No. 5 (December 1961), p. 989.

the Supreme Court denied relief on the ground that control of manufacturing, as distinguished from interstate commerce, had been achieved.

By the time the Supreme Court had receded from this extreme position, the merger movement had given to American industry what Professor Homan called "its characteristic 20th-century concentration of control."

Congress tried to remedy the situation in 1914 by including Section 7 in the Clayton Act. This statute was directed not merely at monopoly but at incipient monopoly. But that act was ineffective in stemming the merger movement of the 1920's because of the much discussed loophole: stock acquisitions were prohibited, but acquisitions of assets could go beyond challenge.

The merger movement of the 1920's firmly set an oligopoly structure in most basic industries. By 1950, in the midst of a burgeoning merger movement, Congress closed the loophole with the Celler-Kefauver Act and made amply clear its intention to prevent increases in concentration through horizontal, vertical, or conglomerate mergers.

Horizontal, Vertical, and Conglomerate Mergers

It is of some interest to discuss for a moment the distinctions between major types of mergers. Horizontal mergers are familiar to all of us. They would involve the joining of competitors manufacturing the same type of product and selling in the same geographical market.

Most mergers which took place during the great merger movement at the turn of the century were of this type. In the classic cases, erstwhile competitors joined forces in an effort to settle the competitive battle between themselves and gain some control of the market.

Vertical mergers, which also appeared as early as the merger movement at the turn of the century, were designed either to insure a source of raw material or a market outlet. The competitive consequences of vertical mergers are not so clear and obvious as those flowing from pure horizontal mergers. Sometimes, vertical mergers are motivated by a desire to gain control of an entire line of supply, extending from the extractive phase through basic manufacturing and fabricating and on through wholesaling and retailing to the ultimate consumer. At other times, partial vertical thrusts are attempted in an effort to shake loose domination of a particular stage in the vertical chain.

The conglomerate merger, which has been of growing concern in recent years to students of industrial organization, is sometimes explained by the single word "diversification." The purposes and implications of the conglomerate merger, however, are usually much more complex than the laudable effort of the forward-looking business executive to avoid putting "all of his eggs in one basket."

The large corporation has an array of advantages which may be exploited in pursuit of conglomerate expansion, including ready access to short-term and long-term credit, discriminations and preferences in buying, control over distribution, etc., which can be used to soften up a potential acquiree. The large corporation can subsidize the sale of products in the newly entered "conglomerate" line with profits made in other phases of its operations. Such a potential threat can be an inducement for small business to "take cover" through quick sale.

We have now had slightly more than a decade of experience with the new antimerger statute—the Celler-Kefauver Act—and we are in a pretty good position to judge its value. Very briefly, the law is quite effective in preventing further increases in concentration in such highly concentrated areas as the steel industry. This was established in the noted *Bethlehem-Youngstown* merger case.[6] In that case, the second largest producer—Bethlehem—with about 15 per cent of the industry capacity, attempted to acquire Youngstown—the fifth largest—with about 5 per cent. The court held that this would violate the antimerger act and concluded that, if the merger were permitted, we might end up with three steel producers controlling the bulk of the industry. The term "tripoly" was added to the court lexicon.

The recent *Brown Shoe* decision of the Supreme Court[7] demonstrates that the antimerger statute cuts even deeper and outlaws mergers which might transform only slightly or moderately concentrated industries into oligopolies.

Thus, in the industrial sphere we find that effective antitrust legislation is sufficient to check the growth in concentration through horizontal and vertical mergers.

Nevertheless, the merger movement has continued unchecked and has taken predominantly the new form—the conglomerate merger.

In a word, then, we find that the antitrust laws failed to stem the horizontal and vertical merger movements of the 1890's and the 1920's and

---

[6] *United States* v. *Bethlehem*, 168 F.Supp. 576 (S.D. N.Y. 1958).
[7] *Brown Shoe Co.* v. *United States*, 370 U.S. 294 (1962).

have had no deterrent effect on the conglomerate merger movement of the 1950's and 1960's.

In the regulated industries, the merger movement has been even more rampant in recent years with a whole series of railroad, airline, and bank mergers, but discussion of merger developments in those areas would take us beyond the scope of immediate concern here, namely, the problem of industrial concentration.

Effects of Industrial Concentration

Thus far we have discussed two aspects of the concentration question: First, the growth in concentration, and second, the causes of concentration.

What are the effects of increasing concentration?

There are many who feel that some of our recent problems—inflation, pressure on the dollar, and stagnation—are closely related to undue concentration.

In explaining the President's tax proposal, Senator Paul Douglas of Illinois attributes much of our underutilization of men and machines and unsatisfactory economic growth to concentration. The tax cut is a substitute measure for industrial price cutting.

The situation was summarized by Senator Douglas as follows:

> To put the problem in economic terms, there is not enough purchasing power in the economy to buy the goods and services which our labor force and industry can produce at the prices charged.
> There are at least two general ways to attack this problem. One of them, and perhaps the preferable one, is to reduce the prices charged to the level of monetary purchasing power. This could be done by an all-out attack on monopoly, semimonopoly, and administered prices, and the structural defects that prevent competition.
> The second way to attack the problem is to increase the monetary purchasing power in the economy to the level of the prices that are charged. This is what a tax cut would do.
> To put it simply, tax cuts would increase monetary purchasing power which in turn would put idle men to work on idle machines producing goods which would not otherwise be produced.[8]

---

[8] *Washington Post*, February 24, 1963, p. E-1.

Is Deconcentration the Answer?

In the midst of the 1958 steel price controversy, Judge Victor R. Hansen, chief of the Antitrust Division, testified before the Kefauver committee. Judge Hansen, at considerable length, traced the behavior of the steel companies just prior to the steel price increase and suggested that a new form of "conspiracy through newspaper announcements" might have been under way in the industry. He went on to point out, however, the difficulties in proving conspiracy under the Sherman Act and suggested that the concentrated structure of the steel industry was the root of the problem of elimination of price competition in the industry.

Judge Hansen made one recommendation—that new legislation be enacted to apply present Celler-Kefauver standards to existing concentration.

Let's engage in a bit of fantasy. Suppose the Congress had seized upon this idea of deconcentration and passed forthwith just such legislation. Make a further set of assumptions—that the Antitrust Division moved with great speed to enforce the new statute, applying the best economic intelligence. A series of divestiture suits would have been filed. Undoubtedly, the steel industry would have received early consideration. No doubt the just recently adjudicated *Bethlehem-Youngstown* merger case would have set the standards. Since the merger involved a combination of the second and fifth largest integrated steel producers, raising Bethlehem's percentage of industry capacity from 15 to 20 per cent, the divestiture suit may have called for a reduction in concentration of United States Steel to something smaller than its own 29 per cent of the industry. Indeed, the court might have entertained any reorganization plan designed to remove the "probable lessening of competition or tendency to monopoly" in the steel industry.

In pressing for the reorganization of the steel industry, the government would have made a full presentation on the characteristics and structure of the industry, together with a historical picture of the United States Steel Corp. during the merger movement of the 1890's and tracing the techniques of achieving price uniformity in the industry through the Gary dinners and the Pittsburgh-plus basing point system. It would further trace the changes which followed the Federal Trade Commission's outlawing of Pittsburgh-plus, and would have pointed out that multiple basing points and the present system of f.o.b. freight equalization, coupled with uniform extra charges, had perpetuated a system of identical pricing at every point of consumption throughout the country. Moreover, an exposition would be made of the system of price leadership under which periodic base price changes are instituted under United States Steel, not only as the price "leader" but also, in the words of one of its own executives, as the price "maker."[9]

It would have been shown that the steel industry is largely concentrated in the hands of the 12 largest integrated producers, but that the key to the concentrated structure lies in the position of the "Big Three"— United States Steel, Bethlehem, and Republic. United States Steel with nearly 30 per cent, Bethlehem with 15 per cent, and Republic with 8 per cent of the industry capacity tower over the other members of the industry. This is the source of most of the concentration.

Below the Big Three, the major producers have only 4 to 5 per cent each of the industry capacity.

The government's presentation, further, would have shown that much of the power held by United States Steel was derived from the fact that it operates on a national scale and has the fullest complement of steel products.

The court would have been reminded of the testimony of an economist in behalf of the defendants in the *Bethlehem* merger case, who stated that United States Steel "is exercising power at least in the short run to control prices. This I would call a kind of monopoly power."[10]

The government's presentation would have bolstered the factual underpinnings of this statement.

The crux of the government's case, however, would center in two questions: (1) Could the steel industry be reconstructed in a more com-

---

[9] This was probably never more clearly shown than in the testimony of William A. Irvin, then president of United States Steel, in 1936 before the Interstate Commerce Commission. Queried by Chairman Wheeler, Mr. Irvin's reply was as follows:

Mr. Irvin. "I would say we generally make the prices."

The Chairman. "You generally make the prices?"

Mr. Irvin. "Yes, sir. We generally make the prices unless some of the other members of the industry think that that price may be too high, and they make the price."

The Chairman. "You lead off, then, with a price charged, either up or down, at Gary: Is that correct?"

Mr. Irvin. "Yes."

(Hearings before the Senate Interstate Commerce Commission, 74th Congress, 2nd Session, on S. 4055, p. 595, reproduced in *Hearings on Administered Prices*, pt. 3, "Steel," pp. 918-919.)

[10] *United States* v. *Bethlehem*, Tr. 2198. See also 168 F. Supp. 576, at 607.

petitive framework through a divestiture program; and (2) given such reorganization, would there be a prospect of vigorous price competition in the industry? Crucial to the government's case would be a showing that such a reorganization could be achieved without adversely affecting productive efficiency in the industry.

Plant Versus Company Concentration

The government's case on this score would have rested primarily on the question of plant versus company concentration. Leading economists, such as Professors George Stigler and Walter Adams, would have been called as witnesses.

Professor Stigler would have testified, much as he had before the Celler committee some years ago, where he had raised the key question: Do large scale production methods require companies so large as to make oligopoly inevitable? Stigler's answer was:

> . . . in most industries, steel among them, the answer is "No." The fundamental fact is that the plants are the units of technology, not the companies. It would be necessary to be an expert on steel technology, which I assuredly am not, to determine whether a steel plant must have 4 or 6 million tons of ingot capacity to be of maximum technological efficiency, but it requires no such technological information to assert that no plant now produces more than 5 or 6 percent of the ingots in America, and that this plant need not be touched in order to make the steel industry much more competitive.

Professor Walter Adams' testimony would have been much as follows:

> On the basis of information which is available it seems reasonable that iron and steel making requires firms of considerable size—firms which are not only significant horizontally (i.e. within any one branch of the industry) but which are also integrated vertically. Vertical integration in iron and steel—by contrast with such industries as tobacco, for example—seems economically justifiable due to the "geographic concentration of the industry, the magnitude of individual operations necessary for efficiency in mining and manufacture, and the economies obtained by continuous operation, which makes possible the immediate use of the end product of one stage of production as the material in the next stage." Thus there are very definite economies to be obtained

from a combination of the operations of blast furnaces and steel works. These economies are obtained (1) by transforming pig iron into steel by a continuous process without permitting the iron to cool, thus using it in a molten state; (2) by recovering the valuable by-product gases from blast furnaces and coke ovens; and (3) by avoiding the cost of transporting pig iron, a cost which is high in comparison to its value.

On the other hand, there is little evidence to indicate that firms must be of Brobdignagian size to be efficient. In fact, much of the evidence points the other way. It indicates that (1) operational efficiency, (2) technological progressiveness, and (3) profitability might best be promoted not by preserving, but by reducing the size of some steel plants.

First, with respect to operational efficiency, it is doubtful if the combination of spatially and functionally separate plant units yield any significant economies. To be sure, there are advantages in integrated steel production at Pittsburgh or Gary or Birmingham; but is there any technological justification for combining these three functionally independent *plant units* under the administration of *one firm?*

Consider for a moment that United States Steel's Gary plant alone is bigger than the total operations of Jones & Laughlin, National, Youngstown, Armco, and Inland. *One* plant of the Nation's largest steel producer is bigger than *all* the plants of the fourth largest producer. This inevitably raises the question, whether Jones & Laughlin, National, and other companies of similarly substantial size are big enough to be efficient. If they are, then certainly United States Steel's Gary plant—standing on its own feet and divorced from the industrial family of United States Steel—should also be capable of efficient operation. The same goes for the corporation's integrated units at Pittsburgh and Birmingham. Divorcement of these plants from the home office should hardly result in a loss of efficiency.

The importance of the distinction between plant concentration and company concentration thus would have been the core of the government's position in pressing for a reorganization of the industry. It would have presented alternative plans, whereby either United States Steel alone, or United States Steel and Bethlehem, or each of the Big Three (including Republic) could be reorganized so as to reduce the "concentration at the top" and at the same time increase the number of effective sellers of steel.

Incidentally, two points may be made here. First, the five largest American steel companies also are the top five steel companies in the free world. In other words, the fourth largest, Jones & Laughlin, and the fifth largest, National Steel—which fall below the level of the highly concentrated "Big Three"—are still very large in the world setting, larger than 113 others on the list of the "largest steel companies in the free world" just issued by the International Metalworkers' Federation. Second, profit studies reveal that such "small" steel companies as National and Inland have, over the years, been by far the most profitable of the American steel companies.

In a word, United States Steel could have been divided up into some 10 companies, Bethlehem could be divided into 4 companies, and Republic into 2 companies without impairing technological efficiency. In each case, the structural organization at each plant site, involving vertical flow from coke, pig iron, and steel ingots on to an array of finished steel products—sheets, bars, and so on—would be left intact.

Increase in Number of Effective Sellers Would Stimulate Rivalry Among Steel Companies

By increasing the number of effective sellers with the bulk of the industry capacity from approximately 12 to some 25, rivalry among steel sellers would clearly be stimulated.

Would such deconcentration and increase in the number of sellers be sufficient to eliminate oligopoly pricing?

It should be recalled that the economic theory of oligopoly hinges very largely on two propositions: (1) the number of sellers and (2) the question of elasticity of demand for the product. Another factor of great importance is overhead costs.

Steel executives have always argued that there is an inelastic demand for steel and that reduction in prices would not stimulate demand.

While this argument might have some merit in regard to the total demand for steel—from an industry point of view—it has no merit in terms of an individual seller. Each seller is concerned with the potential sales for his own company at a given level of prices. If he stands some possibility of gaining a greater market share by reducing prices, he might be stimulated to do so. He is influenced, of course, by the number of sellers. If the number of sellers is so few that he might expect immediate matching of his lower price by his competitors, he might be dissuaded from making the effort. On the other hand, if the number of sellers is sufficient that the "immediate meeting" might not take place and that he stands a chance of gaining a share of the market, he might undertake the effort.

It should not be overlooked that the slope of the demand curve for an individual seller is flat. Buyers are highly informed and alert to any opportunities for cost savings. In other words, an individual seller who had the courage to cut prices might experience an immediate enhancement of sales.

In the words of Professor George W. Stocking:

> . . . In short, even though the total demand for steel is inelastic, the demand for any one producer's steel is highly elastic, purchases expanding quickly at prices lower than rivals charge, contracting quickly at prices higher than rivals charge.

Another crucial factor in the equation facing the individual steel seller is the enormous pressure of overhead costs. As one writer has pointed out:

> Inherent in steel manufacture are the elements of violent competition. . . . When operations fall . . . there is a strong urge to cut prices in order to get volume back to the "break-even" point. Any price that yields something beyond out-of-pocket costs contributes just as much toward overhead. . . .

In other words, the greater the overhead, the more *leverage* is involved in the cost-profit picture; volume of output has a crucial bearing on profitability. As volume falls off unit costs rise sharply, because overhead costs become a heavy burden. Conversely, as output rises, overhead is spread over a greater number of units, with a marked reduction in average costs. It follows, therefore, that for the individual firm there is every incentive to increase volume of production toward the full capacity level to achieve the lowest unit costs and maximum aggregate profits. Under a competitive framework, each member of an industry with high overhead costs would pursue a low price, high volume policy. Only under a monopolistic or oligopolistic structure, would and could the individual firm acquiesce to the reverse—a low volume, high price policy.

Finally, the government's case would stress the argument that any basic industry—particularly one in the producer's goods area—faces, as an industry, an inelastic demand curve. But this is in reality an argument requiring the restructuring of such an industry if it is oligopolistic, to preclude the individual seller from pricing like a monopolist.

Assume all these things happened. Assume that the steel industry and others were reorganized. Would we have had the administered price inflation which occurred subsequent to 1958? The documentation provided by the Kefauver committee and analyzed by Gardiner Means suggests that the steel price increase was largely responsible for the post-1958 price inflation.

Would we have had a balance-of-payments problem? Data developed by the Kefauver committee similarly suggests that much of our loss of exports and increase in imports stems directly from the steel situation.

Would we have had chronic stagnation? Here again, the administered price industries are the very ones where capacity has not been fully utilized. Under competitive structure, these industries might well have cut prices in order to stimulate sales at a higher utilization rate.

In short, the very problem of lagging purchasing power, to which Senator Douglas refers, might have been taken care of within the framework of the competitive system. Then the proposed tax cuts to restore purchasing power would have been unnecessary.

With a restructuring of the steel industry, could there have been the confrontation between Mr. Blough of United States Steel and the President in April 1962?

We think not. Demand conditions at that time were not conducive to a price increase; and if United States Steel had made any premature attempt to increase steel prices, there would have been more than one "Inland Steel" to resist the rise. Indeed, under the conditions that prevailed in April 1962, it is even more likely that prices would have been on the decline and no threatened resumption of the price spiral would have been in the picture.

We return now to our opening inquiry. What basis is there for concluding that we are entering a new era—the era of "superconcentration"? What is the meaning and significance of "superconcentration"?

In a word, our fantasy to the contrary notwithstanding, there is no movement afoot to bring about a deconcentration of industry. The antitrust laws are proving partially effective in holding the line on further increases in horizontal and vertical concentration. But the record shows a clear cultural lag in the fashioning of restraints against the new phenomenon—the conglomerate merger.

The conglomerate merger is being superimposed upon an already highly concentrated economy—an economy struggling under a burden of underutilization of men and machines and the failure of purchasing power.

Thus, the incipient conglomerate merger movement which threatens to break down industrial barriers and fashion new forms of concentrated economic power is carrying us into a new era—an era of superconcentration.

Questions for Thought and Discussion

1. Why is there a concern about industrial concentration? Would you expect concentrated industries to perform differently than unconcentrated industries? Why?
2. Is the American economy concentrated? What would cause an economy to become concentrated?

OLIGOPOLY UNDER THE ANTITRUST LAWS

John W. Snow

American antitrust policy provides a notable instance of the law-economics interface. Antitrust law is an extremely complex and highly developed field of public law containing a vast body of decisions, rules, and principles; but the underlying reality is economics.

One of the most perplexing problems currently facing antitrust policy is how to cope with market structures that are felt to violate the spirit and purpose but not the letter of existing statutes. The most notable and pressing instance of this problem occurs where industries are subject to an undesirable degree of concentration, leading to behavior which is felt to fall short of effective competition. The industry may be entirely immune to sanctions under Section I of the Sherman Act because actual agreement required under the Act as evidence of a violation is not present. Yet the behavior pattern may indicate a notable absence of competition. Section II of the Sherman Act may likewise be ineffective under traditional interpretation unless some elements of monopolization are found. Market shares in these highly concentrated industries often remain approximately constant or may even decline, affording no opportunity for a traditional Section II action. The problem, in a nutshell, is how to cope with established market structures which are unduly concentrated and lead to behavior falling short of effective competition but yet are not violative of either Section I or Section II as currently enforced.

Collective Monopolization

Antitrust policy has been subject to serious criticism for its failure to cope with the highly concentrated, coordinated oligopoly markets where interdependence is effectively recognized and price competition virtually

193

eliminated. The argument is essentially this: The root purpose of antitrust policy is to prevent the exercise of monopoly power in significant industries. Monopoly power is continuously being exercised in many highly concentrated, coordinated oligopoly industries.[1] These industries achieve profit levels revealing large measures of monopoly power.[2] Monopoly power is being collectively or jointly exercised to yield monopoly results for the industry. Under these circumstances, it is argued that the spirit and purpose of antitrust policy is being violated and, therefore, such market structures should be illegal under Section II of the Sherman Act. Section II is violated, because the industry has been and continues to be monopolized by the joint and collective coordinated conduct of the oligopolists.

Some antitrust authorities have suggested that a theory of collective monopolization affords considerable hope of bringing effective antitrust enforcement to the highly concentrated, coordinated oligopoly industries. The starting place for this analysis is always the "new" Sherman Act. The "new" Sherman Act refers to the judicial revitalization of the basic antitrust statute that occurred some 20 years ago in a series of cases that included *U.S. v. Pullman Co.*,[3] *U.S. v. Aluminum Co. of America*,[4] *American Tobacco Co. v. U.S.*,[5] *U.S. v. Griffith*,[6] *U.S. v. Paramount Pictures, Inc.*,[7] and *U.S. v. United Shoe Machinery Corp.*[8] The cumulative effect of these cases, taken together, was to change the basic focus of antitrust action. The good trust, bad trust standard, which had prevailed since the

---

[1] Joe S. Bain, a leading student of American industry, feels that "in these oligopolies, on the average, at least modified monopolistic performance tendencies are consistently noted. Tendencies toward monopolistic output restrictions and profits, moreover, are augmented by elevated costs of nonprice competition, through advertising and product variation." *Industrial Organization* (New York: John Wiley & Sons, 1959), p. 533.

[2] In a well-known study, Bain found a high positive correlation between excessive profits (monopoly returns) and highly concentrated markets. *Quarterly Journal of Economics*, LXV (1951), pp. 293-325. According to Bain, "The simple average of 22 industry profit rates for industries wherein 70% or more of value product was controlled by 8 firms was 12.1 percent; for 20 industries below the 70% line it was 6.9 percent." (p. 314)

[3] 50 F. Supp. 123 (E.D.Pa., 1943), 53 F. Supp. 908 (E.D.Pa., 1944), 55 F. Supp. 985 (E.D.Pa., 1944), 64 F. Supp. 108 (E.D.Pa., 1946), affirmed without opinion, 330 U.S. 806 (1947).

[4] 148 F.2d 416 (and Cir., 1945).

[5] 328 U.S. 781 (1946).

[6] 334 U.S. 100 (1948).

[7] 334 U.S. 131 (1948).

[8] 110 F. Supp. 295 (D.Mass., 1953) affirmed without opinion, 347 U.S. 521 (1954).

United States Steel Corp.[9] and *International Harvester*[10] decisions of the
'twenties, was replaced by something akin to the economist's standard of
monopoly power. Students of antitrust differed on the exact scope and
limits of the new Sherman Act, but none denied that antitrust had significantly extended its hegemony.

The new Sherman Act made the possession of market power the basis
for antitrust violation. Good performance did not exonerate the firm of
possession of monopoly power, for as Judge Learned Hand said in the
Alcoa decision: "It is no excuse for 'monopolizing' a market that the
monopoly has not been used to extract from the consumer more than a
'fair' profit." Possession of monopoly power could escape antitrust liability
only where the monopolist was so inherently superior to his competitors
that his monopoly position was "thrust on." Hand appears to have had
grave doubts that this would ever occur, since "no monopolist monopo-
lizes unconscious of what he is doing." The scope of the thrust on justification was very limited, since it is doubtful that market power could
ever be acquired passively and active deliberate achievement of market
power was illegal. The basic principle of the *Alcoa* decision was extended
in *U.S. v. United Shoe Machinery Corp.* to bring the deliberate maintenance of monopoly power within the ambit of antitrust action.

Alcoa established monopoly power as the core of a Section II offense,
shifting judicial thinking away from the position that abuses of power
constituted the legal wrong toward the view that monopolization as such
was forbidden.

The idea of collective monopolization found even greater support in
the *American Tobacco* decision in which the Supreme Court upheld a
criminal conviction against the Big Three tobacco companies. The government argued in effect that oligopoly per se was illegal when three
firms controlled over two-thirds of a market and assiduously avoided price
competition, preserved their respective market shares, and achieved the
noncollusive results and benefits of collusion. The defense argued that
market forces produced and required parallel action but that the conduct was not collusive and, therefore, not in violation of the Sherman Act.
Argument before the court was limited to the one question of "whether
actual exclusion of competitors is necessary to the crime of monopoliza-

---

9 U.S. v. United States Steel Corp., 251 U.S. 417 (1920).
10 U.S. v. International Harvester, 274 U.S. 693 (1927).

tion under Section II of the Sherman Act." The holding of the court shows an obvious reliance upon Learned Hand's opinion in the *Alcoa* case:

> Where the circumstances are such as to warrant a jury in finding that the conspirators had a unity of purpose or a common design and understanding, or a meeting of the minds in an unlawful arrangement, the conclusion that a conspiracy is established is justified. Neither proof of the exertion of power to exclude nor proof of actual exclusion of existing or potential competition is essential to sustain a charge of monopolization under the Sherman Act.

Undeniably, the language of the court was broad enough to lend some credence to the suggestion that the court had brought tight oligopolies within the scope of the Sherman Act, that the law of monopolizing embraced oligopolists' pricing and behavior.

In his now-famous interpretation of the *American Tobacco* decision and its significance for antitrust enforcement, Dean Eugene V. Rostow of the Yale Law School concluded:

> When three companies produce so large a percentage of market supply, that fact alone is almost sufficient evidence that the statute is violated. Ruthless and predatory behavior need not be shown. The actual elimination of small competitors is unnecessary. . . . Parallel action, price leadership, a reliance on advertising rather than price competition as a means of inducing changes in each seller's share of the market, and, above all, size—the market advantage of a small number of large sellers or buyers—these are now key points to be proved in case of monopoly or of combinations in restraint of trade. . . . Painstaking search for scraps of evidence is no longer necessary. . . . Decisive elements are the power to assert a degree of control over price and output in the market as a whole.[11]

In the *American Tobacco* case, the court had been unpersuaded by the argument of counsel for Reynolds Tobacco Company that:

> . . . The significance of these convictions extends far beyond the immediate consequences to petitioners and the Tobacco industry.

---

[11] Eugene V. Rostow, "The New Sherman Act: A Positive Instrument of Progress," *University of Chicago Law Review*, XIV (1947), 567, 585.

... For, if these convictions be lawful, the pattern of prosecution is applicable—with the results of almost certain and repeated convictions—to every other executive and corporation in a mass production industry ... in which, as a matter of common knowledge, economic forces have produced identities or close similarities in manufacturing, packaging, pricing, advertising, marketing and even raw material acquisition.[12]

Professor Nicholls of Vanderbilt University, writing in a 1949 article, felt that "the conviction of the major tobacco companies suggests at least a presumption in favor of the view that the Antitrust Division's ability to find and prosecute monopolies successfully is now limited only by the extent of its own resources in bringing cases to trial."[13]

Nicholls was echoing the sentiments of many others when he expressed the view that:

> The tobacco case is clearly a legal milestone in the social control of oligopoly. By permitting the inference of illegal conspiracy from detailed similarity of behavior and by shifting attention from the abuse of power to its mere existence (as indicated by the degree of market control), the courts have at last brought oligopolistic industries within reach of successful prosecution under the antitrust laws. This is all to the good.[14]

Other economists expressed similar views, some with much less than Nicholls' full measure of approval. For instance, Galbraith felt that the cigarette companies had been convicted for "the commonplace behavior of firms when the industry is shared by a few giants." Joe Bain interpreted the new Sherman Act cases as having "fairly well established the principle [that] a group of oligopolists acting in concert (noncollusively) may ... violate ... Section 2 of the Act by jointly monopolizing their common market." Wendell Berge felt that the new Sherman Act was a recognition that "monopoly power cannot reasonably be reconciled with the objective of the Sherman Act, because its mere existence constitutes the power to fix prices, exclude competition, and otherwise control a market."

Despite the commentators' almost unanimous view that the new Sher-

---

[12] In the Supreme Court of the United States, October term, 1498, No. 840, *Reynolds* v. *U.S.*, Petition for Writ of Certiorari, p. 14.

[13] William H. Nicholls, "The Tobacco Case of 1946," *American Economic Review*, XXXIX (May 1949), 289.

[14] *Ibid.*, p. 296.

man Act would provide the legal tools to deal with oligopoly, it is now undeniable that this early promise has had little fulfillment. Market occupancy by three or four dominant firms pursuing noncollusively coordinated policies remains as immune from antitrust action today as it was prior to the new Sherman Act cases. Oligopoly is very clearly not a violation per se of the Sherman Act as presently enforced.

Two questions remain to be discussed briefly. First, what is the economic rationale of collective monopolization? In other words, can an economic case be made for an antitrust attack on market structures that give rise to the joint exercise of market power by oligopolists? Second, why has the promise of the new Sherman Act cases, particularly as represented in the *American Tobacco* and *Paramount* cases, been unrealized?

The Economics of Collective Monopolization

Collective monopolization possesses considerable economic appeal because it provides a method of coping with the highly concentrated and coordinated oligopoly industries where price competition is assiduously avoided. There is considerable evidence that concentration exceeds the levels required for efficient operation in many markets.

Economists are in general agreement that the current level of concentration in many industries is too high in the sense that the market could support additional optimum-sized firms. In many industries, entry could occur with no loss in economic efficiency. Under these circumstances, the competitive character and economic performance of the industry would doubtless be improved by the entry of new firms. The only justification for greater concentration than warranted by efficiency considerations in production and distribution is the somewhat dubious and highly speculative notion that high concentration fosters greater innovation and progressiveness. The most forceful advocate of this position was the eminent Harvard economist Joseph Schumpeter, who argued that monopoly position was a prerequisite of innovation and progress—the "process of creative destruction."

According to Schumpeter:

> As soon as we go into details and inquire into the individual items in which progress was most conspicuous, the trail leads not to the doors of those firms that work under conditions of comparatively free competition but precisely to the door of the large concern—which as in the case of agricultural machinery, also

accounts for much of the progress in the competitive sector—and a shocking suspicion dawns upon us that big business may have more to do with creating that standard of life than with keeping it down.[15]

Galbraith seconded the Schumpeter thesis, noting the irony that:

. . . The showpieces [of American industrial achievement] are with rare exceptions, the industries which are dominated by a handful of large firms. The foreign visitor, brought to the U.S. by the Economic Cooperation Administration, visits the same firms as do attorneys of the Department of Justice in their search for monopoly.[16]

The Schumpeter-Galbraith argument is essentially this: The dynamic elements of competition relate to innovation, and only large firms can (1) afford the required research and (2) have the economic incentive to engage in vigorous product competition.

It is difficult to appraise this thesis because so little is known today about the sources of innovation. Economists in the past few years have shown great interest in the question, and numerous empirical studies replete with regressions have been conducted testing the Schumpeter hypothesis. As yet, no conclusive answers have been forthcoming; but clearly, the hypothesis has been reduced to something less than an inviolable law of economic science. In any event, it is unlikely that firms of sufficient size to exhaust economies of production and distribution would be severely handicapped in research and development activities.

While an economic rationale does exist for collective monopolization, application of the standard would be an exceedingly difficult task for any court. The major economic problem would be identification of excessive concentration in a properly defined economic market. The central issue posed by these highly concentrated industries is whether economies of scale do or do not actually require sellers of the sizes found in these industries.

Assuming this identification could be accomplished, divorcement or dissolution would be the only remedy to bring about more competitive behavior, but this would penalize all growth in market power unrelated

---

[15] Joseph Schumpeter, *Capitalism, Socialism, and Democracy* (New York: Harper & Bros., 1950), pp. 80-87.

[16] John K. Galbraith, *American Capitalism* (Boston: Houghton Mifflin Co., 1956), p. 53.

to efficiency (whether achieved internally or by merger), with possible adverse consequences to entrepreneurial activity. This is a potentially serious drawback to any attack on market power per se because:

> In our economy, growth is the badge of entrepreneurial success, and the achievement of growth is an important stimulus to entrepreneurial effort. Any limitation of growth may thus have wide repercussions on the general efficiency of enterprise far beyond the firms directly affected by particular anti-trust proceedings.[17]

Another serious difficulty with a collective monopolization standard of antitrust would be the tendency to lose sight of the economics of oligopoly and, therefore, identify interdependence as the legal evil. We have seen that the theory of oligopoly provides one bright hornbook-like economic gem: Where a small number of firms dominate a market, mutual interdependence will be recognized. Economic theory might not do much more with oligopoly, but it does tell us this in singular fashion. Oligopolists understand their market relationships with one another, and public policy which tried to make firms act as if interdependence did not exist would be clearly unreasonable. However, the higher the level of concentration, the greater the recognized interdependence and, thus, the less uncertainty. The evidence is very persuasive that an industry's coordination of pricing policies becomes tighter and more effective in extremely concentrated oligopolistic markets. Since concentration can be, and probably often is, higher than dictated by efficiency considerations, public policy directed against excess concentration has a respectable economic foundation.

The Legal Demise of Collective Monopolization

The early optimism of the commentators on the new Sherman Act and the promise it held out against the jointly acting oligopolists stand in stark contrast to the achievements of the theory of collective monopolization. Looking at the language in the *Paramount* case opinion, where the court said that "it is enough that a concept of action is contemplated and that the defendants conformed to the agreement," it is hard not to

---

[17] Carl Kaysen and Donald F. Turner, *Antitrust Policy and Economic and Legal Analysis* (Cambridge: Harvard University Press, 1959), pp. 110-111.

agree with the early commentators that at last the legal tools to cope with the coordinated oligopolistic industries had been forged. Yet, the undeniable fact is that collective monopolization never got off the ground as a legal concept to challenge oligopoly. Outside of *American Tobacco* and *Paramount*, one will search the case law in vain for any real application of Section II to a static oligopoly market where power is jointly, but noncollusively, exercised. In short, collective monopolization expired at birth, for following *American Tobacco* and *Paramount*, there have been no significant Section II cases involving monopolization by a group of jointly operating oligopolists.

The question which naturally arises is how to account for the failure of collective monopolization to take hold as a working principle of antitrust. We have seen that collective monopolization has an inherent logic and that many contemporary students of antitrust were convinced that collective monopolization afforded a corrective to the oligopoly problem in antitrust. Yet we know from the record that collective monopolization was stillborn. The problem that remains is to suggest why collective monopolization never reached maturity. All we can do here is point out various contributing factors. No doubt, the explanation is multicausal.

One suggestion is that the only effective remedy under a Section II collective monopolization suit—dissolution and divestiture—would seriously offend the basic philosophical orientation of the courts. Courts may have a strong conservative property bias and concern for innocent parties, such as employees and stockholders, that makes trust busting a last and improbable judicial resort. According to Professor Donald Dewey, an important antitrust scholar, the collapse of the new Sherman Act is attributable to the fact that the courts "are not convinced that the exercise of monopoly which has not been acquired by means either actionable or indictable per se violates the law to an extent justifying its elimination without a sympathetic attention to the position of worker and stockholder whose interests may adversely be affected by trust-busting."[18] Dewey argued that while the *Alcoa, American Tobacco*, and *Paramount* cases held out great promise for the judicial control of oligopoly, the new Sherman Act has become almost indistinguishable from the old because of the inevitable judicial reluctance to disturb private rights in the interest of promoting unspecified public goals. This really

---

[18] Donald Dewey, *Monopoly in Law and Economics* (Chicago: Rand McNally, 1964), p. 247.

amounts to the suggestion that courts applying their own conception of a public welfare have determined that the social gains from a collective monopolization theory are not sufficient to overcome the private losses to shareholders, employees, and management through corporate disruption.

Another factor militating against collective monopolization is the limited resources at the disposal of antitrust agencies and the heavy burden that such an antitrust approach would entail. While the antitrust agencies may suffer somewhat from skimpy budgets, it is doubtful that this alone goes very far to explain the failure of the collective monopolization approach to enforcement.

A third problem with collective monopolization has already been suggested—applying an effective collective monopolization standard would require the court to determine the extent of production and distribution economies in given markets, a most difficult and taxing task from which the ablest economists have continually shied away. Added to this is the gnawing realization that, even if a successful suit were maintained complete with a dissolution decree, interdependence would still be recognized unless the decree went so far as to render the former market almost unrecognizable. Dissolution decrees could not be expected to go this far, but failure to provide such a remedy would mean that interdependence, albeit diminished, would remain an important market factor.

Theory suggests that tight oligopolies produce a greater anticompetitive climate than loose oligopolies, but where a tight oligopoly ends and a loose oligopoly begins is pure conjecture. It is safe to say that 4 firms with 90 per cent of output constitute a tight oligopoly, and 40 firms of approximately equal size controlling 80 per cent of output constitutes a loose oligopoly. However, it is extremely unlikely that any dissolution decree would insure movement out of tight-into-loose oligopoly.

Professor Galbraith suggests that *American Tobacco, Alcoa*, and the other new Sherman Act cases were a reaction to the discovery that traditional norms of competition no longer applied. Antitrust was called on to restore competition, a competition which Galbraith argues was being supplanted once and for all. According to this line of reasoning, the failure of the new Sherman Act stemmed from a growing recognition that "to suppose that there are grounds for antitrust prosecution whenever three, four or a half dozen firms dominate a market is to suppose that the very fabric of American capitalism is illegal. This is a notion which can seem sensible only to the briefless lawyer." [19]

The new Sherman Act cases afforded a latent theory of collective monopolization for later courts to embrace, but none of these cases presented a clear and unequivocal collective monopolization standard. Abuses of monopoly power in one form or another can be found in all the new Sherman Act cases. Ambiguity is a characteristic feature of these cases. This ambiguity, of course, made the new Sherman Act less than a certain precedent in any of the cases and allowed a reluctant court a wide scope of interpretation. Judicial ingenuity played no small part in reducing the potency of the new Sherman Act. This is particularly true with reference to remedies where, as we have seen, dissolution has been almost completely avoided. The cases were easy to limit to their facts.

Whatever the explanation, there can be no doubt that static oligopolistic market structures, even of the tightest and most socially objectionable varieties, remain immune from antitrust action. This history of the new Sherman Act demonstrates the power of a hostile judiciary to limit an unwelcome legal theory.

Questions for Thought and Discussion

1. What is the idea of collective monopolization? Is collective monopolization prohibited by the antitrust laws?
2. What is meant by the "new Sherman Act"? Would you prefer an antitrust policy based on the old or the new Sherman Act?
3. Are large firms more innovative and progressive? Is this a good argument for allowing heavy concentration?

---

[19] Galbraith, *op. cit.*, p. 55.

THE STRUCTURE OF REGULATED INDUSTRY

M. Loe

The rationale of government control of industry lies in multifaceted concepts—some of which have little to do with the elements of economic analysis. One of the basic considerations is the desire of society to have some assurance that they will have to pay no more than a fair price for certain essential commodities. Selection of what is essential is, of course, an "art" rather than a scientifically determinable process. In the United States today, there is substantial question whether automobiles are any less essential than electricity; yet the latter industry is regulated and the former is not. Primarily, however, economic regulation in the United States centers upon those industries that are considered to possess the characteristics of "natural" or "quasi-natural" monopolies.

In general, whether an industry is or is not a natural monopoly depends on the interrelationships of market structure and cost characteristics of the industry. Market structure and pricing cases range from the purely competitive, where no seller has the ability to control the price of his product,[1] to pure monopoly, where one seller has absolute control of his price and output. Under competition, the impersonal forces of demand and supply determine the price and thus "control" the price, obviating any need for a governmental, noneconomic determination of a fair or just price. In addition, pure competition results in the minimum price and the maximum output consistent with demand. Under monopoly, buyers are at the mercy of the seller to an extent alleviated only by the

---

The author is an economist with the Interstate Commerce Commission. The opinions expressed here are those of the author and are not necessarily the official views of the ICC or any other government agency.

[1] A condition under which demand determines price, since the level of demand determines which is the high cost or marginal firm.

monopolist's desire to maximize his profit and to keep possible entrants out of the industry. Furthermore, the monopolist may successfully discriminate among buyers[2] to achieve maximum profits and will restrict output below the lowest cost level of production.

There is disagreement among economists on the definition of natural monopoly and, thus, industries properly subject to regulation. For the purposes of this essay, natural monopoly may be deemed to exist in an industry which operates under increasing returns to scale, i.e., wherever increasing size of plant is accompanied by ever-decreasing unit cost of production. Under this condition, if two or more firms sell in the market, competition will be unstable or collusion inevitable since each seller can supply all or a substantial part of the market. Unstable competition, in turn, is generally viewed as destructive (price wars) and collusion as resulting in output restrictions to bring prices close to the monopoly price. In any case, these conditions are generally accompanied by overcapacity and consequent economic waste of resources, and it is considered economically beneficial to grant franchises to one or a few firms (if the market is sufficiently large) to avoid such waste and to provide control of entry as well as regulation of prices.

It must be remembered that what constitutes a natural monopoly may change as the size of the market changes. If demand increases so that the marginal revenue curve intersects the average total cost curve at or to the right of its lowest point, there may be substantial inducement and economic rationale for another firm to enter the industry. However, technological improvements seem to be on the side of the monopolist, since most provide cheaper means of producing the same or greater output.

Indivisibilities in the application of factors of production constitute a primary factor in capital investment in fixed plant. The implication is that these industries require relatively large capital investment and that smaller investments are either physically impossible or economically unfeasible. The classical illustration of such indivisibilities is that it is

---

[2] Discrimination is encouraged in many regulated industries but is usually called price differentiation to avoid the unsavory connotation of the former term. For example, many manufacturing plants and utilities buy natural gas at rates below normal volume rates on an interruptable basis. That is, the gas company may cut off supplies to the firm if other demands require all its capacity, and the rates are justified on the basis that buyers under "interruptable rates" do not contribute to capacity investment and, on the other hand, permit the gas company to charge generally lower rates by improving utilization of its plant.

not possible to lay down only one rail between any two points and still provide any rail service. Along with a high fixed investment goes a necessity for relatively long life of plant. And, this large capital investment is related to the annual sales it can generate. For industry generally, the ratio of fixed plant investment to annual sales is usually no more than 1.00 to 1.00 or 1.25 to 1.00 (generally lower). In regulated industries, on the other hand, investment in fixed plant to annual revenue ratio ranges upward from about 4.00 to 1.00.

Under this situation, the industry faces high fixed costs (overhead) in the short run. The necessity to meet these costs out of either current cash flow or retained income poses serious problems for price policy.[3] This is one of the prime conditions creating the need for regulation where duopoly or oligopoly exist. In the short run, given price, a decrease in demand for the product will result in the elimination or reduction of profits. If the fall in demand and revenue endangers the firm's ability to meet current fixed obligations, it will have every incentive to lower price, since any price above average variable cost contributes something to overhead. Furthermore, at the lower price, demand may be estimated to be such that one firm will be unable to meet even average variable cost. The situation cannot long exist, since any pre-existing balance of interests between the firms will be destroyed. The other firms, in turn, must make price reductions and will again share the market, leading to further losses. Such actions may lead to insolvency for one or all of the firms, and, where the industry is large and vitally affects the welfare of society, the possible discontinuation of production and disruption of financial markets is not easily tolerated.[4] The excess capacity implicit for these developments to occur is characteristic of industries where there are large indivisibilities of capital, and it is this factor that creates the basic condition for destructive competition among oligopolists.

---

[3] Economic literature is replete with discussions of the short and long runs and particularly the theory that, in the long run, there are no fixed costs. It must be borne in mind that the results of the theoretical analysis of the long run have relevance almost solely in reference to planning for fixed plant investment. With modifications for estimates of the future and the desire for price stability, the pricing policies of business management are primarily determined by immediate conditions and estimates of intermediate term conditions. It is of little consequence to management that, in the long run, fixed costs disappear when it must meet the mortgage at the end of the month.

[4] See Grodinski's *The Iowa Pool* and Josephson's *The Robber Barons* for case histories of the described possible developments.

Other, less esoteric, factors indicate the desirability of regulation of industry. It would be a public nuisance to have more than one transit company operating over the same streets as it would be to have more than one water company or electric company tear up those streets to repair their installations. Food and drugs ought to meet certain minimum standards; and, while this is not economic regulation, per se, it affects the economics of the industries.

There are certain instances in which industries or subindustries that do not display the structures described above are brought under regulation; this occurs where industries affected with the public interest are regulated. An example of this type of regulation is the regulation of motor carriers by both state and federal governments. Motor carriers are at the opposite end of the capital turnover scale, having a ratio of investment to annual sales of about $.20 or $.25 to $1.00. The institution of motor carrier regulation came in the early and mid-1930's when the problems of excess capacity in transportation, particularly railroads, became manifest. Since motor carriers and railroads compete for large blocks of the same traffic, it is clear that their rates should be regulated and some barriers to entry be erected to make enforcement possible.

Substantial problems exist, however, in motor carrier control as well as control of other modes of transportation. Motor carriers of agricultural commodities are exempt from regulation, and even carriers otherwise subject to regulation are exempt in the transportation of such commodities. Barge line rates are also exempt from regulation in the transportation of agricultural commodities as well as other bulk commodities such as coal and ores. In addition, no regulation other than on safety exists for proprietary and exempt trucking, which is estimated to account for up to two-thirds of all motor carrier traffic. These exemptions from transportation regulation are creating serious problems in the regulation of both railroads and motor carriers, and solutions are not yet in sight.

The essential goal of regulation, then, is to create the results that would be achieved by perfect competition were it practical. Whether competition is feasible is in turn determined by the cost structure of the industry. Even where cost structures indicate the desirability of competition, a subindustry may have to be regulated if such competition threatens to destroy an industry that needs to be regulated.

Economic regulation of industries is, in fact, not limited to public utility or natural monopoly industries; and there is always the problem that some industries which are not natural monopolies will seek regulation and public utility status as a legal monopoly to avoid the necessity for competitive effort. When this happens, there is no distortion in resource allocation as long as regulation is effective in eliminating monopoly profits. But even under effective regulation it is improbable that competitive price and output will be achieved, as will be shown.

Geometry of Public Utilities

Any company contemplating the construction of a new plant is faced with choosing the correct size of plant for the market to be served. As we have seen in the utility field, the firm is often faced with increasing returns to scale. Out of the variety of possible plant sizes, the one chosen depends on the estimated size of the market. The properties of increasing returns to scale are graphed in Figure 1, showing a family of short-run cost curves (plant curves) enclosed by the long-run cost curve. If the greatest output consistent with maximum profit is ON, plant "1" will be constructed and produce that output at lower average costs than any other plant.[5] If demand increases, a larger plant could be built which would produce at lower average costs than the next smaller plant and could possibly capture the total market by making the first plant sell below costs or by coming to agreement whereby price would be set to provide both firms with at least some monopoly profit. For example, if demand increased to ON' the first plant would be making very high profits which would act as a lure to other entrepreneurs. New investors could build a plant of the same size as Plant 1 and satisfy that portion of the market not taken care of by the first plant. They would, however, see that investment to build Plant 2 could handle total demand at much lower average total cost. Left to their own devices, Plant 2 would probably be constructed, and the two firms would compromise on output and price, resulting in the waste of scarce resources.

Assuming the demand schedule is continuous and intersects at or to the right of QP', Plant 4 is the optimum size and, from a social standpoint, should be the plant constructed. With unrestricted entry, however, the industry may well develop all plants with consequent waste of resources and generally higher prices than warranted.

The characteristics of the individual firm are shown in Figure 2.

---

[5] This is true only if plant sizes are discontinuous, as depicted in Figure 1. For LRAC to be constructed in a continuous smooth curve as presented requires the opportunity for infinitely small increments in plant size.

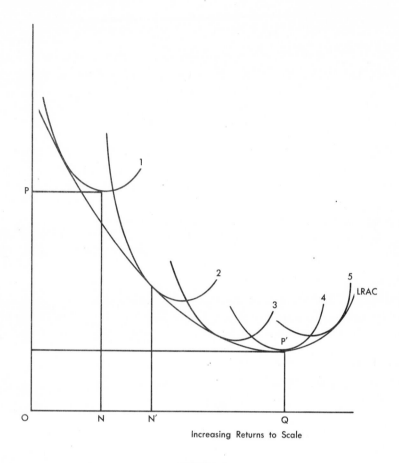

Increasing Returns to Scale

FIGURE 1

Output will be determined where marginal revenue, MR, equals marginal cost, MC, and price will be OP. Excess profit to the firm is the price OP minus OS—the average total cost of the particular output. There are other "losses" to the economy resulting from monopoly price and output. It is desirable for the total economy that resources be utilized as efficiently as possible. That point on Figure 2 is at the intersection of D, MC, and ATC. If the firm was competitive, it would face a perfectly elastic D and price would be at the lowest point of ATC. The sloping demand curve confronting the monopolist permits him to determine price

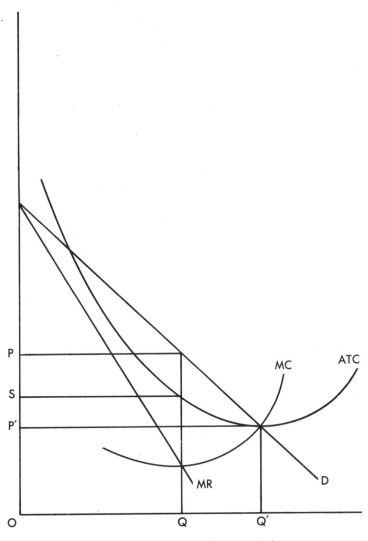

Plant Curve Characteristics

FIGURE 2

and output in order to realize excess profits. The major function of regulation should be to move the price from OP to OP′, and output from ·OQ to OQ′.

Two conclusions follow from the foregoing: (1) An industry of increasing returns to scale (long run) will operate under short-run decreasing costs (spreading overhead), i.e., to the left of lowest average total costs. (2) In such an industry, the existence of more than one firm will tend to create destructive or cutthroat competition leading either to single firm monopoly or collusion resulting in monopoly price and output restrictions.

It has been shown that regulation can produce an economically optimum price, as in Figure 2 where D=MC=ATC. That model represents an ideal solution. There are, however, other situations in which price and output cannot be optimally set. Referring to Figure 2, if demand shifted to the left it would intersect the marginal cost curve below the average total cost curve. From a resource allocation standpoint, these are the optimum price-output coordinates. In practical terms, price cannot be set at that point since the firm would not be covering its total costs. Under regulation, price would be set where D=ATC to insure a "fair" rate of return to the enterprise.

While ideal pricing probably cannot be achieved, regulated pricing is a preferable condition to unrestrained monopoly in industries in which competition is not workable. There are substantial problems in determining the industries that should be regulated. The intercity trucking industry, for example, was brought under regulation to protect the railroads with which it competes rather than to protect the consumer, although the cost structure of the industry indicates competition would effectively regulate the industry.[6] The same applies to taxicabs and some other industries.

The complexity of regulation itself introduces costs and distortions that are avoided in competitive industries and would be avoided whenever competition is a reasonably effective force. In assessing whether an industry should be regulated, these costs must be borne in mind. In cases where investment in fixed plant is large and long-term, i.e., where monopoly is possible or probable, the costs of regulation are probably insufficient to cause serious distortion in the industry structure. However, where such costs are high relative to the fixed costs of the industry, the total cost curve of the industry may be raised substantially. This would be the case in industries with substantial competitive characteristics. Regulation of

---

[6] This does not imply that the Commission does not attempt to protect the consumer in its administration of the Act; merely that consumer protection was not the Act's legislative genesis.

such industries raises the price of the product both by frustrating the natural effects of competition and by imposing social costs which are not necessary to the adequate functioning of the industry.

Questions for Thought and Discussion

1. What are the implications of price regulation of railroads absent price regulation of motor carriers or barge lines?
2. Is there any justification for price discrimination by public utility companies?
3. Many economists hold that individual plants are the primary source of any economies of size that exist. Discuss this view in terms of multi-plant electric power generating companies; the telephone system; and non-utility industry, such as automobile and steel manufacture.

Section VI

THE ECONOMIES OF LABOR
AND UNIONS

THE ECONOMICS OF WAGES

David Ricardo

Labour, like all other things which are purchased and sold, and which may be increased or diminished in quantity, has its natural and its market price. The natural price of labour is that price which is necessary to enable the labourers, one with another, to subsist and to perpetuate their race, without either increase or diminution.

The power of the labourer to support himself, and the family which may be necessary to keep up the number of labourers, does not depend on the quantity of money which he may receive for wages, but on the quantity of food, necessaries, and conveniences become essential to him from habit, which that money will purchase. The natural price of labour, therefore, depends on the price of the food, necessaries, and conveniences required for the support of the labourer and his family. With a rise in the price of food and necessaries, the natural price of labour will rise; with the fall in their price, the natural price of labour will fall.

With the progress of society the natural price of labour has always a tendency to rise, because one of the principal commodities by which its natural price is regulated, has a tendency to become dearer, from the greater difficulty of producing it. As, however, the improvements in agriculture, the discovery of new markets, whence provisions may be imported, may for a time counteract the tendency to a rise in the price of necessaries, and may even occasion their natural price to fall, so will the same causes produce the correspondent effects on the natural price of labour. . . .

The market price of labour is the price which is really paid for it, from the natural operation of the proportion of the supply to the demand;

David Ricardo, *Principles of Political Economy* (1817).

labour is dear when it is scarce, and cheap when it is plentiful. However much the market price of labour may deviate from its natural price, it has, like commodities, a tendency to conform to it.

It is when the market price of labour exceeds its natural price, that the condition of the labourer is flourishing and happy, that he has it in his power to command a greater proportion of the necessaries and enjoyments of life, and therefore to rear a healthy and numerous family. When, however, by the encouragement which high wages give to the increase of population, the number of labourers is increased, wages again fall to their natural price, and indeed from a reaction sometimes fall below it.

When the market price of labour is below its natural price, the condition of the labourers is most wretched: then poverty deprives them of those comforts which custom renders absolute necessaries. It is only after their privations have reduced their number, or the demand for labour has increased, that the market price of labour will rise to its natural price, and that the labourer will have the moderate comforts which the natural rate of wages will afford.

Notwithstanding the tendency of wages to conform to their natural rate, their market rate may, in an improving society, for an indefinite period, be constantly above it; for no sooner may the impulse, which an increased capital gives to a new demand for labour be obeyed, then another increase of capital may produce the same effect; and thus, if the increase of capital be gradual and constant, the demand for labour may give a continued stimulus to an increase of people. . . .

It is not to be understood that the natural price of labour, estimated even in food and necessaries, is absolutely fixed and constant. It varies at different times in the same country, and very materially differs in different countries. It essentially depends on the habits and customs of the people. An English labourer would consider his wages under their natural rate, and too scanty to support a family, if they enabled him to purchase no other food than potatoes, and to live in no better habitation than a mud cabin; yet these moderate demands of nature are often deemed sufficient in countries where "man's life is cheap," and his wants easily satisfied. Many of the conveniences now enjoyed in an English cottage, would have been thought luxuries at an earlier period of our history. . . .

Questions for Thought and Discussion

1. According to Ricardo, why do wages tend towards a subsistence level?

2. Does "subsistence" have a single absolute meaning, or does "subsistence" change from generation to generation and from country to country? What level of income would you estimate as the subsistence income for a family of four in this country if subsistence were defined as meeting the basic needs for an adequate diet?

WAGES AND PRODUCTIVITY

John Stuart Mill

The subsistence theory of wages was a prominent part of classical economics. As Ricardo expressed the idea, wages could rise above a subsistence level in the short run, but higher wages would lead to larger families thus increasing the labor force and pushing wages back down to the subsistence level. The so-called "iron law of wages" contributed to the idea that economics was a pessimistic and dismal science. Of course we know today that subsistence is a very ambiguous term. One age's luxury will be another's mere subsistence. This selection from Mill indicates his belief in man's capacity to continuously improve his material lot. After noting that managers of enterprises commonly earn far more money than other wage earners, Mill goes on to explain why.

. . . To the laborer this large payment to the manager seems to be paid for the possession of capital. This we now know to be wrong. The manager's wages are payments of exactly the same nature as any laborer's wages. It makes no difference whether wages are paid for manual or mental labor. The [only] payment to capital . . . as such, known as interest (with insurance for risk), is unmistakably increasing, even in the United States. And yet we see men gain by industrial operations enormous rewards; but these returns are in their essence solely manager's wages. For in many instances . . . the manager is not the owner of the capital he employs.

To what does this lead us? Inevitably to the conclusion that the laborer, if he would become something more than a receiver of wages, in the ordinary sense, must himself move up in the scale of laborers until he

John Stuart Mill, *Principles of Political Economy* (New York, 1891), p. 523.

reaches the skill and power also to command manager's wages. The importance of this principle to the workingman can not be exaggerated, and there flows from it important consequences to the whole social condition of the lower classes. It leads us directly to the means by which the lower classes may raise themselves to a higher position. . . .

Questions for Thought and Discussion

1. If manager's wages are payments of exactly the same nature as any laborer's wages, why do managers earn more income than other types of labor?
2. According to Mill, what ultimately determines the compensation of labor whether the labor is that of auto mechanics, physicists, lawyers, carpenters, or corporate management?

THE WAGE BARGAIN

Adam Smith

... What are the common wages of labour, depends every where upon the contract usually made between those two parties, whose interests are by no means the same. The workmen desire to get as much, the masters to give as little as possible. The former are disposed to combine in order to raise, the latter in order to lower the wages of labour.

It is not, however, difficult to foresee which of the two parties must, upon all ordinary occasions, have the advantage in the dispute, and force the other into a compliance with their terms. The masters, being fewer in number, can combine much more easily; and the law, besides, authorises, or at least does not prohibit their combinations, while it prohibits those of the workmen. We have no acts of parliament against combining to lower the price of work; but many against combining to raise it. In all such disputes the masters can hold out much longer. A landlord, a farmer, a master manufacturer, or merchant, though they did not employ a single workman, could generally live a year or two upon the stocks which they have already acquired. Many workmen could not subsist a week, few could subsist a month, and scarce any a year without employment. In the long-run the workman may be as necessary to his master as his master is to him, but the necessity is not so immediate.

We rarely hear, it has been said, of the combinations of masters, though frequently of those of workmen. But whoever imagines, upon this account, that masters rarely combine, is as ignorant of the world as of the subject. Masters are always and every where in a sort of tacit, but constant and uniform combination, not to raise the wages of labour above their common rate. To violate this combination is every where a most

Adam Smith, *The Wealth of Nations* (1776).

unpopular action, and a sort of reproach to a master among his neighbours and equals. We seldom, indeed, hear of this combination, because it is the usual, and one may say, the natural state of things which nobody ever hears of. Masters too sometimes enter into particular combinations to sink the wages of labour even below this rate. These are always conducted with the utmost silence and secrecy, till the moment of execution, and when the workmen yield, as they sometimes do, without resistance, though severely felt by them, they are never heard of by other people. Such combinations, however, are frequently resisted by a contrary defensive combination of the workmen; who sometimes, too, without any provocation of this kind, combine of their own accord to raise the price of their labour. Their usual pretences are, sometimes the high price of provisions; sometimes the great profit which their masters make by their work. But whether their combinations be offensive or defensive, they are always abundantly heard of. In order to bring the point to a speedy decision, they have always recourse to the loudest clamour, and sometimes to the most shocking violence and outrage. They are desperate, and act with the folly and extravagance of desperate men, who must either starve, or frighten their masters into an immediate compliance with their demands. The masters upon these occasions are just as clamorous upon the other side, and never cease to call aloud for the assistance of the civil magistrate, and the rigorous execution of those laws which have been enacted with so much severity against the combinations of servants, labourers, and journeymen. The workmen, accordingly, very seldom derive any advantage from the violence of those tumultous combinations, which, partly from the interposition of the civil magistrate, partly from the superior steadiness of the masters, partly from the necessity which the greater part of the workmen are under of submitting for the sake of present subsistence, generally end in nothing, but the punishment or ruin of the ring-leaders.

But though in disputes with their workmen, masters must generally have the advantage, there is however a certain rate below which it seems impossible to reduce, for any considerable time, the ordinary wages even of the lowest species of labour.

A man must always live by his work, and his wages must at least be sufficient to maintain him. They must even upon most occasions be somewhat more; otherwise it would be impossible for him to bring up a family, and the race of such workmen could not last beyond the first generation. . . .

There are certain circumstances, however, which sometimes give the labourers an advantage, and enable them to raise their wages considerably above this rate; evidently the lowest which is consistent with common humanity.

When in any country the demand for those who live by wages; labourers, journeymen, servants of every kind, is continually increasing; when every year furnishes employment for a greater number than had been employed the year before, the workmen have no occasion to combine in order to raise their wages. The scarcity of hands occasions a competition among masters, who bid against one another, in order to get workmen, and thus voluntarily break through the natural combination of masters not to raise wages. . . .

LABOR UNIONS AND THE AMERICAN ECONOMY

R. E. L. Knight

Why should an economist be interested in labor unions? Two principal answers may be suggested. First, economists are interested in whatever affects the demand, supply, and pricing of economic resources. Second, economists in the United States and other predominantly capitalist nations are interested in any forces at work within their societies which may conceivably lead to drastic modifications in private enterprise capitalism or to the eventual replacement of capitalism by some form of socialism.

The organization of workers into labor unions influences the manner and terms upon which an economic resource—human labor—is bought and sold. And, it has long been the rosy dream of those on the left wing of the political spectrum (and the nightmare of those on the far right wing) that organized labor will someday become the rallying force for a movement that sweeps capitalism, at last, into the dustbin of history.

The impersonal description of human labor as an economic resource or a factor of production is correct within the context of the economist's professional interests. Yet, it has seemed cold-blooded and repellent to many people not conditioned to look at the world from the economist's viewpoint. Congress, when it passed the Clayton Act of 1914, felt called upon to assure American workers that "the labor of a human being is not a commodity or article of commerce." Willard Wirtz, Secretary of Labor, decreed several years ago that the term "labor market" was no longer to be used officially by the U.S. Department of Labor. Perhaps the term carried the unpleasant connotation of a slave auction in the antebellum South; in any case, it was uncomfortable to find the Department of Labor rely-

The author is Associate Professor of Economics at the University of Maryland.

ing on the same terminology the Department of Agriculture used to report the marketing of hogs or beef cattle.

The good intentions of the Congress and the Secretary of Labor to the contrary notwithstanding, labor markets do exist—though their boundaries can rarely be precisely defined—and prices are determined in the transactions that occur in these markets. The sale of human labor is unavoidably a subject for economic analysis, even if this analysis may appear excessively clinical.

To some economists, analysis of labor market transactions would be a much more satisfying task if by waving a magic wand they could cause labor unions to vanish. If an economist is wholly devoted to the honored theory that demonstrates the virtues of unfettered competition in a private enterprise economy, then intellectual consistency virtually forces him to deplore the existence of unions. A full-fledged "model" of a competitive economy calls for the prices of consumer goods and services to be determined through the vigorous competition of many individual sellers, each contending against the other, without collusion to fix prices or restrict supply. It also calls for the prices (wage rates and salaries) at which human labor is sold to be determined by comparably vigorous, individual competition on both sides of the labor market—by employers competing against one another in bidding for workers and by each worker competing against the other in offering his labor to employers. In theory, such competition will "clear the market." The competitive struggle among employers to hire the more highly trained, intelligent, skilled workers will bid their wages and salaries up to levels which accurately reflect their value to employers. As for the worker with little skill, competence, or productivity, he too will find employment, provided only that he is willing to accept a wage just low enough to make it economically rational for some employer to take him on. In the purely competitive labor market postulated by economic theory, no one needs to go without a job, and each worker receives economic justice, as an individual, in the form of a wage or salary that corresponds to the value his particular labor services have for the employer who makes the highest competitive bid to hire him.

In this attractive picture painted by theory, a labor union looms up like a snake in the Garden of Eden. When workers come together to form a union, they are flouting the rules of the competitive game. No longer individually competing with each other in selling their services, they have banded together in a combination—or "conspiracy" in the view of

228

some observers—to try to fix a price for their labor. The price they attempt to fix will almost certainly appear to be "unnatural" or "artificial"—that is, one which is higher than the prices they would receive if they continued to compete as individual sellers of labor.

The spectacle of workers joined in a collective effort, through a union, to fix a price for their labor can be deeply disturbing to anyone who is intellectually and emotionally committed to the position that the intensely competitive market place is the proper source from which prices should flow. In the United States, if a group of pharmaceutical companies enter an agreement to fix the prices of prescription drugs or if a group of electrical equipment manufacturers agree among themselves to use identical price lists in submitting bids to a government procurement agency, they have committed a crime under the antitrust laws. If exposed, they will be castigated by the writers of newspaper editorials and prosecuted by the U.S. Department of Justice. Should we, then, allow workers to do what is forbidden to businessmen? If a price-fixing combination formed by business firms is an intolerable economic evil, is not a price-fixing combination formed by workers also intolerable? Economists have been, and remain, in disagreement among themselves on the answer.

Economists will continue to score debating points against each other in their running controversy over the proposition that labor unions exercise a gravely undesirable influence upon the wage-setting process in a private enterprise system. But, as a practical matter, the freedom of workers to establish combinations aimed at fixing a price for their labor rests upon deeply rooted political forces. The field of study now called "economics" was once generally known as "political economy"—and the older title seems the more appropriate as one seeks to explain why workers may legally attempt to fix prices while business firms may not. There is an overwhelming public consensus in our society in support of the formal doctrine, at least, that business firms are obligated to compete, rather than collude to set whatever prices will squeeze the maximum profits out of the buyers of their products. Even a businessman who is engaged with his fellow producers in a *sub rosa* price-fixing violation of the antitrust laws will pay enthusiastic lip service to the virtues of price competition when giving a speech to a Chamber of Commerce meeting. In the years since the passage of the Sherman Antitrust Act in 1890, some groups of business firms—for example, small retail grocers and druggists—have occasionally lobbied successfully in Congress and the state legislatures for laws which give them a limited amount of special exemption from certain general rules laid down by the antitrust legislation. But virtually no political support could be mustered in the United States today, or in the foreseeable future, for repeal of the antitrust laws' central, fundamental prohibition against businessmen's price-fixing conspiracies.

Turning from business firms to labor organizations, we certainly do not find an overwhelming consensus in favor of a diametrically opposite doctrine that workers should form unions for the purpose of wage fixing. On the contrary, a significant minority of Americans would be delighted if state and federal legislation could be passed that would effectively destroy labor unions. Many others feel ill at ease upon hearing or reading accounts—usually much exaggerated—of the power which unionization has given workers to influence the wages they are paid. Yet, there are approximately 17 million union members in the United States as of mid-1968. It is true that an unknown number of these are involuntary members who have been drafted into paying union dues because their employers accepted union shop clauses in their collective bargaining agreements. Workers conscripted into unions against their will are probably a very small proportion of total membership, however, and the great majority of union members—in company with millions of their friends and relatives—could be expected to put up an impassioned resistance against any seriously threatening drive to wipe out union freedom to negotiate wage rates. In view of the present size of organized labor in the United States, there are very few, if any, rational and ambitious politicians who would overtly identify themselves with an extreme antiunion crusade. Union members are a minority of American voters, but political candidates can lose elections by arousing against themselves the intense antagonism of sizeable minority groups. Seventeen million union members constitute a political force formidable enough to evoke respect from office seekers in our democratic society.

One should keep in mind, moreover, that the position organized labor has today in the United States was not generously granted to it by benevolent businessmen and legislators who decided, as a matter of lofty principle, that it was only fair and proper for workers to form unions. If labor's status had been so effortlessly achieved, it would now be less of a challenge to try to take it away. Instead, the American labor movement made its gains through a long, uphill battle against employers who were determined to beat down the efforts of their employees to have a collective voice in the setting of their wages and working conditions. In the majority of the conflicts between individual unions and employers during most of the period since American workers first began to organize, it was the employer—not the union—who could draw support from the newspapers, local government officials, state and federal courts, private detective agencies, professional strikebreaking agencies, and the police. In the occasional strike that blew up into violence on too large a scale for the local police to handle, the employer could usually look to the National Guard or federal troops to intervene against the strikers.

True, the American worker had a legal right to join a union. But, until the 1930's, his employer also had a legal right to fire him if he caught him doing so. Workers had a legal right, with some exceptions, to go on strike for higher wages and better working conditions. But the worker who joined a picket line in exercising that right ran the risk of being dragged off to jail (or to the hospital, if the police were in a mood to swing their clubs freely). Striking workers were not alone in being exposed to risk. Few employers and business executives were ever injured in American labor disputes—except in the pocketbook—but there were numerous casualties among strike replacements, private guards and detectives, and policemen. The era of widespread strike violence in the United States, a period in which deaths and injuries were a much more common feature of American labor disputes than of those in Western Europe, is roughly bounded by the late 1870's and the late 1930's. Its early years are marked by the railroad strikes of 1877, when mobs of strikers and strike sympathizers armed themselves to do battle with state militia for control of several key railroad terminals. Its closing phase can be seen in the "Memorial Day Massacre of 1937"—an episode bloodier than any American labor dispute has produced in the 30 years since—when Chicago police opened fire on a peaceful demonstration in support of striking steelworkers and shot a large number of men and women. No authoritative count exists of those struck down by fists, bricks, clubs, and guns during these 60 years that approximately constitute the peak period of labor dispute violence in America. The sum of the casualties on both sides was probably three to four thousand killed, and certainly many thousands were wounded. This is a trivial number, in comparison with the carnage of even a small-scale modern war, but enough to show the intensity of emotion in the struggle between organized labor and its enemies in the United States.

The definitive breakthrough for labor did not come until the 1930's—still a relatively recent time in American history. More than any other single event, the passage of the Wagner Act of 1935 stands out as the signal that organized labor had finally won a secure position in our society. Senators and Congressmen in office under the banner of Roosevelt's New Deal saw to it that the labor movement, in particular, received a "new deal."

The Wagner Act hemmed in the employer, making it far more difficult than in the past for him to fight off the unionization of his workers. If he tried to carry on the old practice of firing any of his employees discovered to be union members, federal authorities—acting through the newly established National Labor Relations Board and the federal courts —could now order him to put these workers back on their jobs. More painful still, the employer could be ordered to give such workers enough back pay to compensate them for their losses of income as a result of his having illegally discharged them. If the employer rejected a union's demand that he bargain with it, claiming that the union was not actually the choice of his employees, the NLRB would hold a secret-ballot election among the employees. If the union won a majority of the votes, the NLRB would officially "certify" it as the bargaining representative of the employees, after which the employer was legally required under the Wagner Act to sit down promptly at the negotiating table with the union's leaders. If he still attempted to evade the unpleasant obligation of dealing with the union, the NLRB could get a federal court order compelling him to negotiate, under penalty of heavy fines if he continued to drag his feet. Not only was the employer required to bargain, but he was required to bargain in "good faith"—that is, to make a sincere effort to reach an agreement with the union on wages, hours, and other terms of a union-management contract. If he sat at the bargaining table in such a taciturn, sullen, hostile fashion as to indicate that he was not acting in good faith, but was merely going through the motions, he then could be considered legally responsible for provoking a strike the union might call. In such a strike, even if the employer recruited strikebreakers to replenish his workforce and the strike collapsed after a few weeks or months, he could not fully reap the fruits of victory as he could have before 1935. Despite the strike's failure, the Wagner Act still required him to recognize and bargain with the union; and it also required him to reinstate those of his employees who asked for their jobs back, even though this usually forced him to discharge replacements hired for the purpose of breaking the strike.

The Wagner Act of 1935 did not usher in the millennium for the American labor movement. If it had, there would be far more than 17 million union members in the country today. Legislation alone does not enable union organizers to sign up workers who are apathetic, suspicious, or hostile toward labor unions, or who are simply skeptical that a union will bring them benefits worth the cost of the union dues. However, the Wagner Act gave excellent protection to that great number of American workers who could be persuaded to join unions, provided they were released from fear of employer retaliation against them. It also reduced the employer's chance of ridding himself of the costly annoyance of dealing with a union by use of the tactic of provoking a strike and then recruiting a new work force uncontaminated by union sympathies. For this and other reasons, employers were less inclined after the mid-1930's than before to turn to the hiring of strikebreakers—or "scabs," in the language of union members—as the answer to a strike. Particularly after 1937, when the Supreme Court upset the predictions of eminent legal counsel and dashed the hopes of American businessmen by declaring the Wagner Act constitutional, it became the practice of most employers to accept strikes fairly philosophically when they occurred, to renounce any attempt to keep their factories or other business establishments operating in the face of a strike, and to continue negotiating more or less calmly with union leaders toward a mutual agreement on terms to settle the strike. Accordingly, the level of violence accompanying labor disputes in the United States fell in the late 1930's and has remained since then well below that of the earlier era.

The American employer certainly always had a clear legal right to hire replacements, if he could find them, when his employees went on strike and to try to keep his business going without interruption. He has that legal right today, although he no longer commonly attempts to exercise it. This right of the employer, however, has not received the wholehearted acceptance of American workers, whatever the law may be. The worker who has gone on strike does not think of himself as having abandoned a job which his employer should now be perfectly free to give to someone else. He has only left for a time, as a means of putting the employer under additional pressure to sweeten the terms offered the employees. The worker sees the job he has temporarily walked away from as still *his* job, one in which he holds a form of property right. It may not be a property right the courts will recognize, but it is nonetheless real to the worker. Indeed, since he frequently owns little property of the conventional sort, he is likely to value his job as the most precious asset he has. To the striker on the picket line, the strike replacement walking past him to enter the plant is a thief, engaged in a despicable act of stealing

233

another man's job—even though he has a police escort for protection while he carries out the theft. The striking worker's sense of outrage toward the "scab" is akin to the emotional reaction a man might have to a burglar found ransacking his home. It is this deep feeling of the worker that he is entitled to a right of ownership in his job which largely explains why thousands of Americans, perhaps no more inclined to lawlessness than the average citizen under most circumstances, have committed acts of criminal violence in labor disputes with little or no evident sense of guilt over their behavior. An explanation, of course, is not the same thing as an excuse.

Although the Wagner Act helped greatly to civilize the relationships between unions and employers and to make their disputes less bloody affairs, the rules the Act laid down were eventually modified and supplemented by new federal legislation. By the end of World War II, an apparent majority of Americans—including many who were strongly sympathetic to unions—had become critical of some of the organizing and strike tactics which the labor movement had commonly indulged in since the mid-1930's. In 1947, accordingly, Congress replaced the Wagner Act with the Taft-Hartley Act, a lengthy, complicated law which regulated labor relations in much greater detail than its predecessor. Union officials reacted to the passage of the Taft-Hartley Act with high-voltage public temper tantrums. They cried that the old crowd of reactionary Republicans and Dixiecrats had ganged up to thrust the American worker into a legal status comparable to that of a Russian serf under Ivan the Terrible.

Nothing of the sort had, in fact, occurred. The Taft-Hartley Act changed various rules of the game, taking away some of labor's previous freedom to wield almost any weapon that came to hand and giving those employers willing to fight unions a little more elbowroom than they had under the Wagner Act. It also rolled out a splendid vista of employment opportunities before the American legal profession. But, from the vantage point of 20 years later, it is clear that the Taft-Hartley Act of 1947 has done little damage to the labor movement—far less than most of the Act's proponents had hoped and almost all of its opponents had feared.

Since 1947, Congress has enacted no legislation designed to bring a significant shift in the balance of power between unions and employers. In 1959, organized labor claimed—though in much more muted tones than in 1947—that it had received a slap from Congress in the passage of the Landrum-Griffin Act. That Act did restrict union tactics in a few ways which would probably have been incorporated in the original Taft-Hartley Act had Senator Taft been able to foresee the need for them. The Landrum-Griffin Act was aimed primarily, however, at encouraging a higher standard of democratic government within American unions and discouraging that minority of union officials who may be tempted to try to run their organizations like Chinese war lords. These are goals that virtually no one will decry publicly, and criticism of the Landrum-Griffin Act has been confined largely to quibbles over some of its allegedly nit-picking details.

In 1965, six years following enactment of the Landrum-Griffin Act, it looked as if labor were finally going to have its turn in the legislative batting box. The Republican Party's unexpected decision to nominate Barry Goldwater for President helped Lyndon Johnson pull into Congress an unusually large number of liberal Democrats in the 1964 election. Organized labor's priority target, on the convening of the Congress in January, 1965, was repeal of Section 14-b of the Taft-Hartley Act, which authorizes so-called state "right-to-work" laws. This section of the Act has the effect of depriving the labor movement of a substantial flow of money from dues and initiation fees by enabling almost every Southern state, and many Midwestern and Mountain states, to prohibit the inclusion of union shop clauses in collective bargaining agreements. The sum lost to unions is at least several million dollars per year, and despite the well cultivated myth that American union treasuries are full to overflowing, this money would be most welcome for the financing of organizing campaigns and other union activities. The House of Representatives, in 1965, did pass a bill to repeal Section 14-b, with a margin of votes supplied by freshman Congressmen swept in with the anti-Goldwater landslide. Labor also had enough assured votes to get the bill through the Senate, if the Senate could only manage to vote on it. But the time-honored Senatorial custom known as the filibuster proved an insuperable obstacle. Neither in 1965 nor in 1966 did the bill reach the point of a Senate vote.

The November, 1966, Congressional election replaced an unexpected number of Democrats with Republicans, and the 1968 election has put Richard Nixon in the White House. Organized labor's propects for pushing favorable legislation through Congress are murky for the indefinite future.

Nevertheless, the labor movement's failure over the past 20 years to strike out the more onerous provisions of the Taft-Hartley Act should not be interpreted as evidence that established labor unions have been markedly weakened in their negotiations with employers. Nor does it indi-

235

cate much improvement in the employer's chance of escaping unionization if his workers are more than superficially attracted by the appeals of
union organizers. The Taft-Hartley Act superseded, but did not scrap,
the Wagner Act. The essence of the Wagner Act was reincorporated in
the Taft-Hartley Act and lives on. The American employer is still forbidden to threaten or harass his employees in his effort to keep them out
of labor unions. He will still be ordered to reinstate, with back pay, any
employee he is found to have fired for union activity. He remains under
legal obligation to bargain—and to bargain in "good faith"—with any
union certified by the NLRB as the representative chosen by his employees. And if he is one of those who tries to maintain operations in the
face of a strike, he will usually find that an adequate supply of strikebreakers is much harder to recruit than it was before the 1930's.

Labor unions thus remain solidly entrenched in American society.
Perhaps, in accordance with the tenets of many economic theorists, they
should not have a role in the determination of wage rates. But they have
won this role against strong opposition, and they intend to hold fast to
it. Unions may be an intellectually indigestible lump of reality to those
who dream of a world of perfect competition, but there is no visible likelihood of their evaporating.

Why Join a Union?

Since a labor union attracts the economist's professional attention
largely because it influences the price of labor, the economist may be
tempted to explain the formation of a union in the same way in which he
would explain the formation of a businessmen's price-fixing combination.
The motives that drive workers to join together in labor unions may be
interpreted as essentially identical with those that might lead a group of
retail drug store operators to agree among themselves to raise their prices
for prescription drugs. In such an interpretation, the union member is cast
into the mold of a highly calculating "economic man" whose one overriding interest is in the price at which he can sell his labor, and the union
becomes little more than a means for getting its members a higher price.

Anyone who seeks to understand how unions come into existence
must not allow his gaze to become too narrowly fixed on the union's role
as a negotiator of wage rates. As one approach to an explanation of why
workers form unions, consider the following hypothetical situations:

1. A worker is seriously hurt in an automobile accident. He requires six months to recover from his injuries. When recovered, he reports to his employer and asks to be put back to work. He is told that his job was filled long ago and no other job is available for him.

2. Overtime work, at time-and-one-half the regular hourly rate, is occasionally available in a business firm, and the departmental supervisor gives almost all the overtime work to a few favorite employees who have ingratiated themselves with him.

3. An employee is 15 minutes late to work, for the fourth time in a year. The plant manager fires him. The employee protests that he can offer an excuse for each time he has come late and that, in any case, the loss of his job is an unreasonably severe penalty. His appeal is rejected.

4. Since business is slack, a factory must temporarily lay off a large number of men. Workers with as much as 10 years' seniority receive layoff notices; but a foreman's nephew, who began work only a year earlier, is kept on the job.

5. A 55-year-old worker, after 20 years of employment in a factory, is fired because he no longer has the strength and energy to keep up with the assembly line. He asks the company to transfer him to some lighter job, such as watchman or janitor, but is refused.

6. A firm has lost valuable supplies and materials in a series of thefts which it suspects have been carried out by one or more of the employees. The firm orders all the workers, therefore, to submit to questioning with a lie detector. Several of them object to the order as humiliating and degrading but are told that they will lose their jobs if they refuse to undergo the lie detector test.

7. After months of suffering quietly the foul and abusive language of a foreman who delights in browbeating the men under him, a worker loses his temper and threatens to knock the foreman down. The foreman reports him to the plant manager who brushes aside the worker's explanations and gives him a two-week disciplinary layoff without pay, warning him that he will be fired if he raises his voice to the foreman again.

This list of hypothetical, but not wildly implausible, situations could be extended indefinitely. Note that none of the described situations directly involves the issue of wage rates. They involve issues which are fundamentally more important to most workers than a few extra dollars in the weekly pay envelope—such issues as job security, freedom from unfair and arbitrary treatment, human dignity, the desire for a decent and humane approach of one human being to another. Workers do not live by wage rates alone. The rank-and-file worker is subject to the immediate authority of foremen and first-line supervisors as well as to the policies and decisions passed down through a hierarchy of executives. It is virtually impossible for the relationship between those who give orders and those who take them to be continuously and completely satisfactory on both sides. A small minority of executives and supervisors will be petty tyrants, disposed to make life on the job miserable for any underling who displeases them. A great majority—since they are human beings—will occasionally issue an order or make a decision that a worker will consider to be unreasonable, harsh, inequitable, or otherwise unjustified.

What can the individual worker do in the special situations that have been described above or in any of the innumerable other possible situations in which he may consider himself the victim of unfair treatment? Usually, the answer is "not much." Standing alone, as one low-status employee confronting management, he is practically impotent. If he and his fellow employees have banded together in a union, however, the worker's chance of making an effective protest is much improved. As a union song puts it:

> The boss won't listen when one guy squawks,
> But he's got to listen when the union talks.

The union does talk on behalf of the worker—and about a great many things other than wage rates. If management seeks to penalize or discharge a worker for alleged insubordination or incompetence, the union is there to insist that management present adequate evidence and give the worker a fair hearing. If some employees must be laid off, the union-management contract terms rule out selection based on personal favoritism. If a foreman behaves like a Prussian drill sergeant, the union will demand that management straighten him out or replace him. Workers who have organized into a union under alert and vigorous leadership have gained added insurance against being subjected to such practices as: inequitable distribution of overtime work opportunities; speed-ups of the assembly line; arrogant and harsh supervision; discarding of middle-aged workers when their physical strength begins to decline; introduction by management of new machinery and production techniques without provision for

238

the workers displaced; discriminatory wage setting, with some workers paid less than others doing identical work; failure to provide adequate rest periods, comfortable temperatures, ventilation, or other working conditions desired by employees.

Above all, the union protects the worker's individual dignity. It helps him to stand up straight, to escape the danger of degenerating into a boot-licking subservient in order to hold his job or curry favor with a super-visor.

The fact that the employees of a firm have *not* become unionized does not imply, of course, that they will necessarily suffer from any par-ticular form of arbitrary treatment. Indeed, it may imply that the man-agement has been scrupulously careful to avoid any injustices which might spur the employees into forming a union for their mutual protec-tion. Nevertheless, one cannot legitimately gloss over the very real dis-tinction between the position of the worker who hopes to be fairly treated out of the wisdom and kindness of his supervisors and the position of the worker whose prospects for fair treatment are underwritten by terms spelled out in a union contract, with the union standing by to assure that these terms are honored.

There are so many ways in which unions can serve to protect and secure justice for the worker that a society is conceivable in which unions eschew a role in negotiating wages. Theoretically, the determination of wage levels might be left to the interaction of supply and demand in the labor market, while unions occupied themselves with the host of nonwage issues that arise in the relationship between employer and employee. A boundary line of this sort was presumably being considered by one of the best-known critics of labor unions, the late Henry Simons, professor of economics at the University of Chicago, when he wrote:

> I wish I could honestly propose that unions be protected and fostered in their good functions and deprived of their socially bad ones.

However, Professor Simons went on to say:

> Like others, I can *wish* for this solution, but also like others, I cannot honestly propose it, for I have no notion *how* it could be done.

One may or may not agree with Professor Simons' view that the negotia-tion of wage rates is a "socially bad" union function. But one can hardly dispute his view that it seems impossible—at least in a country such as the United States, with its political democracy and predominantly private enterprise economy—to somehow take away from unions the power to bargain over wages while leaving them sufficient power to protect their members with respect to those issues that do not involve the direct setting of wage levels.

The Economic Effects of Unions

When organized labor in a country reaches a stage of large size and apparently impressive strength, it stimulates many questions in the mind of the economist. Several of the most important of these will be raised here. But anyone who expects neat, definitive answers is warned that he will be disappointed. Unions undoubtedly have effects upon the economy, but the techniques of economic analysis have not been, and may never be, sharpened to the point where they can disentangle and measure the precise impact of unions, as distinct from the multitude of other forces that are simultaneously influencing economic activity. Furthermore, unionism, on a large enough scale to warrant the economist's having much concern about it, did not emerge in the United States until about 30 years ago. It is still a comparatively recent development. A generation or two from now, if our present form of society survives so long in this nuclear era, the accumulation of observations may allow more confident answers to be offered concerning the impact of a big labor movement upon the American economy.

Given these precautionary comments, consider the following questions:

1. Do unions change the rate at which productivity rises in the economy?
2. Do unions affect the total level of employment in the economy?
3. Do unions alter the form in which workers are paid for their labor?
4. Do unions raise the wage rates of union members relative to those of workers not in unions?
5. Do unions push up the general level of wages and salaries in the economy? If so, do they indirectly push up the general level of prices?

An identical, but not very satisfactory, answer can be given to all of these: Yes, almost certainly unions do—to some unknown extent. Below this level of sweeping generality, a few brief observations will be presented concerning each question in turn.

Productivity

Labor productivity—or output per man-hour—is measured by dividing an index number representing the real output of goods and services in an economy by an index number representing the input of man-hours of labor used to produce those goods and services. If, from year to year, the index of output rises more rapidly than the index of man-hour input, then labor productivity has increased. For example, if total output increases by 5 per cent, while the input of man-hours increases by 2 per cent, then output per man-hour has risen by a shade less than 3 per cent.

Whatever the influence of unions may be on labor productivity as measured for the economy as a whole, there is universal agreement that it is vastly less important than the influence of technological and managerial innovations—such as new and improved types of equipment, new materials and chemical processes, and ingenious improvements in the way management combines labor and other resources in a production process. Granted, then, that union influence is relatively modest, is it positive or negative?

On this question, no consensus has been reached, although the arguments presented seem to tip the scales toward those whose answer is "negative." They point out various adverse effects unions may have. For example, unions in the construction industry and some other lines of work maintain such jealousy guarded jurisdictional rules that unionized firms cannot deploy their labor with maximum flexibility and efficiency. Unions occasionally delay the introduction of labor-saving machinery and processes, although they very rarely manage to block these permanently. Jobs which should be eliminated as a result of technological change, such as the jobs of firemen when steam locomotives were replaced by diesels, are sometimes kept filled by union pressure on employers. Workers protected by union contracts have also been claimed by some observers to slack off more, to put forth less conscientious effort than nonunion workers whom an employer can discharge without fearing a challenge from union officials. Evidence on this last point is not easily come by, and there is inevitable disagreement in interpreting what evidence is available. Men working at a pace that, in the view of one observer, seems reasonable may, in the view of another, be slave-driven almost to the point of physical ex-haustion. And it would be naive to expect employer and employee to have identical estimates of what is a "fair day's work" on the employee's part.

Defense arguments can be offered against the case for convicting unions of a net adverse effect on productivity. The protection of unions is claimed to improve the morale of workers, assure them that their griev-ances will be listened to, and avoid their building up bitter feelings against repressive management. All this, it is argued, must make the workers more contented and therefore more productive on the job. Recurrent union demands for wage increases are often cited as having a positive effect on productivity—the rather optimistic line of argument being that as labor becomes ever more costly, management is continuously spurred on to success in developing techniques for using that labor more efficiently. Or-ganized labor can also claim to contribute to higher productivity in gen-eral, in an indirect way, through its role as one of the most important political forces supporting public programs to increase the resources de-voted to health and education in the United States. A healthier, better educated citizenry will be more productive.

Whichever arguments may appear to be the more plausible, the sta-tistical evidence is unchallenged on one point: Labor productivity, as it is measured for the private industry sector of the American economy, has risen at a somewhat faster average annual rate in the period since World War II—a period of large-scale, vigorous union activity—than it rose over the period from the Civil War to the early 1930's, when the American labor movement was small and weak. Possibly, in the absence of unions, it might have risen at an even slightly faster rate in the past 20 years, but the postwar gain in productivity has been a very gratifying one by any reasonable evaluation.

The President's Council of Economic Advisers estimates that real output per man-hour in the private sector of our economy has been in-creasing in recent years at an annual average rate of about 3.2 per cent. If we can keep up this fast pace of productivity increase—*and* if we can also maintain approximately full employment in the economy, *and* if we do not devote a substantially increased proportion of our economic re-sources to the Cold War, miscellaneous hot wars around the globe, and the exploration of outer space—then the living standards of the American population generally will rise so rapidly that few people will feel much concern over the question of organized labor's possible effect on produc-tivity.

242

Aggregate Level of Employment

Have unions influenced the American economy to operate closer to, or farther away from, a level of full employment in the years since the end of World War II? Again, there is both general agreement that any effects of unions on the aggregate level of employment have been minor compared to other economic forces and disagreement over what effects unions have probably had.

It is a common experience, of course, to hear dire warnings publicly directed to unions that they are "pricing themselves out of the market" and are destroying job opportunities for their members by their outrageous and insatiable wage demands. It is undeniably true that if a single union should win one wage increase after another, while every other wage rate and price in the economy remained unchanged, the firms employing the union's members would eventually be forced to cut back employment greatly. (It is also true that before this point was reached, these firms would have dug in their heels and begun to put up a stubborn resistance to further union demands.) It is by no means true, however, that a series of wage increases negotiated by a union will necessarily cause unemployment for its members, if wage rates—both union and nonunion —and prices are rising generally throughout the economy.

In the post-World War II American economy, wages, salaries, prices —and, in most years, profits—have been generally rising for more than two decades. Except during the Korean War and the current Vietnam War, however, the unemployment rate has been above 4 per cent almost throughout this period—which is to say that a state of genuinely "full" employment has been the exception, not the rule. Should we assign to union-negotiated wage increases any part of the blame for this failure to maintain full employment? There are some who believe so, but their reasoning has not been widely persuasive.

On the political side, organized labor has been a consistent advocate of vigorous federal government policies to stimulate a high level of employment. It opposed the election of Eisenhower and generally criticized the economic policy of his administration, with its three recessions in eight years and its chronic inability to achieve full employment. (In fairness to Eisenhower, it might be noted that if he had spent American dollars at the rate of $25 billion per year, and American lives at the rate of 10,000 per year, to fight a war on the other side of the world, he too would have pushed the unemployment rate down below 4 per cent.) During the 1960's, organized labor's lobbyists on Capitol Hill worked to enlist support for a number of measures directed toward the unemployment problem—measures ranging from the Johnson Administration's 1964 cut in federal income tax rates, which most economists endorsed, to the AFL-CIO's own demand that the workweek be reduced by law to 35 hours, a shopworn proposal which all but a handful of professional economists unqualifiedly rejected as a means of reducing unemployment.

Since the labor movement is continually leaning its political weight on the side of expansionary federal fiscal and monetary policies, it seems plausible to assume that both Congress and the White House have given somewhat more serious attention to the goal of full employment than would have been the case had there been no highly visible and vocal organizations which claimed to speak for millions of American workers—and voters. But labor's net influence upon government economic policy could easily be exaggerated. There is now widespread support from many segments of our society for the view that the federal government has an ultimate responsibility for keeping employment high. Business executives, for example, may feel less concern than union officials over a one or two percentage point rise in the unemployment rate, but they are well aware of the unprofitability of recessions and are no longer apoplectic at the thought of an unbalanced federal budget. They have far more economic sophistication than their predecessors who stood amidst the debacle from 1929 through 1932, crying out for lower wage rates and reductions in government spending, with the American economy collapsing around them. With or without the pressure of a big labor movement, it seems unlikely that the American citizenry would again allow itself to suffer from a persistent level of severe unemployment.

Employee Compensation: Its
Changing Composition

Has collective bargaining by unions shifted the relative proportion of direct money wages and "fringe benefits" in the total compensation that American workers receive for their labor? To this question, a large majority would agree that the answer is "yes."

Until the 1930's, the issues in union-management negotiations were usually neither numerous nor complex. They could commonly be disposed of in a contract of one or two typewritten pages. When the parties had agreed on a wage rate, the length of the standard workday or workweek, and the extra pay (if any) for overtime work, they had generally taken care of all that was immediately relevant to the question of what the employee was going to get from the employer. This innocent era of blissfully uncomplicated agreements drew to a close as labor unions swelled in size and increased in vigor during the 1930's. Over the past 30 years, union and management negotiators have sat down to bargain about a constantly growing list of different forms of employee compensation.

Today, a collective bargaining agreement may specify not only an hourly wage rate for the employees but also may include: a number of holidays with pay; a paid annual vacation plan, with detailed provisions concerning the length of service required for vacations of varying length; time off for jury service, with pay, as well as for funerals of family members, for voting, and for other purposes; an employer-financed health insurance plan; a pension plan, perhaps with options for retirement at various ages at different levels of monthly pension payments; a group life insurance plan; a plan for employer financing of "supplementary unemployment benefits" to laid-off employees, in addition to their weekly payments of unemployment compensation benefits from public funds; provision for varying amounts of severance pay to workers permanently laid off before reaching retirement eligibility; employer financing of part of the relocation costs of employees entitled to be transferred when operations are moved from one branch plant to another; arrangements for the employer to pay the costs of retraining workers whose former jobs have been eliminated by technological change; provision of "sick pay" to ill or injured employees.

All these items, and quite a few others which may appear today in a collective bargaining agreement, represent compensation in one form or another to the employees and represent "labor cost" to the employer. Their proliferation has made the job of labor contract negotiators more technically challenging and has provided employment for many statisticians, actuaries, lawyers, investment counselors, and other specialists called in to advise unions and management concerning the more complex types of fringe benefits. Correspondingly, it has become more difficult to evaluate just what a union has "won" when it renegotiates a collective bargaining agreement. If the renewed contract provides, in addition to a wage increase, improvements in various fringe benefits, neither the union nor the management may be able to state with complete confidence the precise size of the "package." The usual practice is to try to translate all the fringe benefit changes into the common denominator of a "cents-per-hour" equivalent and add them to the hourly wage increase in order to arrive at a figure which purports to be the addition in cost the employer has agreed to incur for each man-hour of labor he hires. Frequently, after a long and involved contract has been renegotiated, the union and the employer announce substantially different figures as their respective estimates of the total "cents-per-hour" price.

Would the structure of employee compensation in the United States have become quite so complex in the absence of a large-scale labor movement? Probably not. Some observers have not-so-facetiously suggested that American unions appear to be engaged in a contest to determine which can come up with the most esoteric and imaginative fringe benefit. If one persuades an employer to agree to pay college tuition for any employee's child who stands in the top 15 per cent of his high school graduating class, perhaps another will try to top this with a proposal that the employer pay marriage counselor fees for any employee who is beset by marital difficulties. The market for new fashions in fringe benefits is still a lively one.

However, the bulk of employer outlays for fringe benefits goes to finance such almost universally accepted items as group life insurance plans, health insurance plans, pension plans, and annual vacations. Unions have been very active in negotiating for these; but it is extremely probable that each of these benefits—with the possible exception of private pension plans—would have become very widespread by now, even if the American labor movement had remained in a state of coma since the 1930's. A few pioneering, nonunion business firms began providing these benefits to their employees long before it became the practice of unions to raise demands for them, and undoubtedly the example set by these progressive employers would have been increasingly followed by others as the years passed.

With respect to the principal standard fringe benefits, then, the role of unions seems to have been primarily that of accelerating the pace of a development that would have unfolded, to a substantial degree, in any case. To say this is not to minimize the impact unions may have had. In particular, it seems likely that union pressure for the establishment and improvement of pension plans has made, and will make, old age a less depressing time of life for hundreds of thousands of American workers who would otherwise have waited in vain for their employers to take on some of the responsibility for providing them with retirement incomes.

Union Wages Relative to Nonunion

It may seem astonishing that a few economists have professed to be unconvinced that the wage rates negotiated in collective bargaining agreements are appreciably different from those that would have emerged anyway, if workers had never troubled themselves to form unions. Still, if one insists that the wage impact of unions be proven beyond the thinnest shadow of a doubt, he puts himself in a position from which he is not easily dislodged.

Does all the emotion and energy that has been channeled into union activity leave union members with wages no higher, relative to the wages of nonunion workers, than they would otherwise have been? Is it but sound and fury, signifying nothing? Not many people believe so; but precise, indisputable measurements of the relative wage gains won by unions are not available.

A wage rate which a group of workers gets through union-management negotiation is still one which may be influenced by virtually all of the forces which would have determined the level of that wage if the workers had not been unionized. Workers cannot escape from the economic environment by forming a union. The wage the union negotiates for them will be affected by such factors as: the demand for and supply of labor in the occupation or industry the union represents; the wage rates being paid in other occupations and industries; sales forecasts and profit expectations of the firms with whom the union is bargaining; the rate of increase of labor productivity in these firms; the degree of freedom the firms have to pass on wage increases through raising their prices; and the ratio of labor cost to total cost incurred by the firms. Many other factors could be cited.

Although there is no doubt that unionization does not miraculously empower workers to shatter the economic forces that limit the extent to which wages can rise, it would be remarkably ironic if unions were unable—at least on the average—to win something over and above the wage rates unorganized workers would have received. Many economists have carried out studies in an effort to estimate the extra gains that American unions may bring to their members. These studies have been based upon a great variety of wages and other data and have employed many different methods, including the use of complex statistical techniques. In general, they have led to rather tentative estimates that unions have probably pushed up wage rates, in the well unionized occupations and industries in the United States, an average of 10 per cent to 25 percent, relative to wages in nonunion occupations and industries. These are estimates which, of necessity, have been derived from imperfect data by the ingenious but still limited techniques that are currently known. They seem plausible enough, given their limitations, but they are not universally credited.

Someone who has been influenced by hearing unions frequently described as "labor monopolies" might be puzzled to find that those who have most carefully estimated the probable relative wage gains made by American unions have not produced estimates greater than about 25 per cent, at most. If unions really have the amount of power associated with the term "monopoly," would they not use it to bring their members relative gains of 50 per cent, 100 per cent, or even more?

A brief answer is that a union simply does not have the power of a monopolist as that term is defined by economists. True, many people who wish to arouse antagonism toward organized labor in the United States consider it helpful to insist that unions are labor monopolies. Everyone is conditioned to abhor monopoly; and it can be effective, if not overly sportsmanlike, as a tactic to pin an odious label on one's adversary. But the monopoly label is not appropriate for a union. A genuine monopolist can unilaterally set the price of the product he has to sell, since he is the exclusive seller of that product. He, and he alone, decides what the price is to be. Unions, however, do not unilaterally set prices—that is, the wages of their members. They *negotiate* wage rates. They bargain with employers over wages, and the employers whom unions face are not weak and spineless creatures who meekly accept whatever terms unions dictate to them. Collective bargaining is a two-person game, played under rules and conditions which by no means guarantee that the union must always "win." It is not surprising, therefore, that wages of union members have failed to skyrocket to dramatic heights by comparison with the wages of workers outside of unions.

The General Wage Level and Price Level

Even if unions did not have the effect of elevating union wage rates relative to the nonunion portion of the economy, it would still be possible, theoretically, for unions to push up the general level of wages and salaries throughout the economy. Let us suppose, just for the purpose of illustration, that all American unions simultaneously negotiated a 10 per cent wage increase for their members and that all the nonunion employees in the nation promptly reacted by giving their employees an identical 10 per cent increase, either because they considered this to be only equitable, or because they feared their employees also would turn to unions if their wages were allowed to lag behind. In such a hypothetical case, unions would not have changed the position of union wage rates relative to nonunion; but they would nevertheless have been basically responsible for the upward movement in all wages.

The normal level of money wages and salaries in the United States has been continuously moving up since the late 1930's and is expected to keep right on moving up for as far into the future as most economists attempt to look. There is no period in previous American history when the general wage level is known to have risen without a break for as much as 30 consecutive years. Are unions, then, primarily or largely accountable for this unbroken rise that has been going on ever since organized labor first reached mass proportions under the Roosevelt Administration?

Economists differ widely among themselves in their estimates of the influence unions have upon the general wage level. Some believe that wage increases conspicuously negotiated by large and aggressive unions blaze an upward path which is then followed, more or less closely, by other unions and by nonunion firms whose employees might become restless if they fell behind in the procession. Others give little weight to the role of unions and consider movements in the general wage level to be almost entirely determined by such impersonal economic forces as aggregate consumer purchasing power, the economy's demand for labor, the level of unemployment, corporation investment policies, or the rate of increase in the money supply.

After all due homage is paid to the undeniable fact that unions could not continue to negotiate wage increases under harshly unfavorable economic circumstances, several points still remain. The American labor movement has been much larger, and on the whole more aggressive, in the past 30 years than in the previous period of its history. Union members have now generally come to expect that they will receive a wage increase every year without exception—and a wage increase every year is indeed provided in the great majority of union-management agreements. Even if they wished to, nonunion firms could not keep the wage rates of their employees frozen indefinitely while wages in unionized firms continue to rise all around them. Over the past 30 years, the general wage level in the United States has, in fact, risen with a speed and continuity quite unmatched by any earlier period of comparable length. When all these ob-

249

servations are put together, it would not seem very easy to explain unions away as having only a negligible influence on the general wage level.

People are not likely to object to a never-ending upward movement in the general wage level per se, especially if their own wages or salaries are moving along with the rest. They begin to show concern only when they find that the level of consumer prices is also rising. In the United States, the Consumer Price Index has risen substantially—though much less rapidly than wages—and with few interruptions over the past 30 years. Are unions also to be considered largely responsible for this fairly continuous upward movement in the price level?

A fortiori, those economists who see very little union influence on the general wage level deny that unions significantly affect the level of prices. Some who do believe unions push up the wage level point out that wages can rise while prices remain stable, and they turn to a variety of factors other than unions to explain the continuing rise in the Consumer Price Index. The debate among economists over organized labor's share of responsibility for long-term, gradual, "creeping" inflation in the United States seems likely to drag on indefinitely.

One point based on inescapable economic reality and simple arithmetic can be emphasized. In our private enterprise economy, the Consumer Price Index will not long remain stable if the general wage level is rising at a rate faster than labor productivity rises in the private sector of the economy. This, in turn, means that the "noninflationary" average annual increase in the wage-and-fringe-benefit compensation of American workers is slightly over 3 per cent at best and perhaps somewhat less than 3 per cent. Up to now, at least, neither union members nor union leaders in this country appear ready to settle for a rate of increase in compensation of no more than about 3 per cent per year. The prospect for a halt in the upward movement of the Consumer Price Index is not promising.

The American Labor Movement and the Capitalist System

In conclusion, let us return to a question raised at the outset of this essay—the possibility that the organized labor movement will eventually prove to be the doom of the private enterprise system.

Whatever the experience in other nations, American labor has been a terrible disappointment to those who hoped for so long that unions would help lead the way toward the establishment of the socialist state. Within the American Federation of Labor, from the time it was founded in 1886, a minority who felt the capitalist system to be intolerable carried on an unprevailing struggle to convert the rest. The majority of AFL union members and officials were certainly far from satisfied with the living standards of American workers, with the legal status of unions, or with the position of organized labor in American society. They could not be persuaded, however, that labor's best course of action was to rally under the banner of socialism.

Outside the AFL, beginning in 1905, a violently anticapitalist labor organization, the Industrial Workers of the World, tried passionately to stir American workers into open revolution against the system. The colorfully unrestrained language of its proclamations and the mass demonstrations and strikes which the IWW occasionally managed to touch off attracted to it a measure of public attention quite out of proportion to its small membership. During its approximately 15 years of noisily active life, the IWW provoked the intense antagonism of many AFL union leaders—whom it continually attacked as traitors to the working class—and sent tremors of alarm among Americans of the type who is perennially fearful that forces of subversion are on the brink of taking over the country. The entry of the United States into the First World War, which the IWW opposed, was the beginning of the end for the organization. Its principal leaders and many of its members were arrested for continuing to speak out against the war after April 6, 1917. They were tried, convicted, and sent to federal penitentiaries. The IWW remained in existence but never regained the membership or vigorous spirit it had before the war.

In the American labor movement, a great deal of mutual resentment and ill feeling developed, not only between the adherents of the IWW and those of the AFL but also between factions within the AFL who were in bitter disagreement over the goals and tactics organized labor should adopt. Their internal conflicts have a marked resemblance to those that are currently creating a turbulent scene among the members of the NAACP, CORE, the Urban League, SNCC, the Black Muslims, and other organizations who are locked in controversy over the most effective means for winning the Negro a fully equal status in American society. As in the civil rights movement today, there were those in the American labor movement who advocated a calm, careful, step-by-step approach and those who scorned caution and called for an aggressively militant, full-speed-ahead drive toward labor's goals. There were those who advocated a conciliatory approach to employers, designed to persuade them that they could live in reasonable harmony with unions, and those who angrily insisted that the only way a union would ever win concessions from an employer would be by following the advice Theodore Roosevelt allegedly prescribed for dealing with a Congressman: "Take a stick, and hit him on the snout." There were those who believed that unions could win a decent status for the American worker within the existing political and economic framework of our society, given some modest reforms of the system, and those who condemned American capitalism as rotten at the core and exhorted workers to accept no compromise with it.

From the 1880's through the 1920's, a large majority of the leadership positions within the labor movement were held by men who can be loosely classified as belonging to the "moderate" faction. In contrast to the hypermilitant minority, they were very conscious of organized labor's weak position in the United States and of the disasters that could befall unions which rushed headlong into ill-planned strikes. They sought to gain approval from the general public and to allay employer antagonism by trying to build up an image of unions as "responsible" organizations led by reasonable men who could be trusted not to make rapacious demands upon employers. They criticized some aspects of private enterprise capitalism but did not basically challenge the system itself.

Despite their restrained and cautious policies, these "moderate" union officials, who dominated the mainstream of the American labor movement, commonly found themselves under intense fire from the business community at the same time that they were being verbally blasted by the militant opposition within labor's ranks. Like Tennyson's Light Brigade, they found guns to the right and guns to the left of them. From the employer side, the officials were denounced as "labor agitators"—sowers of discord who poisoned the minds of simple, happy workingmen and excited in them the delusion that they needed a union in order to get fair wages and just treatment. From the radical labor side, they were described as deserving of a variety of uncomplimentary epithets: "labor politician," "pie-card," "labor skate," "sell-out artist," "fink," "labor faker," and so on. They were charged with the crime of *not* agitating the worker but instead of smothering the worker's inherent revolutionary tendencies by their unaggressive, complacent leadership. As one of the labor movement's left-wing extremists stated it, about the time of the First World War:

> The workers have no more insidious enemy than the chicken-hearted labor leader who advises them to be patient and respectable. An ounce of direct action is worth more than tons of paid advice of labor politicians.

During the 1930's, it appeared for a time that the American labor movement might at last come under the sway of a style of leadership acceptable to the militant faction. The economic disaster of the Great Depression shook up many workers who had uncritically accepted the capitalist system, and it made them more willing than in the past to follow left-wing leadership. As the number of union members grew rapidly in the mid-1930's, many young, aggressive men emerged to challenge established union officials. In the AFL's notoriously racketeer-infested International Longshoremen's Association, for example, would-be new leaders played on the resentment many members felt toward the union's president, Joseph Ryan. Drawing an annual salary of $15,000—a princely figure in the Depression years—Ryan had reached a *modus vivendi* with waterfront employers which was comfortable enough for both them and himself but which left more than a little to be desired by the rank-and-file longshoremen on the docks. His opponents stirred up rebellion with a steady stream of attacks upon him, including such poetic creations as:

> Here's to Ryan, the longshore king,
> He likes to live in state.
> He gets his fifteen thousand bucks,
> And the workers pull the freight.

Their tactics brought results; the ILA was split apart, and Ryan's Pacific Coast members seceded, to form a new union under militant left-wing leadership.

In several other AFL unions, aside from the ILA, vigorous newcomers either shoved aside the older, "responsible" leaders or succeeded in pulling a large fraction of the membership into a rival organization. A more ominous threat to traditional AFL leadership arose in the 1930's with the formation of the CIO—a federation of unions that advocated the organization of all workers in an industry, regardless of their occupation or level of skill, into one industrial union.

The CIO not only challenged the AFL's position that skilled crafts-men should belong to exclusive unions of their own, separating them from the mass of semiskilled and unskilled workers; it also adopted mili-tant tactics, including mass picketing and sit-down strikes, which alarmed businessmen. The leaders of the new CIO unions were typically intense, determined young men who were angry over the hardships suffered by workers in the Depression years and who felt a sense of mission to reshape American society. The Communist Party, which attracted more followers in the 1930's than ever before or since, made an all-out effort to gain in-fluence over the CIO. It had only a very limited success but one that was nevertheless impressive, in view of the tiny percentage of Communists among American union members. The leadership of about a dozen na-tional CIO unions—most of them relatively small organizations—was won by men who either were Communists of the 14-karat "card-carrying" variety or who followed the twists of the Soviet Union's foreign policy line through the 1930's and 1940's with truly remarkable fidelity for a purported non-Communist. Since the American businessman was already predisposed to see a host of imaginary Communists lurking within the labor movement, the sight of a few unmistakable Communists among CIO leaders was rather unnerving. AFL officials naturally seized the oppor-tunity to further inflame the fears of businessmen that the CIO was Com-munist-dominated. One of the amusing spectacles of the 1930's, accord-ingly, was the headlong rush of many employers to escape the dreaded CIO by encouraging their employees to sign up with respectable AFL union leaders whom, only a few years earlier, these employers had been denouncing as dangerous "labor agitators."

The CIO was indeed a vigorous new element that much enlivened the American labor movement, but it never lived up to the horrendous image which it initially projected in the overexcited imaginations of em-ployers. The cumulative effect of the social and economic reforms of the Roosevelt Administration greatly reduced the resentment the new CIO leaders had felt in the early Depression period. World War II restored full employment in the economy; and, since the end of that war, unemploy-ment has never begun to approach the level of the 1930's. Over the past 30 years, a tremendous improvement has taken place in the ordinary American worker's standard of living as well as in his degree of economic security in the face of sickness and the onset of old age. The worker has fared so well under private enterprise capitalism that most of those CIO leaders who were originally harsh critics of the system seem long ago to have made their peace with it. What influence the Communist Party had within the CIO was shattered in the late 1940's, when the anti-Communist majority of CIO leaders threw out of the federation the small minority who persisted in following the Soviet Union line after the wartime honeymoon between the U.S. and the U.S.S.R. was over. Today, there are only two independent national unions of any significance in the United States which are still believed to be under a notable degree of Communist influence, and employers apparently find the leaders of these unions no more difficult to live with than union leaders in general. In 1955, the AFL and CIO merged to form the AFL-CIO. In the 13 years since, the reunited federation has developed a posture which, on the whole, seems somewhat more reminiscent of the old AFL than of the fire-breathing CIO of the 1930's.

Prediction is always hazardous; but, as of 1968, there is no sign on the horizon of an eventual shift of the American labor movement away from its long-held present position of acceptance of the private enterprise system. There is very little evidence today of basic hostility toward the system among either union leaders or union members. "Business unionism"—with a generous admixture of moderate social reformism—enjoys probably a more unchallenged hold upon organized labor in the United States than at any time in past history. If its hold is to be shaken within the next 20 to 30 years, it is difficult now to imagine how an effective challenge might arise.

Questions for Thought and Discussion

1. From the standpoint of the *economist*, what are the "desirable" and the "undesirable" influences that labor unions might exert upon American society? What criteria would the economist probably use in assessing these influences?
2. Do you think it might be to the advantage of labor unions and labor union leaders, on net balance, if the American economy were transformed to a predominantly socialist economy?
3. American labor unions claim a total membership of about 17 to 18 million men and women. The total number of wage and salary employees in the nonagricultural sector of the economy (in-

cluding civilian governmental employees) is about 70 million. Develop arguments both pro and con the following proposition:

> The present ratio of labor union membership to non-agricultural wage and salary employment in the U.S. is, on the whole, a healthier and more desirable one from the standpoint of our economy than would be either a much larger ·or a much smaller ratio.

AUTOMATION IN PERSPECTIVE

John A. Delehanty

New problems are not created by new words. The problems appear first and the words afterwards, but occasionally new words are invented to make old problems seem new.[1]

In a relatively short span of time, the term automation has evolved from what was thought of as a simple designation of certain kinds of industrial processes to a symbol of a complicated, almost awesome way of industrial life. Through various magazine articles of a sensational nature, the public has had conjured up before it the specter of a future economy run by robots, wherein men are needed only to build and service these automatic devices. Nothing could be further from the truth at this time.

There are real problems associated with the introduction and diffusion of automation—and technological change in general—throughout the economy, but they are not of the cataclysmic proportions sometimes implied in popular writings. In a brief treatment of the subject, we cannot cover all of the possible aspects and implications of automation for the social and economic fabric of American life; but we will attempt to indicate something about the nature and development of automation, its impact on the labor force, and the implications for public policy.

Automation

Automation has nearly as many definitions as it has advocates. The term is used to refer to anything from mere mechanized handling of ma-

The author is Associate Professor of Economics at Kansas State University.

[1] Senator Joseph C. O'Mahoney, in Joint Committee on the Economic Report, Hearings, *Automation and Technological Change*, 84th Congress, 1st Session (Washington: Government Printing Office, 1955), p. 51.

terials to the kind of automatic process in which all phases of production, manufacture, assembly, and inspection are carried out through the use of automatic controls without human assistance or with a minimum of such assistance. Common to the various forms of automation is the concept of automatic feedback control, or self-correction. Such application of the principles of self-regulation is fundamental to an automated process; and although definitions of automation differ, it is commonly agreed that feedback is basic to the concept. A frequently cited, albeit oversimplified, example of this concept is the common furnace thermostat. That device is so contrived that when the temperature of a room goes above or below a preset level, the fuel supply to the furnace is correspondingly reduced or increased. In other words, information about performance is fed back into the mechanism to correct its operation and to achieve the desired result.

As mechanized handling of materials and the principle of feedback are not new concepts, it seems that if we stop here and label all progress in these fields as automation we are merely applying a new term to express evolutionary progress. To a large extent, this is the case; and yet, a closer look at what is taking place in the contemporary economy reveals a particular set of developments that perhaps warrants the use of a new term to describe them.

As pointed out by Professor Weinberg, current technological developments represent a continuation of the search begun in the eighteenth century for mechanical devices to replace man as a source of energy in production.[2] During the first phase of this movement, the Industrial Revolution, there was a significant shift from hand labor to the utilization of power-driven machinery. The next century witnessed the steady improvement of mechanical devices and their rapid diffusion throughout the economy. The mass-production phase of industrial development was introduced in the 1920's, and machine operations were made more uniform and simple. At the present time, automatic technology is adding a new dimension to these past accomplishments by making it possible to eliminate direct human involvement in the controlling of processes and in the operation, guiding, and feeding of machines.

Contemporary innovations leading toward more automatic technol-

---

[2] Edgar Weinberg, "A Review of Automatic Technology," *Monthly Labor Review*, June, 1955. This and the following paragraph draw heavily on Professor Weinberg's article.

ogy include: (1) automatic machinery, (2) integrated materials handling and processing equipment, (3) automatic control systems, and (4) electronic computers and data processing machines. The first two innovations represent advanced mechanization based on well-known engineering principles. The other innovations were largely developed—during World War II—out of experience in the new fields of communication engineering, electronics, and control. In a technical sense, the term automation should be used to refer only to those types of technological changes which integrate the elements of advanced mechanization, automatic controls, and the computer.

The advent and diffusion of automation throughout various sectors of the economy have led some people to believe that the age of the automatic factory (and eventual elimination of all but a few jobs) is near at hand. This view is not supported by the available evidence;[3] and, further, it overlooks one important aspect of the new technology which is still very much in the initial stages of development. In the typical case, the full potential of automation can only be achieved through rethinking the entire production process.[4] For example, the steel industry utilizes many automatic control devices, but steel production is not fully automated. Further, the probability is that it will not become automatic unless the entire process of steelmaking is reformulated. This aspect of automation, but its very nature, will most likely occur in a gradual or evolutionary manner.

Upon closer examination, automation—even if carefully and technically defined—appears to be more evolutionary than revolutionary; and it also seems that its full potential will not be achieved for many years. However, the impact of automation warrants serious consideration and study because its introduction into the economy has been increasing in recent years, and the potential of automatic technology for the future is becoming clearer.

Further, we must recognize that automation does not represent the sum total of technological developments in the contemporary economy. These developments also include such innovations as jet propulsion, nu-

---

[3] *Technology and the American Economy*, Report of the National Commission on Technology, Automation, and Economic Progress (Washington: Government Printing Office, 1966), I, 1-7.

[4] John Diebold, *Automation: The Advent of the Automatic Factory* (New York: Van Nostrand, 1952).

clear power generation, the newer metallurgy (including light metals and a great range of alloys), and a variety of synthetic products. Automation is a technology to be used as a way of increasing this varied and highly productive existing and evolving technology. At the moment, automation may have stolen the spotlight; but society must deal with the broad problem of assimilating the total technology into our social and economic life. One important aspect of the impact of technological change, including automation, is discussed in the following section.

Impact on the Labor Force

The benefits arising from technological change are generally recognized—e.g., increasing productive potential, higher incomes for the employed and their employers, new and better products, less hazardous and arduous work, and more leisure time. However, there has always been a persistent fear that technical improvements will also destroy jobs and result in an increasing level of permanent employment. In one respect, this concern is justified; but in another, more important, respect it is not borne out by past experience.

Technological change has and will continue to eliminate particular jobs, cause problems of dislocation in certain communities, and lead to the obsolescence of particular skills. In general, however, the unemployment connected with these developments will be of a temporary nature if the number of new jobs being created in the economy is sufficient to offset those being eliminated and to account for growth in the labor force. It is strong to focus attention on the job-eliminating effects of technological change and to ignore the demonstrated ability of our economy to create jobs.

A brief look at history will reveal that a great deal of technological advance has taken place over the years—e.g., our technology has moved from the horse and buggy to jet propulsion and from hand tools to automatic machines—but the total number of jobs has risen almost continually. Of course, we have experienced periods of high unemployment. During the 1930's, unemployment averaged roughly 18 per cent of the labor force, and public concern with "technological unemployment" reached a peak. However, the "villain" was not primarily technological change but insufficient economic and job growth in the economy as a whole. This was clearly demonstrated by our experience during the 1940's and early 1950's. Technological innovations were introduced at a rapid pace in this period;[5] but economic expansion and total job growth were vigorous, and unemployment averaged only about 4 per cent of the labor force.

A more recent example of this phenomenon is provided by our experience since 1957. The economy dropped into a period of slow job growth for half a decade after 1957, and average unemployment increased to 6 per cent of the labor force. This revived the talk about technological change—automation, to be specific—as the primary cause of unemployment. However, the unprecedented expansion which began in early 1961[6] eventually sparked a return to rapid job growth, and average unemployment dropped to below 4 per cent of the labor force by early 1966—its lowest level since the early 1950's.

In short, technological advance is entirely consistent with rising total employment (and low level unemployment) when a reasonable balance is maintained between economic expansion and our growing productive potential.[7] The real problems associated with technological change, including automation, are exemplified by the need to maintain this overall balance in the economy while dealing effectively with the specific cases wherein dislocation and skill obsolescence are caused by the forward thrust of technology.

The role of public policy is crucial in this whole matter, and it is to a brief discussion of this subject that we now direct our attention.

Public Policy

It is not hard to understand why the working classes in English society showed such stubborn resistance to technological change in the early years of the Industrial Revolution. Society had neither the economic knowledge nor the social wisdom to attempt to deal effectively

---

[5] Such significant developments as synthetic rubber, television broadcasting, wide-scale use of titanium, and electronic computers were all commercially introduced into the economy between 1940 and 1950. See Frank Lynn, "The Rate of Development and Diffusion of Technology," *Automation and Economic Progress*, ed. by Howard R. Bowen and Garth L. Mangum (Englewood Cliffs, N.J.: Prentice-Hall, 1966).

[6] "The current expansion was in its 72nd month in February 1967. The longest previous expansion in the 20th century lasted 66 months in the period dominated by World War II, between 1938 and 1943"; *Manpower Report of the President* (Washington: Government Printing Office, 1967), p. 11.

[7] The principal determinants of the growth in productive potential are: the rise in productivity (average output per man-hour), the increase in the labor force, and changes in the number of hours worked (annual average hours worked per man).

with the individual costs and burdens associated with mechanization and the emerging factory system. As a result, society—and the working classes in particular—suffered through a long period of bitter adjustment to the new technology.

Fortunately, our economic knowledge is now reasonably sufficient to enable us to deal with the most serious possible problem connected with technological change—inadequate economic and job growth. Further, contemporary society is more aware of the individual costs associated with the almost constant changes that occur in a dynamic economy—from whatever source—and has exhibited an increasing willingness to take specific steps designed to meet these problems as they emerge.

Of course, all of this economic and social maturity does not guarantee that we will handle the problems successfully; but it indicates that technological change, including automation, presents us with a situation that may be looked upon as more a challenge than a threat. The challenge is to maximize the benefits of the new technology while minimizing the costs associated with its introduction and diffusion throughout the economy.

Our recent experience indicates that the single most important contribution of public policy is the appropriate use of fiscal and monetary measures to keep the economy, and the total number of jobs, expanding in line with our growing productive potential.

During the late 1950's and early 1960's, there was a substantial "gap" between the actual and potential levels of economic activity, and the result was a period of slow job growth and high average unemployment. To help reverse this situation, a series of fiscal and monetary measures were undertaken that were capped by a large personal and corporate tax cut which became effective early in 1964.[8] This provided a significant part of the stimulus (1) to raise the actual level of economic activity to its present near-approach to the potential level, and (2) to reduce average unemployment to below 4 per cent of the labor force.

In the years immediately ahead, it appears that our productive potential will be increasing at about 4 per cent yearly.[9] This means that fiscal and monetary measures will have to be designed to insure a comparable

---

[8] See *Economic Report of the President* (Washington: Government Printing Office, 1965), pp. 61-70.

[9] *Economic Report of the President* (Washington: Government Printing Office, 1967), p. 44.

growth in the actual level of economic activity if we are to maintain a low average level of unemployment.

Vigorous economic expansion does not cure all of the problems associated with technological change, but it is essential if we are to deal effectively with the specific cases of displacement and skill obsolescence. In this regard, the federal government has recently instituted several new "manpower utilization" programs provided for in the Manpower Development and Training Act of 1962 and the Economic Opportunity Act of 1964. Complementary measures which have recently been enacted include the Vocational Education Act of 1963 and the Economic Development Act of 1965. In addition, several existing programs have been updated and expanded—e.g., those administered by the Vocational Rehabilitation Administration and the United States Employment Service.

These programs sponsor or provide a wide range of services designed to equip individuals to fill suitable jobs or to provide suitable jobs for those willing and able to work, such as: prevocational orientation to increase the individual's knowledge of alternative occupational choices; training projects for entry level skills and training allowances for individuals while enrolled in these projects; and relocation allowances for individuals in labor surplus areas, together with special incentives for employers to provide jobs for those left in such areas.[10]

The existence of these programs indicates a new determination on the part of society to minimize the costs associated with technological change and other sources of change in the contemporary society and economy. Our experience in these efforts should provide us with valuable information on how to deal more effectively with such problems in the future.

---

[10] See Sar A. Levitan and Garth L. Mangum, *Making Sense of Federal Manpower Policy*, a joint publication of the Institute of Labor and Industrial Relations (The University of Michigan–Wayne State University) and the National Manpower Policy Task Force (Washington, 1967), p. 4.

Section VII

FISCAL POLICY

THE ECONOMIC BASIS OF FISCAL POLICY

Richard C. Barth

According to a well-known phrase of Thomas Carlyle, the function of government is clearly defined: "Anarchy plus the constable." However, from Adam Smith to Keynes to present-day economists, a much broader basis for the business of the state—especially in economic affairs—has been recognized. Although Adam Smith and other classical economists did not advocate fiscal policy as we know it today, they went far beyond Carlyle in their conception of the government's role in the economy and in doing so provided a tradition of advocating a major role for the state within the scope of a market-oriented economy. As an example of some of the classical thinking on the proper government function, a line from J. R. McCulloch is appropriate: "The principle of *laissez-faire* may be safely trusted to in some things but in many more it is wholly inapplicable; and to appeal to it on all occasions savours more of the policy of a parrot than of a statesman or philosopher."[1] And from another leading classical writer, Nassau Senior, we find that the only rational foundation of government is to do whatever is conducive to the welfare of the governed.[2]

It is not the purpose here to enter into a discussion of the legitimate role of government, but to give a brief background to the introduction of fiscal policy as a governmental function. It was not until Keynes wrote in the *General Theory* that full employment was not automatically achievable but that it required deliberate governmental encouragement that fiscal policy was brought into the economic spotlight.

Dr. Barth is an economist with the Department of Labor.

[1] J. R. McCulloch, *Treatise on the Succession to Property Vacant by Death* (1848), p. 156.

[2] Nassau Senior, in a review of J. S. Mill's *Political Economy*, in *Edinburgh Review*, CLXXVIII (October, 1948), p. 294.

Fiscal policy relates to the use of spending, taxing, and debt management of government—both state and federal—although here the concentration will be on the role of the federal government in fiscal matters. Broadly speaking, all of the major economic problems—including level of employment, price fluctuation, and economic growth—provide the context in which fiscal policy operates.

Many economists believe that the tax cut of 1964 firmly established fiscal policy as a major economic tool. This tax cut was carried out in the face of a rising trend of government spending. In earlier years—especially before 1930—this policy was almost unthinkable. The relationship between taxation and government expenditure is the primary focus of fiscal policy, and the remainder of the discussion here centers around that relationship.

In the discussion to follow, the first section will outline briefly the history of government spending and taxing; the next section will explain the theory of income determination and its relation to fiscal policy; finally, some further aspects of fiscal policy will be presented.

The Record of Federal Receipts and Expenditures

In order to understand the extent to which the federal government has participated in the use of the economy's resources, it is instructive to examine the trends in government spending and taxation. Even after allowing for price changes, federal expenditures increased by over six thousand times from 1800 to 1965. This increase has resulted mainly from changes in defense expenditures, especially during wartime. Table 1 shows the level of expenditures immediately preceding, during, and after the major wars since 1800. Federal spending has been relatively constant between wars; but after the sharp upswing during wartime, spending tends to remain higher than prewar levels because of veterans' expenses and interest payments on war-incurred government debt.

Looking only at total government expenditures can be very misleading, because there is nothing with which to compare it. Better perspective can be obtained if government spending is compared to other economic magnitudes. As a percentage of gross national product, federal expenditures were less than 5 per cent until World War I when they increased to 25 per cent. From 1930 to 1940, they rose from 5 per cent to 10 per cent as a result of Depression programs. World War II pushed the figure to over 45 per cent; and since then, they have fluctuated between 15 per

TABLE 1

FEDERAL GOVERNMENT EXPENDITURES
FOR SELECTED YEARS, 1805-1967
(millions of current dollars)

Year	Expenditure	Year	Expenditure
1805	$ 10.5	1915	$ 761.0
1810	8.2	1919	18,514.0
1815	32.7	1920	6,403.0
1820	18.3	1940	9,062.0
1855	59.7	1945	98,416.0
1860	63.1	1950	39,617.0
1865	1,306.0	1953	74,120.0
1870	309.0	1955	64,389.0
1910	694.0	1965	96,507.0
		1967[1]	127,000.0

Source: **Historical Statistics of the United States, Colonial Times to 1957.**
[1] Estimated.

cent and 20 per cent. Of course, war-connected expenditures have made up most of the total; but, especially since 1954, expenditures on health, labor, and welfare have risen significantly. This latter category is composed mainly of Social Security benefits and unemployment compensation. Table 2 gives the breakdown between defense and nondefense spending since 1940, according to the administrative budget; however, this

TABLE 2

FEDERAL DEFENSE AND NONDEFENSE ADMINISTRATIVE
BUDGET EXPENDITURES: AMOUNTS AND AS A
PERCENTAGE OF GROSS NATIONAL PRODUCT

Year	Defense[1]	Nondefense[1]	GNP[2]	Defense[3]	Nondefense[3]
1940	$ 3,106	$ 5,949	$ 99.7	3.1	6.0
1945	92,983	5,320	211.9	43.9	2.5
1950	30,801	8,743	284.8	10.8	3.1
1955	51,655	12,734	398.0	13.0	3.2
1960	60,457	16,082	503.7	12.0	3.2
1965	67,093	29,414	681.2	9.8	4.3
1966	74,873	32,105	739.5	10.1	4.3

Source: **Economic Report of the President,** 1967.
[1] Millions.
[2] Billions.
[3] Percentage.

269

TABLE 3

FEDERAL NONDEFENSE CASH EXPENDITURES
AS A PERCENTAGE OF GNP

Year	Expenditure[1]	Percentage
1950	$12.3	4.3
1955	18.8	4.7
1960	33.8	6.7
1965	55.3	8.1
1966	62.9	8.5

Source: **Economic Report of the President,** 1967.
[1] Billions of current dollars.

budget omits all trust funds and government enterprise. Table 3 shows the percentages since 1950 of nondefense spending on a cash payment to the public basis. These totals include all trust fund expenditures, the major ones of which are Social Security, unemployment compensation, and highway trust funds. Prior to 1930, nondefense expenditures were less than 1 per cent of GNP and except for wartime defense expenditures were less than 5 per cent. Thus, the major trends that appear include increased total government activity in the economy; the large growth in defense spending; and, more recently, the rise in nondefense spending from extremely low levels prior to 1930. This latter trend is due in large part to increases in Social Security payments and to a lesser extent to the recognition that fiscal measures should be assigned a heavier weight in government policy decisions pertaining to the nation's economy.

TABLE 4

FEDERAL GOVERNMENT DEFICIT OR SURPLUS
AS A PERCENTAGE OF GNP[1]

Year	Percentage	Year	Percentage
1900	+ .27	1940	− 3.89
1910	− .06	1945	−25.25
1920	+ .32	1950	− .15
1925	+ .78	1955	− .70
1930	+ .81	1960	+ .39
1935	−3.84	1965	− .69
		1966	− .98

Source: **Historical Statistics of the United States, Colonial Times to 1957,** and **Economic Report of the President,** 1967.
[1] Data prior to 1950 is for fiscal years; 1950-1966 refers to calendar years.

Tax collections, of course, have increased, with personal income tax collections accounting for nearly half of the federal tax receipts. The major change in the trend of tax collections has been the change in political thinking on the relationship of tax collections to expenditures. Table 4 shows federal deficits or surpluses for selected years. Although the size of a deficit or surplus is not always an accurate indication of current fiscal policy, the large number of deficit years following 1930 indicates that the nation is moving away from the balanced budget fixation. Although in 1932 President Roosevelt advocated a balanced budget in the midst of depression, by 1938 he abandoned that view. As the next sections point out, the basis for incurring deficits is well-founded.

The Economic Foundation of Fiscal Policy

The effects of fiscal policy are manifested in the volume of output and employment of the economy. The clearest way to see how total income and product in the economy is determined is to divide the economy into two sectors: a producing sector, which would include all business firms in a market economy, and a consuming or household sector. All final goods and services are produced in the producing sector and then are sold to the consuming sector. Government has been excluded from this simplified economic picture, but it will be added later.

The simplified economy then operates in the following way. The producing sector offers to buy the productive services of the consuming sector. These productive services can be broken into land, labor, and capital. All productive services are owned by the consuming sector and are supplied to the producing sector at a price. Thus, there is a demand for and a supply of factors of production; and, in a market economy, the demand and supply will interact to produce a price for each productive factor. The price that is paid for the use of land is termed rent; the price of labor, wages and salaries; and the price of capital, interest.

Now that the producing sector has hired its productive resources, it combines them according to the current technology to produce goods and services. This production is then supplied to the consuming sector. The consuming sector bids for the production with the purchasing power gained from the sale of its productive services. Thus, a supply and demand situation is set up in the output market analogous to the supply and demand in the factor market. Given the prices formed in the goods mar-

271

ket, consumer expenditures flow into the producing sector in return for the produced output. This expenditure flow is then used by businesses to pay for the factor inputs; thus, a circular flow of expenditures and goods arises. One additional point should be mentioned here, and that refers to the dollar amounts of expenditures for goods and services and the dollar amounts of payments for factor services. Any difference between these two amounts is termed profits, whether a positive or negative amount. Profits are then included as an additional factor payment, the payment for the provision of enterprise as a productive service in a market econ-

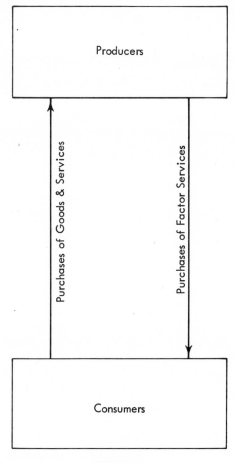

FIGURE 1

omy. By definition, then, the sum of expenditures on goods and services must be equal to the payment for productive or factor services. This process is shown in Figure 1. The left-hand side is known as national product, and the right-hand side is known as national income.

This description of the economy is incomplete in three major respects: (1) Government has been omitted; (2) no allowance was made for consumers to withhold part of their income from the expenditure stream; and (3) it was implied that business firms produce only consumer goods and services.

Government activity in the economy will be represented in two parts. First, part of government activity consists of producing goods and services and selling them to the consumer sector. In the production of these goods and services, government acts very much like a business firm and must purchase factor services—land, labor, and capital—from households. Examples of this sort of government activity are the Post Office and the Tennessee Valley Authority. This type of government activity will be included in the producing sector.

The larger part of government activity, however, takes the form of taxation of income from households and firms, which represents a leakage from the income stream, and the subsequent expenditure whether to business firms (e.g., to build a space capsule) or to households for their factor services (e.g., for the administration of the State Department). This expenditure, then, represents a net addition to the income stream. This withdrawal and addition process is similar to the withdrawal and addition of savings and investment, which will now be discussed.

Although consumers receive a certain amount of disposable income in a given period of time, they may choose not to spend part of it for consumption. This residual disposable income not consumed or spent for consumption goods is defined as saving. It is important now to understand that the saving residual is a withdrawal, or leakage, from the spending-income stream. This is true, no matter what form the saving takes: increases in bank balances, putting saved funds in a hole in the back yard, or even repaying a past debt. In the case of the past debt, negative savings probably occurred when the debt was incurred.

To make the final adjustment to the circular flow model, business firms will now be allowed to produce goods other than for consumption. This nonconsumption goods production takes the form of planned changes in inventory levels and production of capital goods. The total of this nonconsumption production is termed investment and represents

273

an addition to the spending-income stream and thus has the opposite effect of leakage from consumer saving. Investment spending, then, consists of expenditures for capital goods production (the production of goods to be used in the process of producing other goods for sale) and changes in inventory (goods produced but not sold in the current accounting period). On the other hand, consumption goods spending consists of expenditures for consumer goods. Investment is performed by the producing sector, while consumption is performed by the consumer sector. This revised model of income and product is presented in Figure 2. It is still true that expenditures for goods and services, national product, is equal to the income received by productive factors, national income. But now, expenditures for production consist of three types—consumer, government, and investment expenditures and the corresponding types of production.

Now that the key concepts in the flow of goods, services, and income have been discussed, the next step is to examine the factors responsible for the determination of national income and product; once these factors have been analyzed, it will be clear how fiscal policy fits into the national economy.

The total output in any time period—e.g., one year—, or Gross National Product, is determined by total expenditures on goods and services in that time period.[3] In the circular flow model, these expenditures have been divided into consumer spending for consumption goods and services; government spending for goods and services from the producing sector, plus productive services from the household sector; and investment spending for inventories and capital goods. In the process of producing the goods and services that make up the dollar value of Gross National Product, an equivalent dollar value of income is paid to the productive factors in the form of rent, wages and salaries, interest, and profits. Given the value, then, of national product what factors cause this value to change? Assume first that planned expenditures in a given period of time by the three sectors when totalled is exactly equal to the value of production in that period. In this situation—where there is no divergence between planned expenditures in money terms and current output—the economy is said to be in static equilibrium, and there are no internal forces stimulating a change in the economy's output.

This situation may then be contrasted with a situation in which planned expenditures either fall short of current production or exceed it.

---

[3] This analysis omits consideration of the foreign sector which has an impact on GNP.

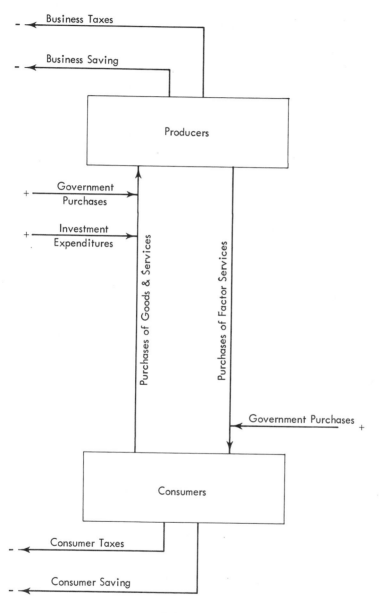

FIGURE 2

For illustration, suppose total production (and, hence, income earned) in the current year for the economy is $1,000 and that households plan to spend $900 of this income on consumption goods and services. Further, suppose that $50 is planned for additions to inventory and new capital equipment and that government plans to spend $25 on goods and services. Then, of $1,000 of production, $975 will be purchased, resulting in an unplanned increase in business inventories of $25. In order to bring inventories down to the planned level, business production must fall in the following time period, thus leading to a decrease in the level of national product and income. The opposite effect on the economy will result from planned spending exceeding production. The foregoing illustrates that the determinant of the economy's output level is planned expenditures for final products by the consumer, government, and business sectors.

To be analytically useful, equilibrium output—where planned expenditures equal production—must be related to a concept called full employment output. For any time period, given the economy's capital stock and the productivity of the labor force employed with the capital stock, there exists a potential level of output. When all labor and capital are utilized in production, this potential level will vary over time—with changes in any of the factors making up the output. For example, as the labor force grows, so does potential output. Now, by comparing total planned expenditure (aggregate demand) of the three sectors, it is possible to ascertain whether the current level of aggregate demand implies full employment output. If aggregate demand falls short of full employment output, unemployment will result; if it exceeds full employment output, a price rise must follow. This latter effect is just an example of demand for goods and services exceeding their supply, the maximum possible supply. In an uncontrolled economy, market forces attempt to induce an equality of demand and supply at a higher price level.

It is now clear how fiscal policy can be integrated with economic welfare. Through changes in tax and spending policies the government can affect total planned spending so as to raise it if unemployment is prevalent or to lower it if inflation poses a threat. A standard income determination diagram, Figure 3, illustrates this discussion.

In Figure 3, planned levels of consumption expenditures (C), investment expenditures (I), and government expenditures (G) are measured along the vertical axis. Production or output (O) is measured horizontally. A 45 degree line divides the quadrant into two halves and any coordinate on the 45 degree line is equidistant from each axis. Therefore, any point on the 45 degree line represents equality between planned expenditures and output. The line labeled C + I + G is the planned expenditure line. Any point on it relates a certain total planned expenditure to a level of output. Thus, the point A indicates that when production (and income) is at the level of O_1 planned expenditures will total S_1. The shape

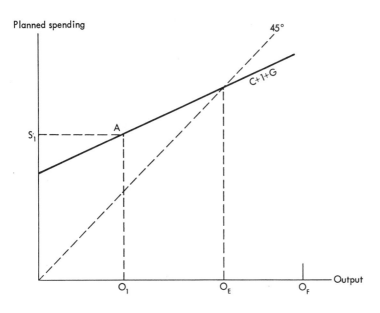

FIGURE 3

of the C + I + G line reflects the generally observed economic phenomenon that planned expenditures are an increasing function of income. The two concepts of income—equilibrium and full employment—in Figure 3 are O_E and O_F, respectively. Thus, equilibrium income falls short of full-employment income—the normal state of the economy, according to Keynes.

Suppose production amounted to O_1 in Figure 4. In this case, total planned expenditure at that level of income—S_1—falls short of output by $S_2 - S_1$. This represents the situation where producers are unable to sell their production. Less will be produced in the following period; and (eventually) for equilibrium to occur, output must fall to O_E. It is now

277

clear that the level of income and output is determined by total planned spending.

Two problems emerge at once from this analysis. Planned expenditure may be less than enough to buy full employment output, thus producing unemployment in the amount $O_F - O_E$ in Figure 3; and planned expenditure may exceed full employment output, thus producing an in-

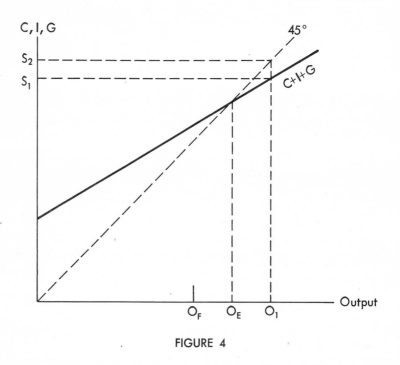

FIGURE 4

flationary situation as measured by $O_E - O_F$ in Figure 4. Fortunately, by employing fiscal policy, the level of planned expenditures can be shifted to achieve the goals of the economy—full employment and stable prices. Since tax collections are withdrawals from the spending-income stream, an increase in taxes will lower the $C + I + G$ line and will produce a drop in output. An increase in government spending will raise the $C + I + G$ line and will produce an increase in output. These changes in government taxes and expenditures, then, are the essence of fiscal policy.

In order to improve the effectiveness of fiscal policy, both President

Kennedy and President Johnson requested Congress to grant the President discretionary tax rate change power. Congress has been reluctant to delegate this authority, thus imposing a constraint on a major fiscal weapon.

Fiscal Policy

Although government spending has increased tremendously since 1800, it was not until the 1930's that a deliberate effort was made to raise the level of total planned spending through government programs. In the 1930's, the emphasis was on public works projects. Since then, as we have seen in Table 4, government nondefense spending has been on the increase. This increase has certainly had a large effect on reducing the gap between full-employment production and actual production. A further indication of the acceptance of fiscal measures to alter production levels is the growing willingness to accept deficits in the government budget when the effect of these deficits will be to add to the spending stream.

Discretionary changes in fiscal policy have typically been very difficult to achieve. The tax cut of 1964 is a case in point. The lag between the recognized need for expansionary or contractionary fiscal policy and its actual occurrence may be so long that by the time a tax or expenditure change takes place the situation may call for a different type of fiscal policy. This lag would be a much more serious problem were it not for automatic fiscal stabilizers.

These fiscal stabilizers are tax or expenditure changes that take place automatically as GNP rises or falls. Their effect is to dampen both increases and decreases in GNP mainly through their influence on consumer disposable income. This dampening effect, then, limits inflationary tendencies during upswings and helps maintain a higher employment rate during downswings.

The two major fiscal stabilizers are (1) transfer payments, the main one being unemployment compensation, and (2) taxes. Transfer payments decrease during rising GNP and increase during falling GNP; and tax collections behave similarly, due to the progressive rate structure. Both of these factors limit increases in disposable income when GNP is rising and limit the decrease in disposable income when GNP is falling. Then, since planned consumer and investment expenditures vary with changes in disposable income, a rise or fall in GNP will be dampened. In 1958,

GNP fell from its 1957 level; but automatic stabilizers—mainly tax collections and unemployment benefits—worked sufficiently to increase disposable income during that period. This increase helped to reverse the falling trend of production and employment by 1959.

Suppose we are interested in ascertaining what type of fiscal policy the government is pursuing. A popular method of doing this is to examine budget deficits and surpluses. A surplus is said to be indicative of contractionary fiscal policy, since more purchasing power is removed from the income stream than is replaced. A deficit is indicative of the opposite policy. This method, however, is faulty, partly as a result of the operation of automatic stabilizers. A contractionary government policy taking the form of decreased government expenditures will lower GNP and will lower tax collections, thus possibly inducing a budget deficit, while an expansionary government policy taking the form of increased government expenditures will increase GNP but possibly not by enough to increase tax collections to avoid a deficit. Thus, a deficit may be the result of fiscal policy in either direction. The same holds true for a surplus.

Whatever form fiscal policy takes, either a budget surplus or deficit will be incurred. Economists have long realized that neither a surplus nor a deficit and the resulting decrease or increase in the national debt create an aggregate burden on the economy in the present or in the future.[4] A planned deficit from either a tax reduction, as in 1964, or an increase in expenditures, as in the 1930's and again in the 1960's, works toward the goal of full-employment production. The danger of a strong inflation is lessened by reductions in spending and increases in taxes. Thus, fiscal policy is inseparable from economic welfare.

The relationship we have been concerned with has been the effect of government spending and taxing on the gap between equilibrium output and full-employment output; but a complication arises as production increases toward the full-employment level. As plants are pushed to full utilization, as less experienced labor is hired, and as more overtime work is necessary, unit costs may rise. Price rises may then occur in the "bottleneck" industries even though unemployment may exist in other parts of

---

[4] There are some situations in which this statement is not strictly accurate, but further discussion is beyond the scope of this article. For a description of possible burden, see James E. Meade's, "Is the National Debt a Burden?" *Oxford Economic Papers*, June 1958, pp. 163-183.

the economy. Thus, as aggregate demand increases, there is increasing pressure on prices even though full employment production has not been achieved. Fiscal policy is limited by a conflict of goals, and a decision as to the appropriate fiscal measures must be made on the basis of benefits and costs of an employment-inflation trade-off.

THE AMERICAN PHILLIPS CURVE

AND THE "CONSENSUAL TRAP"

John Adams

Keynes, in the *General Theory*, and standard interpretations acknowledge that inflationary pressures arise before the economy reaches a full-employment ceiling.[1] The actual degree of money wage change occurring as full employment nears has been measured for the United Kingdom by W. A. Phillips, whose name has subsequently been attached to any in the whole assortment of inflation-unemployment trade-off curves. In the United States, analogous estimates of schedules of wage or price inflation and labor unemployment have been made by Paul Samuelson, Robert Solow and G. L. Perry.[2]

Given the existence of a reciprocal relationship between unemployment and wage and price increases, a balancing of alternative evils—unemployment versus inflation—becomes necessary. The achievement of a nationally acceptable resolution depends directly on the outcome of a political process of bargaining and reconciling public and intragovernmental opinions about prices and employment. The Phillips trade-off relationship

---

The author is Assistant Professor of Economics at the University of Maryland.

[1] J. M. Keynes, *The General Theory of Employment, Interest, and Money* (New York, 1936), p. 301; R. C. O. Matthews, *The Business Cycle* (2nd impression; Chicago, 1962), p. 257; R. A. Gordon, *Business Fluctuations* (2nd ed.; New York, 1961), p. 60.

[2] A. W. Phillips, "The Relation Between Unemployment and the Rate of Change of Money Wage Rates in the United Kingdom, 1861-1957," *Economica* (November, 1958), pp. 283-299. Paul A. Samuelson and Robert M. Solow, "Analytical Aspects of Anti-Inflation Policy," *Papers and Proceedings* of the American Economic Association (May, 1960), pp. 177-194; G. L. Perry, "The Determinants of Wage Rate Changes and the Inflation-Unemployment Trade-off for the United States," *Review of Economic Studies* (October), 1964, pp. 287-306.

thus creates an inescapable dilemma for governmental agents and groups. The President, Congress, the Council of Economic Advisers, and the Federal Reserve Board become engaged in a ceaseless political effort to balance and reconcile divergent valuations of inflation and unemployment. Fiscal and monetary policies and institutional corrections are the two avenues of response and reform open to the policy makers.

There presently exists no elementary framework for analyzing the political economy of inflation, unemployment, and income. Yet the inflation-unemployment curve and some additional constructs can be used to summarize some of the current conventional wisdom of public policy formation. Part I of this article reviews the institutional milieu supporting the Phillips schedule. Part II joins public opinion and political pressures to an inflation-unemployment schedule through use of a device called the "consensual trap." Part III demonstrates how interconnections of prices, employment, and political process affect the determination of national income.

I

Without worrying too much about the specific importance of the various items, it is possible to collect a number of structural and institutional elements which may affect relationships among prices, wages, and unemployment. The list is of interest partly because it indicates the *ceteris paribus* conditions behind the Phillips curve, but mainly because it identifies the institutions public policy will have to modify if the national inflation-unemployment trade-off is to be shifted in response to public preferences.

Labor is currently provided and wages are determined by a differentiated labor market based on a set of institutions mitigating the workings of a perfectly free market system. The size of the national labor market, the degree of labor mobility, heterogeneity and flexibility of the labor force, sex and race discrimination in employment opportunities, immigration policy, and governmental policies at national, state, and local levels—minimum wage legislation, unemployment insurance, wage guidelines—may each cause the overall unemployment-wage rate pattern to vary. Any alteration in labor-providing, wage-fixing institutions is likely to shift the current association between unemployment and wages. The extent of unionization and the mix of unionized industries are two organizational variables. The style of labor leadership and goals of labor organizations are relevant. As an approximate generalization, the more unionization, the

284

greater the strength of unions in concentrated industries, and the more wage-centered the union leadership, the more likely is it that the degree of national unemployment will be unrelated to specific wage demands. The lure of excessive profits ensures wage-increase pressure will be at a maximum.

There are a number of things which affect the prevailing connection between wages and general prices. The pace of technological advance or productivity is among the more important. It is generally assumed that the faster the progress of technology, the more may wages rise without forcing general prices upwards. Another major technological and institutional fact is industry concentration. Monopolistic firms are in a favorable position to correct prices for wage gains; and, they may well overreact. Antitrust policy, informal or formal price and wage controls emanating from the public sector, and suasion are some of the policy ploys which can break existing wage-price ties.

The direction of influence is not always from wages to prices. In a reverse way, the cost of living also affects wage demands. Phillips found that import prices, which reflect conditions totally withdrawn from the internal labor market, could affect money wage demands. A stated or implicit issue in all wage discussions is the prevailing cost of living relative to a desired style of life for the laboring man. Price rises for whatever reasons may tend to increase wage needs regardless of employment conditions.

Wars, grave depressions, and severe expectational shifts can upset the position of the Phillips curve. Perry illustrates that trade-offs differ in different sectors of the economy and it is equally likely that unemployment, wages, and prices are related in a variety of ways in different regions and industries.

It may appear miraculous that a fairly clear, more or less stable Phillips curve can be isolated. There is, however, a certain permanence in the way in which a society institutionalizes its labor provision and price formation. Prevailing institutions are not apt to do much more than slowly evolve into new forms. Even with a high degree of economic change, there exist no reasons to suspect that all forces will affect the Phillips curve in the same way.

II

Figure 1 shows a representative inflation-unemployment trade-off curve, labeled PC. The institutional setting is assumed unvarying relative to monetary and fiscal policy. Monetary and fiscal policy never is neutral, even when active responsibility is temporarily abdicated, and determines what levels of unemployment and inflation on the PC curve the economy must endure, given the prevailing business environment.

The inflation-unemployment interdependence is indicated by curve PC. Inflation, which to the public and politician alike is best summed up

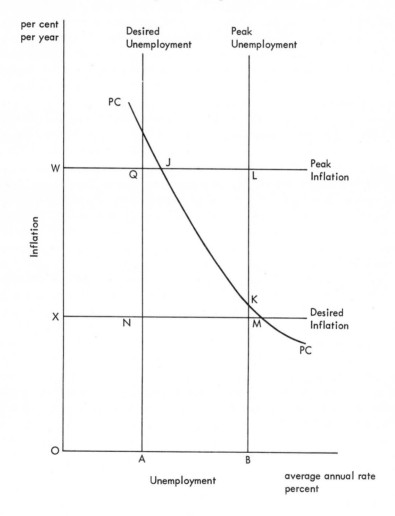

FIGURE 1

286

in the consumer price index, is calibrated on the vertical axis; unemployment is registered on the horizontal axis. For the present, the scales are left bare, and the point of origin (O,O) represents full employment with stable prices. Since the economy must be somewhere on the PC curve, (O,O) is a meaningless target for policy direction.

Political figures and agencies charged with maintaining a satisfactory state of economic well-being in the country must employ their offices to give people what they wish or face growing political antagonism and run an increased risk of losing elections at the polls. With reference to Figure 1, their immediate task is to trade off inflation and unemployment in such a way that the public is reasonably contented. It need not be argued that they must press for an ideal unique solution—e.g., the point on PC nearest (O,O) of any kind. They have other things to concern themselves with and, given the present state of the economic arts, are merely striving for some sort of consensus—most of the people are more or less satisfied much of the time.

The public is apt to have strong preferences about inflation and unemployment, two long-standing national issues. These feelings are transmitted to their representatives through several channels—interest groups, public opinion, and the voting booth. None of these communications systems is infallible, and legislators and administrators are capable of displaying minds of their own. Decentralization of decision making further complicates the process of forging acceptable policy. To the degree that the Federal Reserve, or any other locus of influence, responds differentially to various external interests and to the extent that it (or any other policy making body) feels it has a moral obligation to follow certain ends, the greater will be the discrepancy between public preferences and actual policy. Fortunately, even the most independent policy makers are not totally immune to sanctions; public wishes put overriding constraints on all governmental price and unemployment actions. These constraining boundaries can be estimated for the nation, groups, or regions by the most elementary of polling devices.[3] The effect of these widely held opinions about prices and employment is to draw a "consensual trap" around economic policies.

The consensual trap (LMNQ) in Figure 1 combines four different opinions. The top horizontal line, drawn from OW, signifies the maximum rate of inflation most people feel the economy can bear for any

---

[3] A small-scale exercise along these lines is summed up in the following footnote.

substantial length of time.[4] Underneath at OX is a line which represents the maximum amount of inflation desired by the majority. This shows that the public has some knowledge that to demand no inflation is unrealistic and beyond the bounds of possibility (although some will, of course, distribute opinions to or even beyond that point). Some people may reasonably expect to gain in real terms as a consequence of the redistributive effects of general inflation.

The other two sides of the consensual trap illustrate bounds on policy freedom set up by majority preferences about the peak unemployment thought bearable (OB) and the level of unemployment thought desirable (OA). The desired level is not necessarily the full-employment point. The total elimination of unemployment may be viewed as unattainable or unwarranted by some members of the population.

Because of these political constraints, two things are true. First, some portion of the PC curve must always fall within the consensual trap. Secondly, political pressures will inevitably operate to keep the economy inside points J and K on the PC curve. The first proposition is true because if the PC curve lay northeast of point L for any length of time there would be an obvious inconsistency between levels of inflation and unemployment acceptably bearable and those actually existing. Rudimentary reality-testing would have to induce higher estimates of peak unemployment and peak inflation and, at the same juncture, political pressures to bring the PC curve back into the range of consensus would be especially acute. The argument supporting the notion that the economy tends toward the range JK on the PC curve is similar. Beyond J, the rate of price gain has climbed past the tolerability level for a majority of the people. This indicator has also increasingly diverged from desired levels, and relatively fewer people are much troubled about overly high unemployment. In fact, beyond OA the level of unemployment actually drops below that required to satisfy most of the people. A similar argument can be applied to points beyond K on PC.

On PC within JK, the politicians are comparatively safe. Prices and employment are under control and, within limits, widely believed livable. But, while there is less urgency about policy measures, economic conditions still do not please people. Point N beckons. Here, the spectres of overly high unemployment and prices have long since vanished, and a

---

[4] The four sides of the consensual trap are the median responses to questions designed to draw out preferences on desired and tenable inflation and unemployment. Half the distribution lies on either side of each edge.

majority is satisfied about price and employment performance. Therefore, so long as there is a gap between N and points on JK, political action will work to institute positive policies·designed to move the economy towards that goal.

To illustrate how an American PC curve can be combined with inflation and unemployment preferences, an opinion survey was conducted using economically untrained college students. Drawn in sizeable number from a heterogeneous state campus, they may reflect a fairly wide swatch of the general voting strength either by thinking independently or because of inherited beliefs. Figure 2 summarizes the results. The PC curve is taken from Perry's study.[5] In the diagram, 2 per cent is treated as the full-employment point, but the diagram is otherwise identical with Figure 1. The values for desired and peak unemployment and inflation correspond to median answers to four questions designed to obtain information about the students' feelings. A fifth question offered a choice among alternative positions on Perry's PC curve.[6] Point D (3.5,3) was the median selection.

As predicted, the PC curve falls within the consensual trap, and in late 1966 the economy had been operating on PC within the consensual limits for several years. Nothing is known, of course, about how the respondents felt at any earlier date. The point chosen on the PC curve is not outside the ranges of preference. The students revealed a great willingness to sacrifice price stability to obtain reduced unemployment. The selected position on the PC schedule lies on the upper border of the consensual trap and indicates that inflationary concern was low. A confirmation of this finding appears in responses to a second series of questions.

---

[5] Perry, *op. cit.*, p. 298. Productivity growth is assumed to be 2.7 per cent per annum. The profit rate is 10.8 per cent (the 1953-1960 average).

[6] The sample size was 640. The questions were:

(a) For "desired" inflation, unemployment—

If you were in a position of absolute authority and could control the American economy, what annual rate of price inflation (rate of unemployment) would you enforce?

(b) For "peak" inflation, unemployment—

As a concerned citizen, what is the maximum or highest annual rate of price inflation (rate of unemployment) you think the American economy could bear for several years or longer?

(c) For PC curve preference—

Suppose only the following combinations of inflation and unemployment rates are possible in the American economy. As a concerned citizen, which combinations would you prefer?

In all cases, seven choices were given. Points on the PC curve were rounded off.

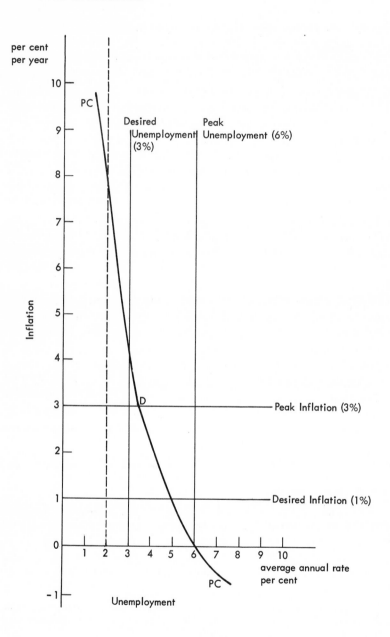

FIGURE 2

Each opinion question was accompanied by a strength of feeling scale.[7] The mode and median intensity of feeling responses were at the second level (b) for both the unemployment and the single PC curve responses. The two inflation questions yielded responses with modal and medial intensity feelings at the first level.

These preliminary results indicate that the consensual trap is an operational concept. There is no reason why the technique cannot be expanded and applied at the national level to the general public and to special interest groupings. Regular collection of this sort of information would do a good deal to remove the need for baseless speculation by the President and his advisers, the Congress, and the Federal Reserve about what people in fact want. The Council of Economic Advisers might be an excellent location for a continuing study of existing trade-offs among economic goals and people's valuations of those goals.

Exactly how permanent are the boundaries of the consensual trap and what conditions are responsible for determining desired and peak levels are unsolved questions. The position of the PC curve itself, the tone of public pronouncements by authoritative figures in or seeking power, the degree of education in economic affairs, and expectations are apt to be worth examination. Another assumption of the simple model is that desires of the public will be proportionately reflected in pressures on politicians and that politicians respond equitably. This is unrealistic to the extent that various groups in the economy have greater access to the ears of power. Consumers and white collar workers are unequally heard in comparison with big business and unionized labor.

The conventional wisdom explaining recent national inflation-unemployment policy may be summarized using the consensual trap analysis. In recent national elections, inflation and unemployment have been major issues. John F. Kennedy's pledge to "get the country moving again" and Lyndon B. Johnson's Populist expansionary sentiments set them apart from their rivals, who paradoxically deplored an active government while pledging themselves to halt inflation. In office, both consciously used fiscal and monetary means to move the country along PC towards lower unemployment and higher rates of inflation. At the same time, they responded to ineluctable forces by espousing institutional policies which were aimed

---

[7] All five opinion questions were followed by:

How strongly do you feel about your choice? (a) I am not very committed to it; (b) I feel fairly strongly about it; and (c) I am positive my answer is superior to others on the list.

at transferring the PC schedule to a more desirable position and thus at reducing inflation at any given level of unemployment. As illustrations, there are: the moribund wage-price guidelines, antitrust enforcement, retraining acts, the Job Corps, stockpile dumping, presidential exhortation, selective government purchasing, area redevelopment legislation, aid to education, and job discrimination acts. Not all were or will be successful. And their bearing on the general levels of unemployment, wages, and prices is not the sole, or even the principal, standard by which most of the institutional adjustments should be evaluated. Unions, concentrated industries, and retraining programs are multifaceted arrangements. Nevertheless, the consensual trap and the PC curve help interpret these variegated actions as an intelligible pattern. It is foreordained that fiscal and monetary attempts to achieve complete consensual accord are necessary but inadequate. Institutional adjustments can be expected as representatives try to act in harmony with community wishes.

III

The Phillips curve and the consensual trap may be employed to supplement the analysis of income determination. The result of doing so is that a full-employment optimum will not ordinarily be the goal of fiscal and monetary policies. The equilibrium income, or what turns out to be an equilibrium range of national incomes, will usually be found below the full-employment state. Figure 3 combines a PC curve, the consensual trap, and a standard income determination diagram. Section 3.1 of Figure 3 includes the PC curve and the consensual trap, QLMN, of Figure 2. Section 3.2 shows income as a declining function of unemployment; 3.4 is an aggregate demand and income diagram with additions as described below.

On the PC curve lie two points of interest in the process of income resolution. A indicates the level of unemployment associated with complete price stability. B represents the full-employment point and the associated rate of price change. In this case, these are: $A(6,0)$ and $B(2,8)$. Dashed lines trace through the diagrammatic ramifications of these pairs. Income levels Y_A and Y_B follow from the 6 and 2 per cent rates of unemployment. In diagram 3.4, these two income levels define the noninflationary level of income $(Y_A,\$Y_A)$ and full-employment income $(Y_B,\$Y_B)$. At Y_A there is no price effect from any source, and money and real income are equal. At any higher level of income, inflation exists in the

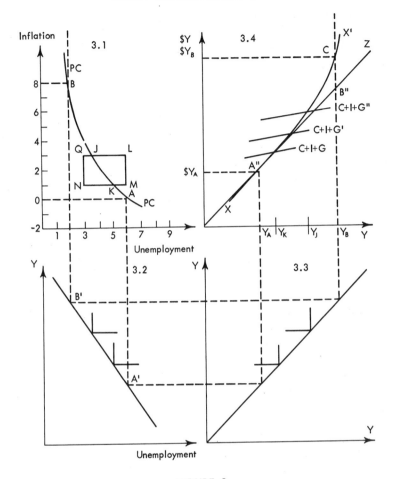

FIGURE 3

amount shown by the PC curve. Beyond Y_A and A'' on OZ, the equality of Y and $Y ceases. Line XX' running through A'' is derived from the degree of inflation (or deflation) indicated by the PC curve. At the full-employment level, Y_B, ordinarily cited as the logical place to operate, there is a sizeable inflationary interval, CB''.

Because of the distastefulness of inflation as Y_B is approached, governmental policy measures will be restrained by public pressures somewhere to the left of full-employment income. The public will begin to complain as inflationary rises accelerate. Y_J is as close to Y_B as the bounds of consensus will permit the economy to travel. This is the level of peak inflation and, by coincidence, the place where the sample indicated the public would prefer to rest. On the other hand, voters would not permit movement towards price stabilization beyond Y_K. The range of tenable income positions is thus set by the argument which concluded that the economy must operate between J and K on the PC curve. Feelings about the gains and losses of inflation and unemployment determine that there is a range of incomes from Y_J to Y_K in which government policies will keep the economy. G, G', G'' are used with fixed I and C to illustrate varying governmental activities. These G's influence the level of income as well as the accompanying inflation-unemployment point on PC. The economy is extremely unlikely to operate at either the zero inflation or full-employment positions. And in recent years it has not.

Institutional policies designed to affect PC will also shift XX'. The ill-fated guidelines, for example, represented an attempt to move PC southwest and to drive XX' down to OZ.

It should not be overlooked that every line on Figure 3 can be ascertained with a modicum of difficulty and uncertainty. PC estimates have become commonplace and the consensual trap is readily determinable for the country or lesser groups inside or outside the government. The diminishing of Y as unemployment rises has been estimated in numerous ways and is widely elucidated in other forms (e.g., the "output gap"). Projections are also available which indicate how selected levels of G will affect Y under various conditions.

Questions for Thought and Discussion

1. What is the Phillips Curve? Why do you think the Phillips Curve relationship exists?
2. What political restraints operate in attempting to move either to very low unemployment or to low inflation?
3. Given the relationship between inflation and unemployment in Figure 2, where do you think the economy should operate? Why?

MONETARY AND FISCAL POLICIES:
A HISTORICAL VIEW

Edward R. Sopiarz

It is now common practice to evaluate how well or how poorly the overall economy is performing according to its degree of success or failure in meeting the general objectives of (1) reasonable price stability, (2) high employment rate, (3) satisfactory growth rate, (4) and equilibrium in the balance of payments.

The federal government, through the constitutional power to regulate the value of money, has long been involved with the first of these—price stability. As the government became increasingly involved in maintaining the economy at full employment, its concern over price level stability correspondingly increased. The second goal became an explicit responsibility of the federal government when the Employment Act of 1946 directed it to "promote maximum employment." The third goal, satisfactory growth, is implicit in the Employment Act of 1946; but the challenge of competing economic systems, particularly that of Soviet Russia, gave this goal additional importance in the last decade. The last of these, equilibrium in the balance of payments, assumed new significance with the balance-of-payments deficits which the United States has experienced in the past several years.

The federal government seeks to achieve the goals by pursuing appropriate *monetary* and *fiscal* policies. Monetary and fiscal policies have already been discussed above, in articles by Mayor, Allsbrook, and Barth. The articles by Havrilesky and Adams also pertain to questions of economic stabilization. The present article will similarly be devoted to these

The author is Professor of Economics at the University of Toledo.

questions. The bulk of the discussion will be carried out in a historical setting, when first monetary policy and then fiscal policy were "feeling their way about" with respect to the proper way to deal with problems facing the economy, and will end with some observations on more recent monetary and fiscal operations.

Monetary Theory and Monetary Policy

Let us begin by making a distinction between monetary *theory* and monetary *policy*. Monetary theory is the analysis of money and money's relationship to other component parts of the economic system. Monetary policy, in a broad sense, refers to the manner in which the sovereign state manages its monetary system. In the narrower sense, the one that is of interest to us in this article, monetary policy refers to the use of government's power to control money for purposes of achieving the macroeconomic goals. Since the supply of money in the United States is largely under the control of the Federal Reserve System, monetary policy in the United States has come to be identified with the monetary policy of the Federal Reserve.

Early Federal Reserve monetary policy concentrated on the movement of the price level. This reflected the monetary theory of the times. Until the severe economic disorders of the 1930's, monetary theory concerned itself primarily with the relationship between the quantity of money and the price level and secondarily with questions of output and employment. The Federal Reserve correspondingly adjusted the quantity of money either to counteract undesirable price level changes or else to maintain desirable ones. The concentration on the price level was not as bad as it may seem, for typically the price level and the level of employment move in the same direction, with high levels of employment accompanying high price levels and vice versa. If, for example, a downward movement of the price level were accompanied by unemployment, any action by the Fed to prevent further falls in the price level would tend to prevent further falls in employment.

The Major Instruments of
Federal Reserve Policy

The oldest of the Federal Reserve's instruments of policy is control over the discount rate. The discount rate (see "The Economics of Central Banking" by Allsbrook) is the interest rate the Federal Reserve banks charge for the loans they grant to commercial banks. When discount rates are raised, commercial banks are likely to borrow less reserves, create less money, and thus tend to dampen expansion. The opposite would be true if discount rates were decreased. In a recession, for example, with unemployment of resourcs, the Fed would lower the discount rate, hoping for the following sequence of events to take place:

1. With lower discount rates, commercial banks would borrow more reserves from the Fed.
2. The additional reserves would make it possible for banks not only to extend more loans but to do so at lower interest rates.
3. More money would be available for expenditures on consumption goods and on investment goods.
4. The end result would be that unemployed resources would be put to work.

If, on the other hand, inflation threatened while there were full employment, the Fed would raise discount rates.

Control over discount rates was the main instrument of policy the Fed had from 1914 until the mid-1930's. In 1935, the Fed was given additional powers, two of which are particularly important. One of these—control over open market operations—gave the Fed virtual day-to-day control over bank reserves, while the other—control over reserve requirements—made it possible for the Fed to adjust reserves to long-run developments and to situations calling for drastic changes (such as would be brought on by war, for example).

Open market operations now consist essentially of buying and selling government securities. Again using a recession for purpose of illustration, use of open market operations as an instrument of policy would follow in a sequence something like:

1. The Fed enters the market and buys up securities.
2. The sellers of securities, which may be either commercial banks or the nonbank public, receive payments from the Fed.
3. These payments make the economy more liquid, since the banks have more reserves and the economy has additional money to spend.
4. Interest rates are depressed, investment stimulated, and unemployed resources are absorbed.

The opposite course would be followed in the case of inflation; i.e., the Fed would sell rather than buy government securities, thus reversing the sequence.

Control over reserve ratio requirements permits the Fed to control

297

the level of bank *excess* reserves simply with an announcement. An announcement that the required reserve ratio is decreased from, say, 15 per cent to 12 per cent would automatically free some reserves that were previously required to be held against bank deposit liabilities. If used as a countercyclical device, the Fed would, of course, lower reserve requirements in a recession and raise them should inflation threaten.

With the discount rate as its only weapon of control, along with the fact that it was relatively new at the "game," the Fed's record from 1914 until the crash of 1929 was not spectacular in the area of economic stabilization. In the contraction that followed the crash of 1929, monetary policy was equally ineffective. A few years of slow and painful recovery followed the 1933 low point, but with the unemployment rate still in excess of 10 per cent, the country found itself in another period of contraction in 1937-38.

A New Framework for Economic Analysis

As the country continued in the throes of the depression, economists began to question some of the precepts that had so long guided economic thinking. The "old" classical economics was unequal to the task of adequately analyzing the difficulties and suggesting remedies that were so desperately needed. The reason was that classical economics tended to concentrate in the area of what is now called *microeconomics*—the analysis of the individual component parts that make up the economy, being involved with such questions as the demand and supply behavior of firms within an industry and industries within the economy. *Macroeconomics*—economics dealing with the operation of the economy as a whole—was given less attention, for the classical economists believed that the natural state of affairs was one of full employment and that such deviations as did occur would be corrected by forces of competition within and between the units comprising the total economy.

Microeconomic theory, however much it contributed toward the understanding of the various segments that make up the total economy, was unable to deal with the broad problems facing the United States, such as the widespread unemployment and reduced total output. The macroeconomic theory of the day also proved to be deficient. "The old orthodox economics," according to Hansen, "left economists completely unprepared to cope with the problems of the Great Depression."[1] A new

---

[1] Alvin H. Hansen, *The American Economy* (New York: McGraw-Hill, 1957).

298

framework was needed; and, as it happened, a "new" economics was about to be born—one that would use the new framework and concentrate on problems facing the total economy.

The framework for this new economics was provided by an English economist, John Maynard Keynes, in a book published in 1936, *The General Theory of Employment, Interest, and Money*.[2] So rapidly were Keynes' ideas assimilated into the mainstream of economic thinking that the decades or so following publication of the book are now referred to as the "Keynesian Revolution," and the economic thinking built on the new framework provided by Keynes is called the "new economics."

Of the many ideas introduced by Keynes, the one of significance to us at this point is his concept of interest rate, because it relates directly to monetary policy.

Prior to Keynes, any given interest rate level was viewed as resulting from the fact that at any given time individuals who need funds are willing to pay a price—i.e., interest—to get the funds, while other individuals have funds which can be coaxed out of them only at a price (interest). The level of interest rate was thus thought to be determined by the demand for funds and the supply of funds.

Keynes took a different position. He viewed the interest rate as a monetary phenomenon. In his analysis, the interest rate is determined by the demand for and the supply of money. If the supply of money is increased, the interest rate is likely to decline; if the supply of money is decreased, the rate of interest is likely to rise, assuming in both cases that there is no change in demand. And who controls the supply of money in a modern economy? In the United States, the Federal Reserve has this power. Could not this power be directed toward a macroeconomic goal, such as full employment? The answer is *yes*, and the sequence of events would be something like:

1. The Fed increases the supply of money.
2. The increases in money supply drive down the interest rates.
3. The lower interest rates mean that the cost of credit is lower.
4. The lower cost of credit results in investment spending that would otherwise not have occurred.
5. More spending means increased employment.

In the case of an overheated economy with danger of inflation, the reverse would hold: The Fed would decrease the supply of money or at least

---

[2] J. M. Keynes, *The General Theory of Employment, Interest, and Money* (New York: Harcourt, Brace, 1936).

tighten up on the increases; this would tend to force interest rates up, cost of credit would rise, and spending would be discouraged.

The Apparent Failure of Monetary Policy

Let us take a brief look at Federal Reserve monetary policy during the 1930's, particularly the latter part. The reader should keep in mind here that in 1935 the Fed was given power to vary reserve ratio requirements and officially took over open market operations; prior to that time, control over discount rates .was its only important control.

Lowering discount rates in the beginning years of the depression proved ineffective. But even when given additional powers, the Fed was unable to pull the country out of the depression. This is understandable, for even under less dramatic conditions, monetary ease does not necessarily guarantee an increase in total spending; making money more available does not necessarily increase the demand for goods. Moreover, another circumstance, relating to the flow of gold, had already achieved a result which Fed action might have been directed at—namely, an increase in bank reserves. The international conditions following World War I and the decade of the 1920's had already resulted in a flow of gold into the United States and an increase in bank reserves. In the second half of the 1930's, conditions in Europe and throughout the world increased the flight of gold into the country, with the result that bank reserves reached an all-time high and correspondingly, interest rates an all-time low. Should the Fed have increased bank reserves even more in the hope that interest rates would be further depressed? There was little reason to believe this would happen or that it would do any good if it did happen, since the interest rates were already so low. The nation was caught in what has since been called a "liquidity trap"—bank reserves were so high and interest rates already so low that even substantial changes in bank reserves and the quantity of money would leave the low rates unaffected. Was there nothing to be done?

The new economics of Keynes did have a prescription. If monetary policy would not work—and Keynes himself held little hope that it would in a severe depression—then turn to fiscal policy.

Fiscal Policy

In discharging its fiscal functions, the government receives funds either from taxes or by borrowing and then spends the funds so received.

The receipt and expenditure of revenue can be organized in a way to help steer the economy toward the macroeconomic goals of price level stability, high level of employment, adequate growth, and an acceptable balance-of-payments equilibrium. *Fiscal policy* is, in other words, the use of government's taxing, borrowing, and spending powers for the purpose of achieving the macroeconomic goals.

Unlike monetary policy, which seeks to change total expenditures through the regulation of money and credit, fiscal policy is aimed directly at total spending. Total spending is the sum of (1) the expenditures made by the private sector for consumption goods C and investment goods I and (2) the expenditures made by the government G. In other words, total expenditures consist of $C + I + G$. (See "The Economic Basis of Fiscal Policy" by Barth.) The government can bring about changes in total spending either by changing G; by inducing changes in C or I by means of tax rate changes; or, of course, by any combination of the methods.

In general, when government expenditures exceed taxes, the result tends to be expansionary insofar as employment is concerned, and inflationary insofar as prices are concerned. On the other hand, if taxes exceed government expenditures, the results tends to be contractionary insofar as prices are concerned. The wider the gap between government expenditures and taxes, the greater the effects on employment and price levels.

Fiscal Policy During the Great Depression: Insufficiently Applied

The first few years of the Great Depression saw an assortment of measures taken by the government in order to promote recovery, among them providing funds to government corporations and agencies to be used in fighting the depression; examples were: the Reconstruction Finance Corporation; offering higher and higher prices for gold and finally devaluing the dollar; outright relief; and, surprisingly enough, attempting to balance the budget by passing additional taxes to take care of the additional government expenditures that arose from fighting the depression. The concept of a *discretionary* fiscal policy, one that takes action against developments that might hinder the achievement of macroeconomic goals, had not yet taken clear form. The economics of Keynes, however, pointed directly to the use of such a policy.

The United States was not yet willing in the latter part of the 1930's to apply fiscal policy in full force, probably because its leaders were not

301

yet sufficiently convinced of its merits. The idea, of course, was new. Willy-nilly, however, a "fiscal policy" of sorts was used, for in the end, relief and expenditures for public works rose more rapidly than receipts, resulting in mounting government deficits. The national debt increased by an amount in excess of $25 billion during the decade. The United States economy was soon to become a war economy as well.

The Effect of World War II on the Relationship Between Monetary and Fiscal Policies

The demands of World War II at long last brought full employment to the economy—but with deficits, it should be noted, that were undreamed of before the war. The problem now became one of a rising price level. Proper *fiscal* policy would be to narrow the gap between expenditures and taxes, either by cutting expenditures or increasing taxes. The former course was certainly an unacceptable condition when fighting a war; the latter was in fact done, although, according to many, not to a sufficient extent. Lacking other controls, appropriate *monetary* policy would make money and credit less and less available, keeping a damper on private expenditures. As it worked out, private spending was dampened far better by other means—rigid price, wage, and production controls and the use of rationing of certain consumption goods. This freed the Federal Reserve from having to do so through strict manipulation of the availability and the cost of credit.

That circumstance was satisfactory to the Treasury, which, finding it necessary to finance higher and higher deficits, was pleased that the funds were readily available at very low rates of interest. The Federal Reserve agreed to continue to accommodate the Treasury in this respect by keeping interest rates at the already low levels.

The agreement between the Federal Reserve and the Treasury was a workable arrangement as long as prices and wages were under control. But when the war ended, the Treasury wanted the Federal Reserve to continue a low interest rate policy despite the fact that Congress removed wage and price controls. With controls off, the price level started moving sharply upwards. Should the Fed capitulate to the Treasury and continue to be an "engine of inflation" as some put it, thus relinquishing the powers given it? The Fed found itself in a dilemma: On the one hand, there was the question of increased interest costs of the national debt if the Fed unpegged government security prices, as well as capital losses for security holders who only a short time before were encouraged by the government to invest in these securities. On the other hand, there was the question of reduced purchasing power of money as the price level increased. A choice between two evils had to be made.

After much controversy and discussion, the "Accord of 1951" was reached between the Federal Reserve and the Treasury, following which the Federal Reserve was once again able to follow either expansive or restrictive money and credit policies based on general economic conditions rather than on the needs of the Treasury. As expected, prices of government securities did drop, but not as much as many had feared they would. Shortly after being freed of its dominance by the Treasury, the Fed made a decision which plunged it into still another controversy, one that revolved around the type of securities the Fed should buy and sell in its open market operations.

A Change in Basic Philosophy: "Bills Only"

Maintaining bank reserves at levels that help achieve macroeconomic goals is, of course, a constant concern of the Federal Reserve. But beyond that, should the Fed (a) be primarily concerned with the availability of credit, letting interest rates adjust to a level reflecting the actions of borrowers and lenders in the money and capital markets, or (b) take an active role in determining the level of long-term interest rates, in addition to overseeing bank reserves?

To see why this makes a difference, recall three of the macroeconomic goals: full employment, adequate growth, and price level stability. Suppose there is unemployment and inadequate growth—what could the Fed do to help? One way to help absorb the unemployed resources is to put them to work creating capital goods. Expenditures for capital goods will not be made, however, or will be insufficiently made if the cost of long-term credit is too high—i.e., if long-term interest rates are too high. In this situation, the Fed could step in and, by buying long-term securities on the open market, bid up their prices, thereby depressing long-term interest rates. Capital spending that was previously shelved might now be made. The result: *both* unemployed resources are absorbed *and* growth induced. The price level need not go up, although pressures to do so could develop because of imperfections in the markets.

It seems clear that in an unemployment and inadequate growth case, as just described, the Federal Reserve should have no qualms about taking an active role in interest rate determination. Yet, in 1953 and lasting until 1960, the Fed embarked upon a policy of making the availability of credit the dominant concern when it announced that open market operations would be confined to the "short-end of the market," that is, to short-term securities. As it happened, open market purchases and sales in this period consisted almost exclusively of Treasury bills, and thus the name "bills only" was given to the Federal Reserve policy of this period.

The question of why the Fed adopted this policy arises. It was not pressured into this course by the administration and was, in fact, severely criticized by individuals within the administration as well as by others, notably many professional economists.

One reason sometimes given for the Fed's decision to go "bills only" was the memory of its domination by the Treasury prior to the Accord of 1951. In buying and selling long-term securities the Fed, of course, does influence the level of interest rates, particularly long-term rates. Might there not be a danger of once again finding themselves involved in programs of supporting government securities? A "bills only" policy made such involvement more remote.

The above explanation for the adoption of "bills only" is in terms of the psychological reaction of the Federal Reserve to the Treasury. Another explanation that might be given is in terms of a shift in the basic philosophy of the Fed—a shift which, in turn, reflected a shift in attitudes of the citizenry itself.

In 1952, Eisenhower was elected President, and along with him the voters elected Republican majorities in both houses of Congress. The country as a whole seemed tired of hot and cold wars, of regimentation, of rules and regulations. It was "time for a change."

Was it also time for the Fed to change? Had the Fed been interfering too much in the operation of the "free" economy? If so, it was time to back off some. "Bills only" is in accord with such an attitude; and, right or wrong, the Fed proceeded with a policy of controlling reserves predominantly through open market operations limited to Treasury bills. To the critic who charged the Fed with paying too much attention to the availability of credit and too little attention to the cost of it, the Fed would answer: "Oh, but you are wrong. We *are* involved in the cost of credit, for if we make reserves scarce, for example, the rate of interest at the commercial banks will tend to rise. This upward trend will be diffused throughout the market, and the result will be the same as if we had done it directly. But instead of our doing it, the market will do it. We are in this way contributing to the maintenance of economic freedom."

There is nothing wrong with this reasoning. But one can ask if it is appropriate. Just as it might be wrong for the Fed to interfere *too much* in the operation of the economy, it could be equally wrong for it to interfere *too little*. If a certain rate of growth is considered to be a desirable goal for the economy, then why wait for the private economy to bumble along if it is within the powers of the Fed to do what it claims the market will later do? In other words, why wait for the market to respond to a Fed policy of increased bank reserves designed to lower short-term rates; why not take a short cut and directly depress long-term rates by buying long-term securities?

The Fed did not respond to this criticism, holding firm to its position that the market and *not* the Fed should determine long-term interest rates. But a development involving short-term rates rather than long-term rates finally forced the Fed to abandon its "bills only" policy.

"Operation Twist": The Fed Reassumes Its Role in Long-Term Interest Rates

In the latter part of the 1950's the position of the United States in the world economy changed significantly. From the end of World War II until the latter 1950's, the demand for dollars was so great that a "dollar shortage" existed. In order to get dollars, countries were willing, or else forced by economic circumstances, to surrender gold in payment, with the result that the gold supplies of the free world tended to be concentrated in the United States.

For whatever the reasons—although certainly our far-flung operations and aid programs are significantly responsible—the picture changed in the latter part of the 1950's. The dollar shortage became a "dollar glut." The gold stock of the United States decreased from approximately $23 billion in 1957 to $18 billion in 1960 and then dropped by another billion in 1961.

In the meantime, the domestic economy was in fairly good shape, with the exception of 1957-58 when a recession occurred. As conditions improved following the upswing in the spring of 1958, the Fed pursued an overall policy of tightness to keep the price level from rising too rapidly. Then, in the summer of 1960, there occurred another downturn.

Now to head off a serious recession, the Fed would, of course, want to pursue a policy of monetary ease, forcing interest rates downward.

305

This, hopefully, would result in additional spending and cause income to increase or at least not to decrease as much as it otherwise might have. The Fed used all three of its major weapons in combatting the contraction: reserve requirements were lowered, discount rates were lowered, and the Fed purchased securities on the open market. But committed as the Fed was to "bills only," the immediate effect was to raise the prices of short-term securities and lower their yields. As expected, the level of short-term rates was depressed.

To the extent that the lower short-term rates would drag down the long-term rates—and this is what the proponents of the "bills only" policy would argue—the action would be countercyclical. The lower long-term rates would induce capital expenditure, raise income, and help absorb unemployed resources.

Short-term interest rates in other countries at this time were already higher than in the United States, encouraging the flow of gold from the United States to foreign countries with the higher rates. A further reduction in short-term rates would further encourage such flow and aggravate the gold problem, a problem over which many people showed increasing concern.

The obvious solution for the Fed was to remove the downward pressure on short-term rates, allowing them to become competitive with foreign rates, thereby stemming the outflow of gold. But what about the domestic unemployment situation—it called for a *decrease* in rates, especially long-term rates. How could the Fed manage an increase in short-term rates and a decrease in long-term rates at the same time?

One way to handle this was to *stop buying* Treasury bills on the open market, for this tended to increase their price and depress short-term rates, and to *buy instead* long-term securities, for this tended to raise their price and lower long-term rates. The higher short-term rates would tend to diminish the outflow of gold, which is what the country wanted, and the lower long-term rates would encourage investment expenditures, aid growth, and absorb unemployed resources, which is also what the country wanted.

Stop buying Treasury bills? Buy instead long-term securities? Deliberately depress long-term rates relative to short-term rates? This the Treasury urged and the Fed did, and "operation twist" as it is sometimes referred to, spelled an end to the "bills only" policy. The Federal Reserve once again assumed an active role in the manipulation of long-term interest rate levels.

A New Application of Fiscal Policy

In 1961, the economy—undoubtedly aided a little by operation twist—went into an expansion phase that was to be the longest sustained expansion in the country's history. But a difficulty showed up: Even with deficits following year after year, the economy was never quite able to make it to a "full" employment level. Unemployment did drop from 6.7 per cent in 1961 to 5.2 per cent in 1964, but the latter rate was still intolerable in terms of modern standards. Should the deficit be *increased* in an *expansion* phase? In other words, should the same kind of fiscal policy, i.e., deficit spending, be applied in an expansion phase as is applied in a contraction phase of the business cycle?

The answer appeared to be *yes, under certain conditions,* such as a condition of continued unemployment in a period of sustained expansion. There seemed to be a "built-in" unemployment factor in the economy in the early 1960's that stemmed from the relationship between federal taxation and full employment. This is explained as follows: As the economy expanded, the taxes collected by the government correspondingly increased; but because of the progressive tax rate structures, taxes collected increased at a more rapid rate than did national income; the deflationary effect of the increased tax collections was strong enough to persistently prevent the expanding economy of the early 1960's from reaching full employment.

If that were the case, why not reduce taxes just enough to allow the economy to reach full employment? This, in fact, is what was done with the tax reduction bill passed by Congress in 1964. The unemployment rate did fall, from 5.2 per cent in 1964 to 4.6 per cent in 1965 and then to 3.9 per cent in 1966. This new application of fiscal policy—lowering taxes in a period of expansion—was hailed as a success. The "new" economics ushered in by Keynes had scored a decisive victory.

Price Stability and Full Employment
Cannot Always Be Simultaneously Attained

However decisive the victory was, it was not complete, for as unemployment was reduced, the price level showed uncomfortably sharp increases. Need one macroeconomic goal be sacrificed for the other? Need the decrease in unemployment be "traded off" for an increase in price level? (See "The American Phillips Curve and the 'Consensual Trap' " by Adams.)

Furthermore, why was monetary policy not able to step in at this point and buttress fiscal policy measures, thus ensuring both stable price and full employment?

If the price level increases were simply a case of "too much money chasing too few goods," or a *demand-pull* inflation as it is called, monetary policy could help. The Fed could head off price level increases by tightening up on bank reserve positions and on the quantity of money that banks create.

But there is another type of inflation—one resulting from strong elements of monopoly in American industry and which should properly be called "sellers' inflation" but is more commonly called "cost-push inflation." Two groups of sellers foster this type of inflation: (a) sellers of products who have a great amount of control over the prices they charge for their products and which include such industries as auto, steel, electrical equipment, construction, and others and (b) sellers of labor services who, through unionization, have a great amount of control over wages and which include such unions as the United Auto Workers, United Steel Workers, International Brotherhood of Electrical Workers, the building trades unions, and others. With one group in control of prices and the other in control of wages, the following situation develops:

1. Industries with control over prices raise them in order to improve profit positions.
2. The high profits attract the attention of unions, who demand a "fair share."
3. Union strength forces the industry to give in to union demands, knowing that to recoup the cost they have only to further raise prices.
4. A "spiral" develops leading from one round of increases to another.
5. Monetary and fiscal policies are unable to maintain *both* price stability *and* full employment in such a situation.
6. A trade-off has to be made—some unemployment must be traded off for price level stability, or else some price level stability must be sacrificed in exchange for full employment.

This does not mean that a solution to the problem does not exist. But the solution does not lie in the areas of monetary and fiscal policies; the solution lies in the areas of antitrust legislation, and union responsibility and, in general, with what the citizenry wants to do about the question of the extent to which power groups will be allowed to interfere with the free operation of the market.

The Federal Budget Brings On
Another Inflation Threat

With the escalation of the Vietnam war, the demand-pull forces of inflation became stronger and stronger. This type of inflation, of course, is subject to some counteraction by the Federal Reserve, and the Fed properly started to tighten up on money and credit. Interest rates increased and soon reached the highest level since the Civil War. But inflation still threatened.

The Fed, it is true, could have taken successively more drastic actions in order to check further increases in the price level. But the "credit crunch"—the severe tightening of the supply of money and credit—was already being felt and was thought to be excessively harmful to the construction industry, in particular, and hurtful, in general, to the macroeconomic growth goal. Moreover, although the Fed could treat the symptoms of the inflation, it was difficult if not impossible to treat the cause, for the problem in the period following the middle 1960's was one of growing deficits superimposed on a full employment economy, which was just the opposite of the built-in unemployment factor present in federal finance in the early 1960's. The deficit gap which appeared to be too narrow in the early 1960's suddenly became too wide as the government stepped up expenditures to finance the Vietnam war. The increase in government expenditures outpaced the increase in tax collections.

This inflation factor could, of course, be quickly removed either by cutting down on government expenditures or by increasing taxes. Which should it be; or should it be a little of each? Three positions are taken on this matter:

1. Those who vehemently oppose the war in Vietnam say "Cut down on government expenditures; remove the inflation factor by ending the war in Vietnam."
2. At the other extreme are those—consisting of both opponents and proponents of the war—who say: "Whether we like it or not, we are for the time being committed to high government expenditures. Let us not compound our troubles by adding inflation to the country's problems. Narrow the deficit with increased taxes."
3. In the middle are those—including, among others, the tax-writing

Ways and Means Committee of the House—who say: "Let's narrow the deficit gap from both ends—reduce government expenditures and increase taxes."

The official position of the Federal Reserve and the Treasury has been the second of those just listed. The Fed has already implemented its anti-inflation posture. The Treasury, as the executor of the country's fiscal policy, must await action by Congress. What action Congress takes remains to be seen.

Some Additional Issues

Before summarizing, it should be pointed out that this discussion has left out many problems involving the relationship between monetary and fiscal policies. Omitted, for example, was such an important consideration as the "monetary policy" of the Treasury. Through its debt management and through the way it chooses to hold its cash receipts, Treasury monetary policy can either reinforce or neutralize Federal Reserve monetary policy.

Also omitted was a discussion of the feasibility of combining the Federal Reserve and the Treasury into a single agency, as is frequently proposed. The proposal stems from the fact that the two do not always analyze and view a macroeconomic situation in the same way, with the result that each goes its own—and often conflicting—way, although both are committed to seeking solutions to macroeconomic problems. Combinations of monetary and fiscal policies, or the proper "mix" of the policies, is similarly slighted, as are other problems involving monetary and fiscal policies. The interested student would do well to look at a report issued by the Commission on Money and Credit which deals in some detail with various aspects of the question of how best to use monetary and fiscal policies to achieve macroeconomic goals.[3]

Summary

As now used, monetary and fiscal policies refer to the explicit use of government powers to achieve the macroeconomic goals of price stability,

---

[3] Commission on Money and Credit, *Money and Credit* (Englewood Cliffs, N.J.: Prentice-Hall, 1961).

high levels of output and employment, adequate growth, and an acceptable balance-of-payments equilibrium. By monetary policy is meant the use of government's power to control money and credit for purposes of economic stabilization.

Historically, monetary policy is the older of the two, although early monetary policy—even after the establishment of the Federal Reserve System—was concerned primarily with the price level. The economic disorders of the 1930's pointed out serious shortcomings of monetary policy in coping with unemployment. In the meantime, Keynes and his followers presented strong arguments in favor of using fiscal policy to fight the depression.

The macroeconomic goals became subordinate considerations during the Second World War, when the exigencies of war brought on full employment and the price level was controlled by the government. The Fed, by keeping the economy sufficiently liquid, cooperated with the Treasury to help finance the large deficits. In the inflation following World War II, the Fed and the Treasury disagreed over the issue of interest rates—the Treasury wanting to continue with low rates and the Fed taking the opposite view.

After the Accord of 1951, the Federal Reserve pursued a policy of "bills only," a move directed toward the availability of credit and disengagement from direct manipulation of long-term interest rates. However, the business recession of 1960—coupled with the gold drain from the United States—compelled the Fed to abandon the policy and to become once again involved directly with interest rate determination.

The expansion, beginning in 1961, was unable to hit the full employment mark. The fiscal policy measure of tax reduction was successfully used to drive unemployment rates downward. The reverse problem, however, occurred in the years just after the mid-1960's, when the Vietnam war was escalated and resulted in budget deficits. Monetary policy was used forcefully to head off inflation. Whether fiscal policy will be equally forcefully applied remains, at the time of this writing, undetermined.

Questions for Thought and Discussion

1. How have the mechanics of monetary policy changed over the past 40 years?
2. What is the proper relationship between monetary and fiscal poli-

cies? How has the relationship between monetary and fiscal policies changed through time?

3. Do you think the Federal Reserve System should be fused with the Treasury, or should the Fed remain independent? What arguments exist for each position?

Section VIII

ECONOMIC DEVELOPMENT

THE ECONOMICS OF ECONOMIC DEVELOPMENT

Robert L. Bennett

If an opinion poll of the world's population were conducted to determine which country at any time in history had attained the highest level of economic development, the virtually unanimous choice would be the present-day United States. This opinion would be based on the fact that with few exceptions people use annual production per person as the yardstick for measuring the level of economic development of a country. It is likely that world opinion would be divided as to whether or not attaining a higher level of economic development should be a nation's major goal. Relatively rich persons might place a higher value on maintaining the *status quo* (which made possible and protects their wealth) and less value on attempting to increase the nation's output per person. Relatively poor people, on the other hand, might be more likely to place higher value on increasing national output per person, since they might reasonably expect to obtain a part of the increase and since the *status quo* is less desirable from their point of view. Many people might feel that economic development is too "materialistic" a national goal, particularly if they think it is attained only through sacrificing important cultural or spiritual values. This paper will discuss various definitions, measures, and aspects of economic development to provide a framework for considering these issues.

When economists measure the level of economic development by the level of output per person, it is usually with several qualifications. It is common for economists to say that if Country A has a higher level of output per person than Country B, then Country A has a higher level of

---

The author is Associate Professor of Economics at the University of Maryland.

economic development than Country B, *other things equal*. What are some of these "other things"?

First, the number of hours of leisure available per person in the two countries should be approximately the same. If two countries are producing the same output per person, Country A with 50 per cent of the population working 40 hours per week and Country B with 50 per cent of the population working 60 hours per week, we would rate Country A higher on the economic development scale.

Second, the two countries should be using approximately the same percentage of their capacity to produce. If two countries are producing the same level of output per person and have the same number of hours of leisure available per person, but Country A has more idle factories than Country B, we would rate Country A higher. For if both countries try to increase their output by inducing more people to work, Country A could be more successful in producing output since its new workers would be aided by more machines.

An economist would also want the usefulness of a unit of output to be approximately the same before he accepted output per person as the measure of the level of economic development. For example, if two countries produce the same output per person, but the climate of Country A is milder and less variable, it is likely that Country A has the higher level of economic development. Calorie requirements to produce the same amount of energy would be lower in Country A; hence, for a given amount of satisfaction from food, the people of Country A would require less food than those of Country B. Country A's people could also get the same amount of protection from the elements with less clothing and less costly housing than are required in Country B. If Country A is more able to coexist peacefully with its neighbors and hence devotes a smaller share of its output to armaments, then the average usefulness of output would probably be higher in Country A. Again, we would classify it as having the higher level of development (and perhaps also as being a "better" country in some moral sense).

Finally (because the list is potentially inexhaustible), the degree of inequality in the distribution of the output among the persons of the two countries should be approximately the same. Assume that countries A and B produce the same output per person; Country A divides its output equally among its citizens while Country B gives half of its output to Mr. Rich and divides the remainder equally among the other citizens. Country A would be assigned the higher position on the economic development scale if this situation has persisted for years. However, we are not sure how to rank the countries if the situation has not persisted unless we know something about the difference between what Mr. Rich does with his differential income (the part of his income that is more than that of other B citizens) and what Country A citizens do with their differential incomes (the part of their incomes which is more than that of nonrich Country B citizens). It is possible that Mr. Rich will do something which Country A does not do that would make Country B's future income more than twice that of Country A. (For instance, he might obtain machines and factories which Country B workers can use to help them produce more output.) Then we would find the curious situation of Country B having a higher output per person, nonrich B citizens having higher incomes than A citizens, and Mr. Rich being even more able to do whatever he does with the large income.

When the level of output per person is used as the basic indicator of the level of economic development, a static definition of economic development is implied. One is looking at the state of one aspect of various countries at some point in time (or that aspect of one country at several points in time) and ranking the countries (or the time periods) on a scale from least developed through more developed to most developed economically. He is, therefore, implying that economic development is defined as producing output per person (subject to some qualifications such as the four discussed). Such a definition may be adequate for many purposes; for other purposes, a different definition may prove more useful.

A more dynamic approach would be to define economic development as the process of increasing the level of output per person. When this definition is used, countries are classified as rapidly developing, slowly developing, stagnant, or regressing, rather than being classified as more developed or less developed. The most often used measure of this dynamic type of economic development is the percentage change per year in output per person. As an example of the difference between the static definition and the dynamic one, note that during the great depression of the 1930's the United States was the most developed country (static) in the world; however, it was far from being a developing country (dynamic), since annual output per person was significantly below that of 1929.

If one is interested in studying the experiences of different countries with a view to learning what, if possible, must be done in order to increase the level of output per person, it is especially important to use the dynamic definition of economic development. This makes it possible to group the countries into those which are developing very rapidly, those developing moderately rapidly, etc. One can then study these groups of countries in an attempt to determine those activities which enhance economic development and those which hamper it. This type of study is not so fruitful when the static definition of economic development is used, since the countries with relatively high (or medium or low) output per person are grouped together—even though some might be increasing rapidly and others might be reducing their output per person.

At first glance, one might be tempted to consider both the static and dynamic definitions of economic development as rather materialistic, since attention is focused either on the level of output per person or on percentage changes in that level. Should we not give more consideration to the quality of the output? Before answering this question, it is necessary to discuss briefly the way in which output is usually measured and the things which are included in output. In measuring output, physical units cannot reasonably be used, since so many different products are produced and one cannot meaningfully add dozens of oranges to tons of steel and numbers of houses. An attempt is made to avoid this problem by initially measuring output in terms of the number of units of money (dollars, for instance) paid for the dozens of oranges, tons of steel, or numbers of houses. For a country, this measure of output is called Gross National Product (GNP). A problem is encountered when one compares the GNP of one year with that of another, since they could differ because of a change in the number of physical units of products produced and/or because of a change in the prices paid for the products. An attempt is made to adjust the GNP figures so as to eliminate the effects of price changes; the resulting measure of output is called real GNP.

Real Gross National Product includes not only goods such as automobiles, furniture, bananas, machines, etc., but also services such as symphony concerts, sermons, lectures, etc. All of these items are valued at the price for which they are sold or at the cost of producing them if they are not sold. Hence, many of the finer, cultural, or spiritual things of life are included in output. Measuring output in terms of the prices which are paid for products results in our taking into account most of the quality differences among products. One usually pays more for attending the performance of a good orchestra than for one of poor quality. Of course, sometimes he finds that he got a bargain, and at other times he finds that he was "robbed." Thus, one can legitimately deplore the fact that, in a particular country, very few people attend orchestra performances; and one might legitimately refer disparagingly to that country as "materialistic." But one does not legitimately complain that economic development is "materialistic" as it is usually measured, since an increase in the output of concerts is registered as readily as an increase in the output of automobiles.

Let us now shift the focus of our attention away from the goods and services such as automobiles, furniture, factories, machines, symphony concerts, sermons, and lectures, and let us concentrate on the human activities such as driving in the country, lying on a soft bed, working in a pleasant environment, typing a poem, and listening to a concert, sermon, or lecture. Obviously, the goods and services just mentioned are indispensable technical prerequisites of the human activities mentioned. For the remainder of this paper, a definition of economic development—which differs from the dynamic definition only in that it focuses attention on human activities—is used: Economic development is the process of increasing the range of technically possible activities of the people involved in the process. In using this definition, one loses a substantial amount of apparent ability to measure economic development precisely, but he can gain a very substantial amount of additional insight into the process of development.

There are very specific, observable technical prerequisites for a given human activity—prerequisites which, in all important respects, are the same in all places and at all times. The technical prerequisites for my flying 200 miles in an hour are, among other things, the airplane and airports (and the industrial complexes necessary to construct them), the trained crew (and the educational complex necessary to make it available), my knowledge of the availability of this activity, and my ability to devote an hour to this activity. These same things would have been required 200 years ago and would be just as necessary in the Amazon Valley as they are in College Park, Maryland.

If one analyzes the almost infinite number of technical prerequisites of flying 200 miles in an hour, he finds that almost every part of the modern United States industrial society plays some role at some stage in the process. For example, if I must devote all of my energy to the production of sufficient food to provide me and my family with adequate energy to continue to provide this food, then I would not be able to spare an hour for flying. It is precisely this situation in which most of the world's inhabitants have traditionally found themselves. But today in the United States, one can rely on specialists from all parts of the world to provide him with all of the things he uses. This specialization in production plays a vital role in making a wide range of activities available to the participants in our industrial society.

Almost all parts of the present society and many parts of past societies have contributed to my being able to fly. The knowledge necessary for constructing the airplane developed gradually over a long period of time. For instance, in order to make the necessary metals, one must use knowledge of metallurgy which has been accumulated at least since the Bronze Age. Past societies educated my pilot, built the airplane, accumulated the knowledge, constructed the various necessary industrial complexes, etc. Similarly, the range of activities that will be available in the future in the United States depends on what we actually do now. If we build more airplanes and airports, train more crews, etc., people in the future will have more possibility of flying. The range of activities available now to people in the Amazon Valley depends on what they (and we) have done in the past; what they will be able to do in the future depends also on what they (and we) are doing now. More generally, the range of technically possible activities limits the activities in which a society actually engages; these, in turn, determine the range of technically possible activities in the future.

The activities in which one actually engages are limited not only by the technical prerequisites discussed above, but also by cultural limits. Flying 200 miles in an hour is technically possible in the United States today, but a cultural requirement restricts this activity for those who cannot afford to pay for the ticket. One can imagine an almost infinite variety of cultural limits to the ability to fly—people who have particular political beliefs might be prohibited, or people with brown eyes, or people who believe the "wrong" set of superstitions. These cultural limits cannot immediately add to the number of seats on a plane, but they can cause seats to be empty. During the Great Depression of the 1930's in the United States, approximately one-fourth of the workers who wished to perform the activity of producing output—with the help of the machines which were available—were prevented from doing this by our cultural limits. This is, admittedly, an extreme example of the possibly perverse effects of cultural limits on economic development. A more developmental set of cultural rules would permit actual activities more nearly to approach the limit of those technically possible.

Whereas the technical prerequisites for an activity are the same for all times and places, the cultural prerequisites are limited in their applicability by both time and space. The cultural limits of the United States and of the Soviet Union are quite different; we find theirs odd, if not obnoxious, and the feeling is mutual. An argument about the technical prerequisites of an activity is easily settled by an appeal to the facts; but an argument about cultural limits is rarely settled since these limits are largely matters of taste, habit, or custom. Particularly important sets of cultural limits, such as the rules under which workers will be permitted to use the machines that are available, are usually part of a package of ideology (such as capitalism, socialism, free enterprise, or christianity) which is defended against change quite vigorously, not by appeals to facts but by appeals to emotions.

Fortunately, it is not necessary for one country to adopt the cultural rules of another in order to experience economic development. The history of Western Europe, the United States, the Soviet Union, and Japan (all of which have experienced tremendous economic development) has demonstrated clearly that economic development can occur under widely differing cultural rules. However, if a country is to experience economic development, it is necessary for that country to have and to use the technical prerequisites of economic development; this may entail substantial changes in its cultural rules.

One usually has these changes in cultural limits in mind when he complains that a concomitant of economic development is some change in the values of a society. For instance, for some years in the United States there has been controversy over whether or not the entire country will be required to observe Daylight Saving Time simultaneously during the summer; Congress finally passed a law on the subject. Such an issue would not arise in a country which has no intercity communications and transportation; only when people provide themselves with the freedom to travel between cities by rail, bus, or air or to use nationwide television or radio does synchronized time become an issue worthy of attention. But many people see in the determination of official time by the federal government some loss of states' or counties' or cities' rights—a change in the cultural limits on the activities of local officials—and they complain of a supposed loss of freedom.

Perhaps the most significant freedom which is lost in the process of economic development is the freedom of individuals to refrain from observing a time schedule. So long as people work and play separately and are relatively unspecialized in their production activities, there is little need for them to observe time schedules. But when people produce in groups, as they must when they become specialists (and, hence, vastly more productive), they must be in particular places at particular times in order to avoid having the group wait for individuals. Many people think fondly of an earlier, less complicated period when clocks and watches were regarded as luxuries rather than necessities. They forget that in this period a folk saying developed to the effect that "man works from sun to sun, but . . . work is never done." Today, the average U.S. manufacturing worker has 3 hours more leisure for every day in the year than did his counterpart in 1900 (the work week has declined from more than 60 hours in 1900 to approximately 40 hours today). Furthermore, he enjoys several more years of formal retirement than was the case in 1900. These increases in freedom from the time clock, together with the increased availability of alternative ways in which to use the leisure, should be considered as at least partially offsetting the increased regimentation during working hours. It is true that most modern, organized leisure activities—such as attending sports events, watching television or attending concerts—also require a person to observe a time schedule. But one has the alternative of less organized activities—such as reading a book, working on a do-it-yourself project, or driving in the country.

The human beings who are participating in a process of economic development are continuously increasing the range of technically possible alternative activities available to themselves. But they are not increasing the number of hours in a day; hence, an individual finds himself, as time passes, either engaging in more and more activities for shorter and shorter periods or engaging in a smaller percentage of the activities which are technically possible. He finds economic development continuously increasing his freedom of choice and, simultaneously, imposing the necessity of choosing.

In the United States today, an individual, since he is likely to be literate and since books and television are both available, often will face the choice between reading a book or watching television. One may legitimately deplore the fact that so many people spend so much time watching poor quality television shows rather than reading good books. This does not mean, however, that the situation was better 25 years ago when the alternative of watching television was not available; in 1942, a smaller percentage of the population was literate, there were fewer books available per person, and there was less leisure available per person. One should deplore the choices which are actually made rather than the fact that the alternatives are available. It is certainly well within the range of choice today to improve the quality of television shows (and of books); that this is not done is evidence, perhaps, of some shortcomings in the cultural rules which determine our actual choices.

The problem of choosing also becomes more important at the group level during economic development. In the United States today—even though more alternatives are available to the citizens than at any time or place in the history of the world—one also finds more of the air and water polluted. We have chosen, in the process of our economic development, to permit our technical ability to breathe fresh air and to swim in clean water to become more restricted. However, polluted air and water are not necessarily concomitants of economic development. We have the technical capability of eliminating and preventing such pollution. This technical capability was created, along with the pollution, in our process of economic development; the same is true of most of the things which are often listed as disadvantages of economic development. We could choose, if we would, to have pure air and water in much the same way that we have chosen to try to have relatively pure food and drugs; this requires restricting, through cultural rules, the activities which pollute air and water and engaging in the activities which purify them. One can quite legitimately deplore the fact that, as yet, we have not made these important choices; but he is not thereby objecting to economic development.

In this paper, the reader's attention has been focused on the human activities which are made possible in the process of economic development. Freedom of choice has been increased tremendously in those countries and at those times which have experienced economic development; this is certainly a worthwhile national goal. But along with the increased freedom of choice during the process of economic development goes an increased necessity for making choices. For in the United States, which today is the leader in making these alternatives available, the citizen is continuously presented with choices which were never before available to human beings. Through the process of trial and error and success, we have already learned quite a lot about the process of making intelligent choices among alternative courses of action; and we have every reason to expect that our decision-making processes will continue to improve in the future. In studying the economic history of Western civilization or of any part of the world—in formulating policy recommendations for the world today—it is most fruitful to analyze the bases on which a society makes its choices. Choices which have actually been made in the past or which will be made in the future are better to the extent that the choices themselves are made on the basis of the scientific method of analyzing the facts and consequences of the choices; the choices are worse to the extent that they are made on the basis of culture-bound custom, habit, inertia, and superstition.

Questions for Thought and Discussion

1. What is economic development? How is economic development related to income and population?
2. What is the relationship between economic development and human welfare?
3. How can economic development be portrayed by a production frontier curve? (See Phaup article.) Would economic development cause the production frontier to move to the left or to the right?

ECONOMIC DEVELOPMENT AND ITS LONG-RUN ENVIRONMENTAL IMPLICATIONS

John H. Cumberland

During the past two centuries, the efforts of Western man to solve his economic problems have met with extraordinary success. By developing new technologies, embodying them in massive industrial complexes, and re-organizing his society on the bases of initiative, efficiency, and accumulation, the Western world has achieved vast acceleration of industrial output. Although pockets of poverty remain for some disadvantaged groups and regions, even the working man in most industrialized nations enjoys a wide range of products and luxuries which would have been unavailable to even the wealthiest of individuals in earlier centuries.

Thus, Western man appears to be well on his way to achieving his major objective in the area of economics—providing a comfortable living for most members of society. Ironically, however, evidence is beginning to emerge that progress towards solution of the economic problem is creating a critical new problem which may turn out to be the greatest challenge man has faced on the earth. This is the problem of environmental deterioration.

In the powerful drive to overcome all obstacles to expanding production, society has tended to ignore the fact that industrial production is accompanied by waste production and environmental modification in a way which is literally changing the face of the earth. Water pollution is spreading from streams into major lakes, rivers, estuaries, and even into the oceans of the globe.

The author is Professor of Economics at the University of Maryland.

Siltation from poor agricultural practices and soil erosion, washing away land bulldozed for roads, and other developmental practices are fouling waterways and filling channels and harbors. Thermal pollution from mushrooming power generation facilities is heating nutrient-laden water bodies, hastening the growth of algae and threatening vital links in the delicate ecological balance of this water.

Smog and air pollution—no longer isolated phenomena—are spreading over the globe, steadily increasing the carbon dioxide content of the atmosphere. Some scientists are concerned that this may create a greenhouse effect which will melt the polar ice caps and submerge the coastal areas and their major cities.

The deliberate use of powerful agricultural fertilizers, herbicides, pesticides, fungicides, and other chemicals is poisoning the land, polluting the water, killing many forms of wildlife, and accumulating in the tissues of plant and animal life (including human) all over the globe.

Since World War II, subtle new environmental threats to the earth have emerged in forms which—because they are invisible, cumulative in their action, delayed in taking effect, and diffused in nature—are even more lethal in their implications. Invisible but deadly radioactivity has been spread over the globe deliberately through explosions and inadvertently through leakage from reactors and buried atomic waste products. Increasing noise levels in the audible range of frequencies pose psychological threats to living organisms, while additional threats are created by the ever-increasing spread of electromagnetic transmission throughout the electromagnetic spectrum from radio, radar, TV, microwave, satellite, and other transmissions.

In the production and economic development process, modern industrial man converts so much of nature and natural resources into waste and pollution that he is running out of the open space and ecological resiliency that he formerly relied upon to absorb and reconvert the unwanted waste products of the industrial, urbanized processes.

These environmental phenomena pose the threat of disaster not only to Western capitalism, but are linked by present technology to large-scale industrialization wherever it occurs. It is not just Lake Erie which is becoming a dead lake, but also the Soviet Lake Baikal is threatened by water pollution. China and the developing nations of the earth can and soon will face similar problems, despite their different ideologies, if they are successful in their aspirations to create for themselves the industrial technologies of the advanced nations.

A few simple relationships considered together in the form of what economists regard as a model useful for systematic projection of probable future events will indicate why deterioration of environmental quality poses such an ominous threat for the future of civilization.

1. With current technology, industrial output is accompanied by output of waste products, pollution, and environmental change.
2. Economic development in industrial nations is characterized by upward trends in the amount of industrial activity per capita.
3. The economic development which is sought by underdeveloped nations, with the encouragement and support of developed nations, will require vast increases of economic activity per capita.
4. Population in most developed and underdeveloped nations of the earth is growing at unprecedented rates.

If these four relationships remain constant, the environmental problem brought about by pollution will be an ominous threat indeed, and the earth may soon become uninhabitable. It is therefore important to examine the extent to which any of these relationships can be modified by society so that it can continue to enjoy the fruits of economic development without suffocating and drowning man in his own waste.

First, the relationship between human aspirations and industrial activity is not likely to be changed. Humans, in both developed and underdeveloped nations, will continue to strive for even more of the fruits of industrial output and affluence in the foreseeable future.

With respect to population trends, there may be some opportunity for more rational human behavior. There is some evidence and some room for hope that, as incomes and educational achievement increase and as technically and culturally acceptable means for family planning become available, the rate of population increase may be retarded. However, this is a critical problem, since optimum levels of population have already been exceeded in most nations, and continued growth of population aggravates most social problems.

Therefore, the major hope for civilization in safeguarding the habitability of the earth is to modify the current technological linkages between industrial activity and environmental pollution. The essential task of society is to develop a pollution-free technology, both in order to maintain the viability of already industrialized nations and in order to insure that the vast surge of industrial activity which is sought by the developing nations will be a technology which will not corrupt the earth with waste and pollution.

It is not yet clear whether technology can offer civilization the means for correcting its own technological abuses of the earth. The problem is

327

to find new ways of recycling some of our vast outputs into efforts to abate pollution, recover by-products, recycle wastes, and convert dangerous outputs into useful inputs such as waste heat from nuclear production of electricity into desaltation of sea water. In order to achieve maximum internalization of external wastes and diseconomies, it may be necessary to plan—from the ground up—new combinations of advanced technologies in optimal relationships for recycling of pollutants, recovery of by-products, and prevention of environmental damage. Advanced planning of the location and structure of massive industrial and urban complexes of the future for minimum damage to the global environment will become necessary, requiring international cooperation for maximum benefits. Recognition of the global nature of watersheds, windsheds, ocean currents, and atmospheric phenomena will indicate the necessity of extending current areas of international agreement, such as those pertaining to world fisheries, peaceful development of polar regions, and use of outer space.

Human society in the future will necessarily be more concerned with the qualitative, as opposed to the merely quantitative, aspects of economic development as it affects the environment and conditions of life. In this endeavor, the economist, using traditional and newly emerging tools of analysis, will pay a significant role in identifying objectives and in evaluating efficient methods for the achievement of objectives. But in addition to improved technology and more sophisticated economic analysis, protection and improvement of the human environment will require extensive modification of our legal, political, and other institutions.

If man has lost control of both his numbers and his technology, then his time remaining on the earth is running out rapidly indeed as he repeats the biblical role of destroying an earthly paradise through his own actions. How long and under what conditions he can continue to enjoy life on earth depends upon the extent to which he will be able to bring his reserves of knowledge and wisdom to bear upon restoring and protecting the quality of his environment.

Questions for Thought and Discussion

1. What conflict exists between economic growth, as that term has generally been used, and the quality of the environment?
2. Would you regard all increases in GNP as beneficial or true economic growth?

THE ROLE OF

TRANSPORTATION IN ECONOMICS

Hale C. Bartlett

Transportation is an important branch of economics. As a process, transportation involves the movement of products and people from one place to another. Transportation, therefore, creates what economists call time and place utility in goods and services. In creating time and place utility, or usefulness, transportation makes possible the implementation of several fundamental economic principles that are vital to the satisfactory performance of any economic system. It is the purpose of this article to indicate how transportation is critical to the economic well-being of any country or region by showing the role of the transportation process in making possible the operation of these basic principles.

Basic Economic Principles and Concepts

The study of economics is founded upon the fact that economic resources are scarce and accordingly must be brought together and used in the most efficient manner possible. Consequently, economists are concerned with the production and distribution of goods and services in any economic society. The ultimate goal is that the economic resources of a society are combined in such a manner that the highest level of material well-being of that society is attained. Through the years, economists have developed a body of principles and concepts which explain the processes of efficient production and distribution. Among the more important of these are the principle of division and specialization of labor, the law of

The author is Associate Professor of Economics, University of Illinois (Chicago).

comparative advantage, and the concept of free trade in competitive markets. Adequate implementation of each of these underlies the wealth of any country or region.

Division and Specialization of Labor

A fundamental determinant of the productivity and hence the economic wealth of any nation, region, or organization of individuals is the principle of division and specialization of labor. Adam Smith was one of the earliest economists to discuss this principle. In his famous example of pin manufacturing, Smith demonstrated how output per worker could be increased several hundredfold if the work necessary to produce a pin were divided among several workers rather than performed by one worker alone. This great increase in productivity was the result of three separate forces at work. First, by specializing in the performance of one or a few tasks, each worker would become much more proficient in the performance of his work. Second, by assigning a limited number of tasks to each worker, much time formerly required in moving from one job to another would be saved. Third, with each worker concentrating on a limited aspect of the job, his attention could be better directed toward how to improve the means of accomplishing that job. This would lead to the invention of labor-saving machines, by either the workmen themselves or by those who were in the business of manufacturing machines. It is this principle upon which our present-day mass production economic system is founded and from which our economic well-being is derived. The reason for this is clear. Division and specialization of labor result in higher output per worker than would otherwise be the case. This means that each worker can earn more income, thereby improving his personal economic situation. The entire society is similarly better off. With greater output per worker, there are more goods to be consumed, and the unit cost of each is lower than it otherwise would be. Assuming competitive markets, this means that the members of society have more goods to consume at lower prices. Clearly, the wealth of any nation is dependent upon that nation's ability to produce goods in an efficient manner.

Now, this principle of division and specialization of labor cannot function without adequate transportation. There are two reasons for this. First, mass production techniques necessitate the amassing of large quantities of men, material, and machines at specific locations. In most mass production industries, relatively few points of production serve a national market. The transportation lines feeding into these production centers can be considered an extension of the production line itself. In some instances, · the gearing of transportation to production is so close that a one-day curtailment of transportation service would result in a shutdown of the production facility.

Secondly, as noted by Adam Smith, the operation of this principle is limited by the extent of the market. Mass production techniques cannot be fully developed unless there are mass markets to be served. The volume of output simply would be too great to be consumed in a local or even regional area. To develop a mass market fully, there must be an adequate system of transportation available to the manufacturer. Further, it is interesting to observe that as transportation facilities become more efficient over time and this efficiency is reflected in lower shipping rates, the marketing area of a manufacturer is increased still further.

Law of Comparative Advantage

The law of comparative advantage explains why nations and regions engage in trade. Such trade exists because nations and regions specialize in certain types of work in much the same way as individuals. To understand the operation of this law, it is desirable first to consider a situation involving absolute advantage of one nation over another in the production of a specific commodity. Let us assume that Great Britain is more efficient in the production of tractors than is India, but India is more efficient in the production of hemp than is Great Britain. Each country has an absolute advantage over the other in the production of a specific commodity. Therefore, it is to the advantage of both that Great Britain produce tractors and India produce hemp and that trade between the two nations in these commodities takes place. Each country will be able to · obtain these two commodities at lower prices, assuming no artificial barriers to trade exist.

Comparative advantage, however, involves more than this. Under the law of comparative advantage, one nation or region may be more efficient than another in the production of *all* commodities. Still, it will be to the advantage of both nations or regions if each specializes in the production of those commodities in which the greatest comparative advantage exists and then trades with the other. Here, let us assume that the state of Michigan is more efficient in the production of both automobiles and furniture than is the state of North Carolina. Also, assume that furniture can be produced in North Carolina more efficiently than automobiles. With no trade between the states, Michigan would produce sufficient quantities of both automobiles and furniture to meet its needs. However, the income earned in manufacturing by the state of Michigan would be lower than in a situation where trade between the two states took place. If Michigan is *more* efficient in the production of automobiles than furniture, then it will be to the advantage of Michigan to devote its resources to the production of automobiles and engage in trade with North Carolina to obtain furniture. In this way, Michigan will be using its resources *most* efficiently and, hence, its income will be higher. North Carolina, too, will gain, since it will be able to devote its resources to the production of furniture rather than automobiles, thereby employing those resources more efficiently. Also, both states will benefit by being able to serve expanded markets, gaining the advantages of increased output and lower unit costs.

Together with the inherent advantage of a nation or region in the production of a specific commodity, transportation must be present if the law of comparative advantage is to function. Since the cost of transportation is one element in the cost of producing a commodity, the rates charged for the transport of commodities from one region to another must be sufficiently low for movement to occur. Otherwise, trade will not occur, since the delivered price of the commodity will be too high in the final market.

Free Trade in Competitive Markets

The economic well-being of a nation or region is dependent upon the ability of products and people to move freely from one place to another. If one region is suffering from a shortage of a commodity, additional amounts of that commodity desirably are moved into the region from an area having a surplus of the commodity. In this way, the quantity supplied is better matched with the quantity demanded, both in the area experiencing a shortage and in the area experiencing a surplus. This improved balance between supply and demand results in more stable prices for both regions. This is a desirable result, since consumers in the deficit area will not be faced with spiraling prices for commodities in short supply and since producers in the surplus area will not experience the bottom falling out of their market for the commodity that is in surplus. Further, with freedom of movement, producers from many areas can bring their products into an area and thereby increase the competition for sale of those products in the area. This breaks down local monopolies, giving consumers lower prices and a greater selection of products. The ability to move a product into an area from a distant point of production is essential to the maintenance of a healthy level of competition. Again, it is clear that without an efficient means of transportation, the balancing of supply and demand for a product in one region and the maintenance of a satisfactory level of competition in that region would be difficult to attain, if not impossible.

A Case in Point: The U.S. Automobile Industry

This discussion has presented in general terms the role of transportation in the implementation of certain basic economic principles and concepts. A review of the nature of automobile manufacturing in the United States will serve to highlight this general discussion.

The U.S. automobile industry represents an advanced stage in the development of the art of mass production. In 1965, 9.3 million passenger automobiles were built and sold in the United States. If one considers the motor trucks and busses produced by this industry, almost 11.1 million vehicles were built that year. This represents an average output of 42,700 vehicles per day. The rate of output for a single assembly line is about 560 vehicles per eight-hour shift, or slightly more than one vehicle per minute. Even more astonishing is the fact that in certain plants one will find completely different makes of automobiles produced by a manufacturer being assembled on the same line, one after the other, in a wide variety of models.

The productive process that generates this output is a highly specialized, mechanized, and coordinated one. At present, more than 740,000 persons are directly engaged in the production of automobiles in the United States. The skills used in this industry range from physicists and engineers working on the development of new powerplants to finishers who wet-sand automobile bodies by hand during the painting process. With approximately 15,000 parts to build and assemble into an automobile, the process of designing and building a modern automobile is a complicated one. By necessity, the total job is divided into many different functional areas which, in turn, have smaller segments of work being performed by specialists.

This division of work has led to a high degree of mechanization. Total investment per worker in the automobile industry now averages about $17,800. Many areas of production are highly automated. For example, engine blocks are automatically bored, honed, drilled, and tapped. The blocks move through long banks of multiple drilling machines, carried by automatic transfer control equipment from one work station to the next. In body manufacture, electric spot welding machines now permit multiple welds to be made upon one application of the machine. This is done either manually or by automatic equipment. The result of such mechanization is greatly improved output per man-hour of production. This is reflected in the fact that automobile workers have consistently earned significantly higher-than-average wages as compared to other industrial employees.

With the development of mechanized manufacturing, production tends to become located in a relatively limited number of places. The reason for this is that specialized production machinery is very expensive. Manufacturers cannot afford to have large numbers of automated engine-machining lines spread throughout the country. Nor is there any real need for this, since a limited amount of automatic equipment can produce large volumes of output very rapidly. For example, one major automobile manufacturer in the United States produced 3.1 million vehicles in 1965. The engines for all of these vehicles were manufactured in four plants located in three cities. Transmissions were produced in three plants located in two cities. Stampings for bodies and other parts were made in five cities. All of the cities involved, except one, are located in the Midwest.

Products from these relatively few production points flow by rail, truck, and air to 17 assembly plants serving the United States. After assembly into finished products, the vehicles are moved by railroad and motor carrier to over 7,000 dealers, where sales to the ultimate consumer take place. Clearly, transportation plays an essential role in this process of production and distribution. In an industry such as this, the transportation network is really an extension of each firm's production line. Without transportation, production is halted at each plant in from one to three days, depending upon the inventory level of each plant. During a recent trucking tie-up where operations were halted for three days, some 15,000 automobile workers were laid off by the end of the second day. Other industries were similarly affected.

On the distribution side, transportation promotes market competition in the sale of automobiles. There are more than 33,000 dealers handling domestic and imported automobiles in the United States. This averages approximately 10 dealers per county. Sales and servicing of vehicles produced by major manufacturers are readily available throughout the country. Competition is brought to the local level through this organization of dealerships. The transportation of used automobiles from one market to another further serves to increase competition in the sale of both used and new automobiles. Finally, domestic manufacturers are continually subject to competition arising from foreign imports landed at coastal and Great Lakes ports of entry and transported to every market in the United States. In 1965, for example, about 560,000 foreign-built automobiles were imported by this country. While this is only 6 per cent of the domestic output, the variety from which consumers may choose is effectively increased. Products from West Germany, the United Kingdom, Sweden, Japan, and other countries are now found in the U.S. automobile market.

Summary

The economic well-being of mankind is dependent upon the efficient use of scarce resources. Certain basic economic principles and concepts relate directly to efficiency in production and distribution. These include division and specialization of labor, the law of comparative advantage, and the concept of free trade in competitive markets. None of these principles and concepts could operate properly without adequate transportation. Hence, if any economic society is to develop to the fullest potential, it must give adequate recognition to the importance of transportation in the operation of its economic system.

Questions for Thought and Discussion

1. What economic characteristics of a developed economy are implemented by transportation?
2. How is transportation related to economic development?

Section IX

ECONOMIC SYSTEMS

THE NATURE OF ECONOMIC SYSTEMS

Allan G. Gruchy

The Definition of an Economic System

An economic system is an evolving pattern or complex of human relations which is concerned with the disposal of scarce resources for the purpose of satisfying various private and public needs for goods and services.[1] Man does not work *in vacuo*. In all geographical areas, he joins with his neighbors and fellow citizens in the work of converting scarce human and natural resources into a supply of useful goods and services. In the United States, the Soviet Union, and India, as elsewhere, men take advantage of the division of labor to cooperate in the important task of making a living. Labor, land, and capital are combined in intricate ways to form different economic systems. These systems or patterns of human relations are cultural processes which have historical origins, undergo development, and move towards the various goals set up by individuals and groups. Like all other cultural processes, economic systems incorporate the past, the present, and the future. As they move from one era to another, economic systems retain many of their older institutional arrangements to form the emerging pattern of economic organization. Economic systems do not stand still. Nothing is more obvious than the changing nature of the world's major economic systems. Our own capitalist system has undergone profound change in the past one hundred years. What the

---

From *Comparative Economic Systems*, by permission of the publisher (Boston: Houghton Mifflin Co., 1966). The author is Professor of Economics at the University of Maryland.

[1] Manuel Gottlieb, "Theory of an Economic System," *The Frontiers of Social Science* (London: Macmillan and Co., Ltd., 1955), pp. 315-339. See also Allan G. Gruchy, *Modern Economic Thought, the American Contribution* (New York: Prentice-Hall, 1947), pp. 550-557.

American capitalist system will be like a hundred years from now no one can accurately foretell, but one can safely predict that, under the pressure of technological change, it will be different in many respects from the welfare capitalism of the first half of the current century.

Diversity

A distinguishing characteristic of the world's major economic systems is their great diversity. There is no single pattern of economic relations. Instead, there is a wide range of patterns—from the unplanned democratic free enterprise or capitalist system at one extreme to the rigorously planned totalitarian communist system at the other extreme. Yet, in spite of their great diversity, all economic systems have some features in common. They are all confronted with the same basic problem of the scarcity of goods and services. Furthermore, the world's major economic systems all make use of the same large-scale industrial technology. And consumers react to changes in the supply of consumer goods in very much the same manner throughout the world. But beyond these common features, a comparison of capitalism, socialism, communism, and fascism reveals wide variations in institutional arrangements and national goals—variations which reflect differences in stages of economic and political development, in cultural and historical backgrounds, and in ideological preferences.

Allocation of Resources

The second part of our definition of an economic system calls attention to the fact that the complex or pattern of human relations which constitutes an economic system is concerned with the disposal or allocation of scarce human and natural resources. Our total social system is made up of many different patterns of human relations. Some patterns have religion as their major interest, while others are concerned with the problems of government, national defense, amusement, education, or some other human interest. The pattern of human relations which makes up the economic system has as its major concern the provision of an adequate supply of goods and services. No nation has an abundance of these items. Everywhere, supplies of raw materials, capital goods, and labor are limited. Every nation, no matter how advanced industrially, is faced with the economic problem of making the most of its scarce supply of human and natural resources. Men are organized in economic systems to overcome this scarcity problem as effectively as possible. In the Soviet Union there are not enough goods and services to meet all the needs of economic growth, national defense, and personal consumption. The complex of economic relations known as the Soviet communist system is designed to meet this problem of spreading scarce resources over many needs. Similarly, in the United States, the country with the world's highest standard of living, there are not enough goods and services to meet the numerous demands coming from private consumers, business men, and governments at various levels. Even though in 1964 we produced $622 billion of goods and services, we were still faced with a scarcity problem (as was made quite clear when the nation came to decide how it should use its available output for various private and public purposes). Whether we look at a country such as India with a very low per-capita national income or at a country such as the United States with a very high per-capita national income, we observe the same fundamental problem of how to meet a vast array of private and public needs with a limited total national output.

Private and Public Goals

The third part of our definition of an economic system relates to the private and public goals which are to be satisfied by the production of goods and services. Every economic system operates to satisfy human wants of both an individual and a collective nature. Individual wants include such personal items as food, clothing, shelter, and amusement. Collective wants are those that fall in the category of public capital facilities, such as roads, schools, hospitals, and sewage disposal plants, and, also, those wants that fall in the category of public services such as national defense, civilian governmental services, education, and various welfare services. Many of the private and public needs, which economic systems are designed to serve, are the same under all types of systems. Human nature being, in essence, the same the world over, the same basic wants must be provided for under all "isms." The demands for food, clothing, and shelter are as insistent under communism as under capitalism. But beyond these basic human wants what goals an economic system shall serve is determined by political and cultural factors which differ widely from system to system. The division of output between investment and consumption and the kinds of producers' and consumers' goods that are to be produced are problems that are settled quite differently in capitalist United States, socialist Norway, and communist China. Differences in rates of economic growth, in international and domestic political objectives, and in class structure influence greatly the size and the nature of the flow of total national production and play a crucial role in determining the shape and direction of the world's major economic systems.

The Technological Basis of Economic Systems

Associated with a nation's supplies of land, labor, and capital is its industrial technology which determines the economic significance of what is described as "land," "labor," and "capital." Whether or not land and the various resources associated with it are useful in an economic sense depends upon the technology available to those who possess the land. Uranium did not become an important material resource until scientific progress had given it a significant place in the new industrial technology based upon atomic fission and nuclear fission. Similarly, the skills of labor and the nature of the nation's capital equipment reflect the basic industrial technology of the nation. Every change in industrial technology requires new skills on the part of labor and new types of capital equipment for the better production of goods and services. As nations move into the new electronic and atomic age of the mid-twentieth century, they find it necessary to have their workers acquire new skills, to alter greatly the nature of their capital structure, and to reassess the availability of land and its raw materials.

Today all the world's major economic systems make use of the same large-scale industrial technology. What is common to the United States, the Soviet Union, the United Kingdom, and other industrialized countries, and increasingly to India and China as they become industrialized, is not any method of organizing economic activities or any set of ideological views. Their common feature is an industrial technology which emphasizes large-scale or assembly-line production. It is this technology which in a sense is their ultimate resource. Today economic systems make progress to the extent that they are in a position to take advantage of the new efficiencies made possible by scientific and technological progress. But it should be noted that industrial technology is ideologically neutral. Capitalist, socialist, and communist nations may make use of the same industrial technology. The engineer, whether in the United States or in the Soviet Union, is faced with the same basic technological problems and, in a technological sense, he could be equally at home in both countries.

342

Although there are many areas of the world today where either the handicraft technology or the simple factory technology based upon steam power continues to be the mainstay of national production, all of the world's major economic systems, as already pointed out, have the same technological foundation. Differing from economic system to economic system are the institutional and ideological bases of these systems. These two aspects of economic systems will claim the major share of our attention in this study, since it is widely agreed that all nations should, as far as possible, avail themselves of the advantages of the assembly-line technology which appears to be moving into a new era of great development as the techniques of automation are improved and atomic energy is effectively exploited as a new source of power.

The Institutional Basis of Economic Systems

Our definition of economic systems points out that they are all evolving patterns of human relations. These cultural patterns, which are made up of institutions of many kinds, constitute the institutional basis of economic systems. It is by means of these institutional patterns that nations coordinate or organize their various economic activities as they endeavour to make what in their opinion is the most effective use of their limited supplies of human and natural resources. When we speak of the economic organization of a country, we have in mind the various economic institutions, such as property, the money system, production units, labor organizations, and governmental agencies, by means of which the country produces its output of goods and services. It is with the aid of these institutions that a nation copes with the primary problem of securing maximum production from its limited supplies of land, labor, and capital.

National patterns of economic institutions have changed greatly over the centuries. If we examine the economic organization of England from the Middle Ages to the present, we see a wide range of institution complexes, running from the manorial system of the period prior to 1500 to the complicated British capitalism of the twentieth century. In each era since the decline of the Roman Empire, the United Kingdom developed a different way of organizing economic activities to meet the same fundamental problem of reducing economic scarcity. Similarly, the economic system of the United States has undergone significant changes in the past two and a half centuries as new economic problems have arisen and new methods of organizing economic life have been devised to meet these problems. Today we have a variety of patterns of economic institutions spread throughout the world. In the United States, the United Kingdom, West Germany, Canada, and other free enterprise nations, we find the capitalist method of organizing economic activities with its emphasis upon private property and private enterprise. In the Soviet Union, the satellite eastern European countries, and the People's Republic of China, the communist complex of economic institutions differs in many important ways from the capitalist economic pattern. Whereas private property and private enterprise bulk large in the institutional pattern of capitalism, public property and state enterprise play major roles in the institutional complex of communism. The institutional pattern of the Scandinavian countries and other socialist countries, such as India, offers considerable contrast to both the capitalist and the communist institutional patterns. In the democratic socialist institutional pattern we find both private and public property and private and public enterprise existing side by side in a manner which no theoretical socialist of the nineteenth century could have envisioned.

The kind of economic organization or pattern of economic institutions which a nation develops reflects two fundamental forces, one technological and the other ideological. Every type of industrial technology and its associated method of production are necessarily reflected to some extent in the economic organizational structures of nations. For example, all countries with a handicraft technology tend to establish large-scale production units. Although the United States and the Soviet Union are poles apart in terms of ideological preferences, both countries employ essentially the same large-scale technology, with its accompanying large-scale productive organization, in turning out their annual supplies of goods and services. It is not surprising, therefore, that the large private corporation in the American capitalist institutional complex has its opposite number in the form of the large state industrial trust in the Russian communist institutional pattern. But industrial technology is only one factor which influences the shape of a nation's economic organization or system. Another significant factor is the inherited ideology or constellation of economic, social, and political ideas which each nation comes to possess as the result of the interaction of individuals and groups and their cultural environment. What explains the fundamental differences between the American and Soviet economic systems is not differences in industrial technology or production methods, but rather the very different systems

344

of political and economic ideas or ideologies which are subsumed by the terms "capitalism" and "communism."

The Ideological Basis of Economic Systems

The satisfying of the individual and collective wants of a nation is greatly influenced by the basic ideology which guides the thinking and value choosing of the general population and their leaders. An ideology is a systematic set of beliefs, opinions, and doctrines about social phenomena, primarily economic and political phenomena, which is possessed by individuals, classes, and nations.[2] Ideologies are complexes of ideas which guide individuals and groups in their interpretations of social phenomena and in their selection of courses of action as they meet various problems. As is quite clear, an ideology is above all a basis for action. An ideological set of values or preferences constitutes a general framework of reference for those who possess a common ideology. For example, the ideology of the capitalist nations of the West leads these nations to prefer parliamentary forms of government under which basic issues are settled through majority decisions. In the realm of economic affairs the capitalist ideology shows up in a strong preference for private property, free markets, and a highly restricted area of public enterprise. For most people in capitalist nations, these preferences are embedded in their inherited premises or assumptions which are generally not open to question on their part. Since all ideologies are inherited schemes of ideas or values which constitute a point of departure in the settling of economic and political problems, they may be described as cultural imperatives. As imperatives, ideologies successfully canalize both economic and political action.

Ideologies, like all other cultural products, may change substantially over the decades. The ideology of twentieth-century capitalism is different in many important ways from the capitalist ideology of the nineteenth century. We have witnessed in the past century a considerable shift from the laissez-faire capitalist ideology dominant in that century. Although these two ideologies have many fundamentals in common, the ideology of twentieth-century capitalism provides a place for a belief in, and an acceptance of, a much wider role for state action in the economic sphere than did the ideology underlying the laissez-faire capitalism of the nine-

---

[2]Talcott Parsons, *The Social System* (Glencoe: The Free Press, 1951). See also Talcott Parsons, *Essays in Sociological Theory* (Glencoe: The Free Press, 1954), pp. 134-135 and 266-268.

345

teenth century. In the capitalist countries of the West, people have now widely come to accept the government as a guiding factor with the major responsibility for achieving such basic national goals as full employment, sustained economic growth, and price stability. While, under the welfare or guided capitalism of today, the major reliance is still placed upon private property, free markets, and private enterprise, there are many more limitations on the ownership and use of private property than prevailed in the nineteenth century.

During the nineteenth century Karl Marx laid the foundations for the set of beliefs and attitudes which together comprise the communist ideology. This ideology has come to emphasize the importance of public property and public or state enterprise. In the same century, but at a somewhat later time, the Fabians and other moderate socialists fostered the development of a laboristic or socialist ideology which lies between the capitalist and communist ideologies. In the first half of the current century the fascist ideology gained wide acceptance in Italy, Germany, Japan, Spain, and other countries where political and economic power fell into the hands of small groups of individuals.

Ideologies play a very important role in the development of economic systems. It has already been pointed out that the use of a large-scale industrial technology by both the United States and the Soviet Union has resulted in the setting up of large-scale productive enterprises in these two countries. Although there is no basic difference in the technological bases of the American and Russian economic systems, there is a fundamental ideological difference between these two systems which is revealed in the official and popular attitudes towards the institution of property. In the United States large-scale enterprises are usually privately owned, whereas in the Soviet Union such enterprises are publicly owned. Also, in the United States the large private corporation operates in a free market, whereas in the Soviet Union the large public enterprise or trust functions in a controlled or planned market. These basic differences in the method of organizing American and Soviet economic activities are to be ascribed to the possession of fundamentally different ideological preferences.

Ideologies also give shape to the political and economic goals which nations seek to achieve. In the Soviet Union the political and economic systems reveal the heavy imprint of Marxian thinking out of which the communist ideology has arisen. The private economic goals of Soviet citizens are subordinated by the Communist party to public goals—in accordance with the basic principles of the communist ideology which regards the current Soviet era as a short-lived transition from socialism to communism. In Scandinavia, although public economic goals are important, the overriding consideration as determined by the laboristic or socialist ideology is the achievement of a rising standard of living for the individual. In capitalist America and Great Britain the current ideology stresses the importance of private economic goals as against public economic goals. Public economic goals in these two countries look forward to establishing only a national minimum, beyond which individuals are expected to go in accordance with their respective capacities to take advantage of the opportunities provided by a primarily private enterprise system. A full understanding of the American, Scandinavian, Soviet, and other economic systems cannot be had until the ideological bases of these systems are fully investigated and revealed.

Economic Systems in Practice

The Capitalist System

There are today in actual practice four major types of economic systems—the capitalist, socialist, communist, and fascist systems. The current capitalist economies preserve many of the features of nineteenth-century capitalism, but at the same time they have moved far beyond the small-scale, laissez-faire capitalism of that century. Twentieth-century capitalism, as found in various western European countries, the United States, and Canada, is a form of regulated or controlled capitalism. The state has come to play a much larger and more positive role than was the case prior to 1900. The private enterprise system has been preserved in its basic essentials, but the government is not satisfied to stand aside while the impersonal forces of the market place largely determine the direction of economic activity and the allocation of scarce resources. A partnership has been established in recent decades between public and private enterprise, with both the government and private business operating in separate but mutually related sectors. In present-day capitalism the government assumes responsibility for the general direction and level of economic activity, while private enterprise meets the specific needs of both individuals and groups for various commodities and services. The "collaborative guidance" of our contemporary welfare capitalism stands in marked contrast to the largely unregulated market guidance provided by private business in the model of theoretical competitive capitalism.

347

The Socialist System

The second important type of current economic system is the Socialist system found in the Scandinavian countries, in India and in other countries of southern Asia, such as Ceylon, and in the United Kingdom, Australia, and New Zealand when the Labor party is in power in these latter countries. This type of socialism is best described as democratic partial socialism and is far removed from the "pure" socialism about which socialists theorized in the past century. In today's partial democratic system, the state takes over only a few key industries, such as transportation; the public utilities, such as gas, electricity, and communications; and in some cases the coal and steel industries. In this type of socialism, agriculture and the great majority of non-agricultural enterprises are left in private hands. As long as private industry and agriculture perform satisfactorily, no move is made to nationalize the economy on a wide front. But the government has a more positive role under democratic partial socialism than it does under controlled or regulated capitalism. What distinguishes partial democratic socialism from welfare capitalism is the extent to which national economic planning is carried out. In those countries where Labor or similar parties, as in India and other countries of southern Asia, hold the reins of government, economic activities are carried on within the framework of annual and longer-term national economic plans. These plans set forth broad annual economic goals in terms of production, employment, and investment, but no specific targets are established for individual private enterprises. Like the capitalist nations, the democratic socialist countries use fiscal and monetary controls as aids in achieving their national economic goals, but they go further—with the aim of controlling or influencing both prices and wages. While the system of democratic partial socialism preserves more of the features of capitalism than would pure or theoretical full socialism, it is still much to the right of full socialism and at the same time it is much to the left of welfare capitalism.

The Communist System

The third important concrete system of the current century is the communist system found in the Soviet Union, Central Europe, the People's Republic of China, and a few other Asian countries. In actual practice, the so-called communist systems of these countries turn out to be examples not of pure communism as it was theorized about in the nineteenth century, but of something which is closer to full socialism. Pure communism of the abstract or theoretical type was constructed on the assumptions of the absence of a strong central government, no private property of any kind, payment of income according to need and not ability, and abundant consumer and occupational freedom. The communist economic systems found in actual operation today are characterized by a one-party political system, a strong central government, a detailed form of national economic planning, the limitation of private property primarily to consumer goods, the payment of income according to ability to produce, and severe limitations on consumer and occupational freedoms. Consequently the communist systems of the Soviet Union, eastern Europe, and the People's Republic of China can be classed neither as pure socialism nor as pure communism. Like controlled capitalism and democratic partial socialism, present-day communism fits neatly into no theoretical category, but reflects instead the special economic, political, and cultural circumstances of the individual nations in which it has taken root.

The Fascist System

The fourth type of actual economic system which is found in the modern world, but which today plays a minor role alongside of welfare capitalism, democratic partial socialism, and communism, is the fascist system. This is the type of economic system which was once dominant in Germany, Italy, and Japan and which is now found in Spain, Portugal, and various Middle East, Asian, African, and Latin American countries. Under this type of economic system, private property and private enterprise are preserved, but within the framework of a broad overall national planning program. Private enterprise is fitted into a general national economic plan under the direction not of a democratic government, but of a small clique of policy makers who are dominated by an established leader. Trade unions are replaced by other labor organizations that do not operate independently. Since the national leader plays such a major role under fascism, the pattern of the fascist system is greatly influenced not only by the special conditions of the country involved, but also by the idiosyncrasies of the dictatorial head of the government. It is for these reasons that fascism in action does not readily lead to any concept of pure or theoretical fascism. If one regards fascism as a debased form of capitalism, he may conclude that there is no separate theoretical type of fascism.

From this point of view, fascism is only an authoritarian deviation from the capitalist model. Historically, fascism has emerged where there has been a breakdown in the capitalist system, as in the cases of Germany, Italy, Spain, and Portugal. Or it has appeared in countries, usually under-developed, where democratic traditions have been either weak or absent and where other cultural circumstances have favored economic and political control by one man or by a small clique.

From the broadest point of view, the world's major economic systems may be classified into only two groups: those with what may be called the western democratic ethic and those with the eastern totalitarian ethic. The western ethic regards the welfare of the individual as the proper ultimate goal of national existence. This individual welfare is enhanced where there are extensive economic and political freedoms, that is to say, where individuals are free to choose their own governments and where they enjoy both consumer and occupational freedoms. Both western capitalism and democratic partial socialism function in accordance with the demands of the individualistic western ethic. The eastern ethic, by contrast, is a pro-state or collectivistic ethic which elevates the state over the individual. The ultimate value, from this eastern viewpoint, is not the welfare of the individual, but the welfare of the state. Although the eastern ethic gives some consideration to the individual's welfare, the ultimate criterion in the light of which final decisions are made is the progress and advancement of the state. The pro-state ethic finds wide acceptance in the communist nations of eastern Europe and Asia, where traditionally the individual has been subservient to the state. In the final analysis, the ultimate conflict between economic systems is between two basically different ethics, the one espoused by democratic capitalism and democratic socialism and the other by totalitarian communism and fascism. It is this deep conflict between two rival ethics that sharpens the struggle among economic systems and makes the march towards international coexistence painfully slow.

All economic systems rest upon two basic flows, the flow of real output or national production and the flow of national income by means of which this production is purchased or distributed. The main problem of each economic system is how to coordinate or mesh these two fundamental economic flows so that output and income are in balance at high and rising levels of production and employment. Economic systems are differentiated one from another by the different ways in which these systems seek to secure this balance. The ways in which the western capitalist nations coordinate their product and income flows are different in many fundamental respects from the methods adopted by the communist nations. And the same is true of the democratic socialist and the totalitarian fascist systems. The main objectives of our comparison of economic systems are to bring out these differences in the ways nations integrate their real and financial flows, and to inquire into the many important consequences that result from the different methods of securing national economic coordination.

Questions for Thought and Discussion

1. What is an economic system?
2. In what sense are all economic systems similar? All developed economic systems?
3. Discuss the principal characteristics of each of the four major types of economic systems outlined in this article.

ORGANIZATION AND OPERATION

OF THE SOVIET ECONOMY

Norton Dodge

Many of the Soviet economy's institutions and mechanisms sound deceptively familiar to us: factories and farms, wages and prices, money and credit, profit and loss. Despite this apparent similarity, the organization and operation of the Soviet economy differs in significant respects from a market economy such as our own. Economic activity in our own economy is guided by private persons making a myriad of individual decisions which are coordinated through the competitive market mechanism. Consumers seek to spend their incomes to maximize their satisfactions or benefits. Entrepreneurs, acting on their own initiative, attempt to maximize their profits by stimulating and shaping consumers' wants and satisfying these wants as cheaply as possible. To this end, they bid for the productive services of labor, land, and capital. Individuals, responding to the wages and salaries offered, tend to choose the employment offering the highest return. Investors, responding to alternative opportunities, will employ their capital where they expect to receive the highest return. Throughout this simplified capitalist model, the search for profit drives the system forward and competition provides the discipline leading toward an optimal use of resources as determined by sovereign consumers who cast their "dollar ballots" for final goods.

The Command Economy

In a collective economy, such as the Soviet, productive resources are owned by the government rather than by private individuals. More im-

The author is Associate Professor of Economics at the University of Maryland.

portant, however, are the operational differences between a collective and a market economy. To understand these differences, one must ask several questions: What are the motivating and discipling forces of an economic system? How is the allocation of resources determined? What makes the system work?

In the Soviet economy, the allocation of resources is determined by a central, sovereign authority and is controlled largely by commands and directives, hence the label "command economy." The competitive market mechanism plays no directive role.

For many years the sovereign authority in all matters in the Soviet Union was Stalin. He made the ultimate decisions on how much of the economy's effort would be devoted to the satisfaction of consumers' wants, to the creation of capital, and to the provision of arms. His allocation of resources unquestionably differed widely from that which consumers with free choice would have made.

Although the present leadership is more responsive to consumer demands, consumers as yet have no direct or effective way of influencing basic economic decisions. The ruling oligarchy, like Stalin, continues to give the consumer what it thinks is good for him regardless of whether or not the consumer would have so chosen himself. Only if the economy were governed by truly democratic political processes, would the ultimate economic sovereignty lie with the voter. Even then, however, elected officials would, of necessity, make the basic economic decisions with voters passing judgment upon their desirability or wisdom only after the fact. Detailed and continuous control of the economic decision-making process always would lie beyond practical possibility for the consumer.

In addition to basic decisions regarding the allocation of the Gross National Product among consumption, investment, and armaments, the Presidium of the Central Committee of the Party and government agencies under its political direction, such as the State Planning Committee (*Gosplan*), make more detailed decisions about the operation of the economy. Areas in which central decision making plays a very important role are, to mention a few: the state budget, the allocation of investment resources among various projects, the distribution of key materials and products among enterprises, the setting of basic manpower and wage policies, the determination of prices, and the planning of exports and imports. These are all areas in which state agencies or enterprises are directly involved.

In other areas of economic life, control is exercised less directly. This is particularly true with respect to relationships between state agencies or enterprises, on the one hand, and households or individuals, on the other. For example, although detailed overall plans for the supply and utilization of manpower are drawn up, most persons of working age are not directed to work in this or that specific job. They are free to choose among various alternative employment opportunities for which they are qualified. Current graduates of factory schools, specialized secondary schools, and higher educational institutions, though, are assigned to jobs for several years after graduation. At the end of the prescribed period, usually three years, they are free to find employment elsewhere if they so desire. While it is true that workers in some critical categories may be influenced or pressured in their choice of place of work, for the great majority of workers this is not true. Also, since Stalin's death, the importance of forced labor in the economy has been sharply reduced.

Although most workers are free to choose their employment today, the terms upon which employment alternatives are offered (wages, benefits, and working conditions) are determined by the state, acting as the only buyer (monopsonist). Similarly, the consumer normally exercises free choice in selecting among the various goods made available to him. But the terms upon which these commodities are offered (prices) are also determined by the state, in this instance acting as a monopolist. The managers of the Soviet economy stop short, then, of telling most citizens specifically what job to take or what to buy. The state, in its dual role as a monopolist and monopsonist, normally can expect its citizens, in their roles as consumers and workers, to adjust to its terms and to perform as expected without the state having to resort to direct, detailed orders and supervision.

Not everyone in the Soviet Union derives his entire income from the state or is employed in the state sector. Outside the state sector are several millions of persons who produce on small private agricultural plots a high percentage of the fruit, vegetable, dairy, and meat products. Although these plots account for only some 3 per cent of the crop land, they account for about a quarter of the agricultural output. Also, doctors, dentists, and lawyers have some private clients, and other individuals provide private services in the form of housework, repairs, and handicrafts. Transactions between such individuals and their consumers are neither planned nor directed by the state, although the state may attempt to influence the terms or manner in which these products or services are provided.

Soviet Economic Planning

Following the Russian revolution in 1917, the Soviet leaders were faced with the task of developing new and different ways of organizing and operating their economy. Critics of socialism, such as Ludwig von Mises, made the dire prediction that in the absence of the regulating force of competitive markets the tasks of coordinating, controlling, and directing a collective economy would be so overwhelmingly complex as to render it a practical impossibility. It is true that Marx had provided no blueprint, nor had Lenin come to grips with the practical problems of running a collective economy before his seizure of power. Nevertheless, within a decade of the revolution, the Soviet economy—by trial and error—was brought back to the prewar level of production. When the first Five-Year Plan was introduced by Stalin at the end of the 1920's, the major features of Soviet economic planning, which have prevailed in their general outlines until the present, were worked out.

Soviet national economic plans are of several types: (1) long-term perspective plans of 15 to 20 years which, of necessity, are very general; (2) the much better known and more specific five-year plans; and (3) detailed annual plans which actually direct the operation of the economy. The last are the most significant in guiding the day-to-day operation of the Soviet economy and will be discussed in some detail.

The annual plans are composed of several subplans. The most important and basic are those which deal with: (1) material balances—the supply of material inputs to industry, including materials used up immediately in production and construction as well as capital goods which are used up over a longer period of time; (2) capital construction programs of various types; (3) the introduction of new technology; (4) the supply of labor; and (5) financial balances. The basic features of the planning process in connection with each of these subplans will be outlined briefly.

Material Balances

The State Planning Committee (*Gosplan*) is in overall charge of the planning process, but the planning of material supplies is developed from the bottom up as well as from the top down. The cooperation of the producing enterprises which carry out the completed plan is essential in drawing it up. The main elements of this plan are "material balances" showing the sources and uses of the centrally allocated products in balance sheet fashion. The products for which these balances are drawn up have varied over the years but have always included the most essential products and those in shortest supply, such as coal, petroleum, ferrous and nonferrous metals, and chemicals. In formulating the plan, *Gosplan* sets provisional production targets for the year ahead in late spring on the bases of previous production levels and future objectives. With these targets in mind and guided by past experiences and input norms, each enterprise calculates its expected requirement of each input. These estimates are then transmitted up the planning hierarchy and consolidated by Gosplan into estimates of total demand for each input. Estimated total demand can then be compared with the production target set for each input to see if they agree.

The material balance of a product shows total demand, including demand for use in production, end uses, year-end inventory, special reserves, and exports. On the supply side, the balance shows not only planned production but also beginning inventory, special reserves, and any imports. If the material balance shows greater anticipated demand than planned supply, *Gosplan* must begin a process of adjustment—pushing and pulling, persuading and browbeating—in an effort to bring the two into balance. Normally, *Gosplan* tries to achieve a balance by squeezing promises of higher output out of producers without increasing their inputs. Frequently, however, more inputs are absolutely essential to achieve increased output. This properly should lead to adjustments in the material balances of these inputs. Second and third generation adjustments or "iterations" are seldom made, however, which invariably increases the tautness of the plan. When there are shortfalls in production as a result, lower priority uses of the products—usually consumer uses—are customarily sacrificed.

However imperfectly, *Gosplan* achieves a formal balance in the supply and demand of planned products some time in the fall. The plan is then approved by the Council of Ministers (ideally before the beginning of the new plan year on January 1), and the production targets and material allocations become law. These are transmitted down the administrative hierarchy to the individual enterprises which then make the plan concrete by signing contracts with other enterprises covering the details of purchases of inputs and sales of outputs.

From this point forward, the actual fulfillment of the plan is in the hands of management at the enterprise level. When the plan calls for fulfillment in quantitative terms, such as tons or yards, the plan can be formally fulfilled, but the quality of coal or the weave of cloth may not be up to standard. When the plan is expressed in rubles, not only the quality but also the assortment of output may be quite different from that which the planners intended. For these reasons, it is very important that "success indicators" showing the degree of plan fulfillment be meaningful so that the plan will be fulfilled in fact not fiction. The perennial difficulties of achieving genuine plan fulfillment have led to the reforms that are now being introduced by the Soviets. New "success indicators" measuring fulfillment have been introduced and managerial incentives tied to them. Although novel in some respects, these reforms appear designed to improve the operation of the existing system rather than to alter it fundamentally.

Capital Construction

Investment planning in the Soviet Union is also carried out by *Gosplan* under directives from the political leadership. Since major investment projects—such as factories, railways, and power plants—normally take several years to plan and complete, the time horizon for investment planning is much longer than a year. For this reason, the Five-Year Plans give special emphasis to investment. Nevertheless, the actual supply of construction materials and equipment going to investment projects is provided for in the material balances of successive annual plans.

While broad investment objectives are set at the highest political level, expert guidance and advice is provided by scientists, engineers, and economists. The Soviets also have taken advantage of the experience of the West, particularly the United States, in planning new factories and other projects. They have borrowed and adapted ready-made technology to their special circumstances. In planning investment projects—particularly for their basic production processes—the Soviets have tended to adopt the most advanced, up-to-date Western techniques and methods. Although borrowing is advantageous in most fields today, it is not the case in some, such as armaments and space, where Soviet technology is on a level with the most advanced countries of the West.

Their Marxist heritage has prevented the Soviets from openly using the interest rate to discriminate among investment alternatives involving different gestation periods, outlays, and returns. As a result, the Soviet penchant for excessively large-scale and ambitious projects has not been restrained by explicit capital costs as it would be in our system. Similarly, failure to recognize time preference has encouraged the devotion of a larger share of Gross National Product to investment at the expense of current consumption than would otherwise be the case.

358

Introduction of New Technology

Despite the advantages which relative technological backwardness provides, the Soviets have experienced rather uneven success in introducing new technology. Major advances were made in the 1930's, but the Soviets missed a good opportunity to catch up during the reconstruction period following World War II. Technological advances tend to be concentrated in the high priority sectors of the economy, while others—such as the consumer sector—have lagged miserably. This has produced what can be termed a *split-level* economy.

Under our economic system, there are powerful forces working for technological advance. Successful innovation can bring rich rewards, while failure to keep pace technologically can mean economic disaster. To a considerable extent, the Soviet System also rewards those responsible for successful invention and innovation while penalizing the researcher or innovator who fails. However, the Soviet mixture of incentives and penalties thus far has not made technological advance with all its risks sufficiently attractive. In practice, fulfillment of the annual output plan has invariably overridden fulfillment of the plan for the introduction of new technology when the two were in conflict. The current reforms tying the bonuses of management and technical personnel to sales and return on capital rather than to production are aimed at encouraging technological advance.

Labor Balances

Gosplan and other government agencies, such as the Ministry of Higher and Specialized Secondary Education, are concerned with planning the labor force. As we have said, persons normally may change their jobs if they so wish. Of course, many of the jobs vacated are soon filled by others seeking jobs, permitting the planners to concentrate on satisfying the net demands for manpower of the various occupations, skill levels, branches of the economy and geographical regions. Persons just completing their training and entering the labor force are most readily available to fill these net demands. Hence, the planning of enrollments and graduations of training and educational programs is a most essential aspect of labor force planning. Effective educational planning is the first step toward assuring the appropriate numbers of properly trained young men and women ready for assignment each year where they are most urgently needed.

Since preparation for the effective performance of most jobs takes a considerable amount of time today, it is vital that substantial lead time be employed in labor force planning, particularly in planning the supply of specialists. In determining the number of future engineers, chemists, physicists, and others who will be admitted to higher educational institutions each year, planners try to look at least five years ahead to the demand for the different types of specialists which will exist upon their graduation. *Gosplan* and the Ministry of Higher and Specialized Secondary Education draw up projections of demand by using coefficients for specialists per 1,000 workers or staffing norms for various sectors of the economy. These projected needs are then compared with the current stock of specialists, adjusted by expected attrition over the intervening years, to determine the required additions of newly trained specialists. Such assessments serve as the basis for admission quotas for each field of study in each higher and specialized secondary educational institutions.

Manpower planning is much less exact and less developed methodologically than the planning of materials supply because of the longer time element as well as the less predictable human element involved. Indeed, in 1959, Khrushchev complained:

> We do not have any scientifically reliable method of estimating how many and what kind of specialists we need in different branches of the national economy, what the future demand will be for a certain kind of specialist, and when such a demand will arise.[1]

Nevertheless, imperfect as Soviet projection methods may be, the planners must try as best they can to assure that there is a man or woman properly trained to fill every job as it is vacated or newly created. Proper planning of the labor balance also calls for adjustments in wages, salaries, and other incentives so that sufficient people will want to do the work which has to be done with as little intervention as possible by the planners in direct assignments to jobs.

Financial Balances

In a command economy, the government would be free to allocate workers, capital equipment, materials, and other things needed in the production process directly without any payment in money. Such an econ-

---

[1] *Pravda*, July 2, 1959.

omy would be very difficult to administer because of the detailed direction required and the absence of adequate incentives. Also, in the absence of money and prices, it would be almost impossible to determine whether it was being operated efficiently or not. As a result, the Soviet Union decided to retain the use of money and prices, realizing that the administration of a socialist economy would thereby be greatly simplified.

Nonetheless, money and prices perform functions in the Soviet economy different from those in our own. Under economic individualism, prices are the mechanism through which the free choices of consumers and producers are expressed and reconciled. Under economic collectivism, on the other hand, prices are employed to accomplish the purposes of the supreme authority. If the authority wishes to check the consumption of a commodity, it raises the price; if it wishes to encourage the consumption of another, it lowers the price. If too few young people with suitable talent want to enter a certain profession, the salary can be raised relative to those of other occupations. If too many seek a particular type of employment, rates of pay can be lowered to discourage entrance. The command economy, therefore, is not the servant but rather the master of prices which are used to further its objectives.

The Soviets have found stable prices to be as desirable for a planned socialist economy as for a free capitalist economy. Otherwise, many of the advantages of using money and prices as aids in directing and operating the economy would be lost. The need for price stability has required the Soviet government to maintain a proper balance between money flows to and from the government and the public sectors. When the state pays wages and salaries, money flows out of the state sector. When the public buys consumer goods, it flows back. However, because many workers and employees are involved in producing goods and services other than consumers goods, total wages and salaries paid out far exceed the production cost of the consumer goods available for purchase. Therefore, some method is required to mop up this excess purchasing power. Otherwise, inflation would result, destroying much of the usefulness of money as a measure of value and in other ways disrupting the effective operation of the economy.

Essentially three alternatives exist for the government to mop up the excess purchasing power: (1) levying a tax on consumers' goods themselves; (2) taxing the enlarged revenues of enterprises producing consumer goods sold at prices raised sufficiently to clear the market; or (3) a tax on incomes of workers and employees. Of course, some combination of these methods also could be used. Indeed, the Soviets have done precisely this.

361

Historically, they have placed greatest emphasis on a sales (turnover) tax on consumer goods. More recently, the levy on enterprise profits has grown in importance. Sometime in the future, however, the low yielding income tax is to be eliminated. For the past two decades, the Soviet planners, using such techniques, have been largely successful in keeping inflationary pressures under control. This was not the case during the prewar and wartime periods when conditions were more difficult and credit to enterprises inadequately controlled.

The Future of Soviet Planning

Will these five major elements of the annual plan continue to guide and direct the operation of the Soviet economy in the future as they have in the past? In a broad sense, yes; but change is already in the making in two respects. The planning and operation of the economy are being improved through better *computation*, on the one hand, and more *competition*, on the other. The first involves the development and application of new and improved mathematical planning techniques, such as input-output and linear programming methods. The second is being furthered by the present economic reform which gives enterprises greater powers of decision.

When Kosygin first announced the reform in the fall of 1965, it seemed to many—particularly to Western journalists—a turning point in Soviet economic development. The reform, like the New Economic Policy (NEP) of the 1920's, was interpreted as a step backward toward capitalism. But it falls far short of the more fundamental reforms taking place in the socialist countries of eastern Europe and in no sense introduces *market socialism*. Since the new mathematical planning techniques are yet to be employed on more than an experimental basis, we must conclude that, on both counts, the model of Soviet planning outlined will remain in effect for some years to come, so far as its fundamental features are concerned. Such changes as are now being introduced are directed more toward improving the operation of a centrally planned economy than replacing it with a fundamentally different type of economic system.

Questions for Thought and Discussion

1. How does the organization and operation of a command economy differ from that of a market economy?

2. How are the basic economic decisions of what to produce, how to produce, and how much to invest made in a command economy?
3. What reforms are taking shape in command economies, such as the one of the Soviet Union? Do these represent a convergence with a market economy or improvements in the operation of a command economy?

GLOSSARY

A GLOSSARY OF ECONOMIC TERMS AND BIOGRAPHICAL SKETCHES OF SEVERAL GREAT ECONOMISTS

Stephen Merchant

This glossary of economic terms is provided as a handy reference for the student unfamiliar with the terminology of economics. It is hoped that as the student reads the essays in this book, the existence of this glossary will be justified and, further, that the need for this reference will continually diminish.

The glossary will best serve the student's interest if the concepts lying behind the term are carefully thought through. Memorization of the definitions is both dull and of little utility. After reading each definition, the student should attempt to put it in his own words—a practice which may prevent the definition from getting lost in the darkest nooks and crannies of the mind.

Economic Terms

ARBITRAGE—The act of buying at one price in some market and selling at the same time in another market at the higher price prevailing there. The difference is the profit from arbitrage.

ASSET—A tangible or intangible object which has exchange value. A house is a tangible asset; and IOU's, bonds, or other claims are intangible assets.

The author is Instructor of Economics at the University of Maryland.

BALANCE OF PAYMENTS—The relationship between the total inflow of receipts from foreign nations and the total outflow of payments to foreign nations. The relationship between foreign claims on a country and that country's claims on the rest of the world.

BALANCE OF TRADE—The relationship between a nation's exports and its imports. A surplus balance of trade means that a country has exported more than it has imported in terms of product value.

BEAR—A slang term usually referring to a stock market speculator who believes that stock prices will fall, as opposed to a *bull*, who believes the opposite.

CAPITAL—In the sense of *capital good*, it is property (a factor of production) from which income is derived. The term *fixed capital* refers to durable, often stationary, capital goods, such as heavy machinery or factory buildings. *Circulating capital* denotes capital goods which are transformed in the production process, such as raw wool and cotton in the production of clothing. *Money capital* is money or bank deposits. Securities, bonds, and other claims on *assets* are also capital.

DEMAND—A relationship between the quantity of a commodity consumers are willing and able to purchase and the price of the commodity. With each of various alternative prices for the commodity, there is associated a *quantity demanded*. The *Law of Demand* postulates an inverse relationship between price and quantity demanded. That is, in the aggregate, consumers will purchase more of a commodity as its price is lowered, *ceteris paribus*.

DEMAND DEPOSIT—A checking account deposit from which the holder may draw at any time, as compared to a *time deposit* (savings account) which earns interest, and for which advance notice may be required to accomplish a withdrawal.

DEPRECIATION—The reduction in the value of a national currency in international trade. The relative fall in the international price of a nation's goods.

DEVALUATION—The reduction of the gold content of a nation's international currency which means a rise in the price of gold in terms of that currency.

DISCOUNTING—The practice of deducting the interest payment due on a loan *at the time* the loan is made. For the borrower, the sum received is less than the amount of the loan, the difference being the *discount*.

DISEQUILIBRIUM—The condition in a market when either excess demand or excess supply exists. Price in the market will be under pressure to rise if excess demand exists or to fall if there is excess supply.

DISPOSABLE INCOME—The aggregate take-home pay of all households in the economy. Income taxes, plus corporate taxes, plus undistributed corporate profits, when subtracted from total income, yield disposable income.

ECONOMICS—The study of how people, as individuals and as aggregates, make choices in allocating resources to the production and distribution of goods and services.

ELASTICITY—A measure of the responsiveness of quantity to price changes on a demand or supply schedule. Where the percentage change in quantity is great in relation to a given percentage change in price, the demand or supply schedule is *elastic*. The schedule is said to be *inelastic* where the percentage change in quantity is smaller than the given percentage change in price.

ENTREPRENEUR—An individual who assumes the risk of loss of his own or borrowed capital in organizing one or more firms with the expectation of making a profit.

EQUILIBRIUM—A condition in a market when the price is such that there exists no excess demand or supply. Market forces, if allowed to operate, will tend to establish this price if the market is in *disequilibrium*.

EXCHANGE RATE—The price of one currency in terms of another. The British pound exchanges for $2.40 of U.S. currency at the official rate.

FACTOR OF PRODUCTION—Any input used in the process of production, usually referring to either land, labor, or capital.

FISCAL POLICY—The use by government of its spending and taxing powers in an attempt to obtain some desired goals, such as full employment, price stability, a high rate of economic growth, etc.

GOLD STANDARD—The international adjustment mechanism based on gold flows under which a nation establishes an exchange rate in terms of gold and meets any international deficits through gold exports or short-term capital flows.

HOARDING—The postponement of consumption or investment in order to acquire money balances.

INDEX NUMBER—A ratio formed for the purpose of finding the percentage change in such numbers as prices, costs, etc. A price index is a ratio less than, equal to, or greater than unity, if prices have decreased, remained the same, or increased from the base year to the year in question.

INVESTMENT—Capital formation, or the creation of capital goods or acquisition of other income earning assets, made possible by saving.

LAW OF DIMINISHING RETURNS—A phenomenon occurring when *additional* amounts of a variable factor, such as labor, are combined with, or applied to, a *fixed* factor, such as land, to produce additional amounts of a product, say food. Some point will be reached after which each successive unit of the variable factor produces a smaller additional amount of product.

LIQUIDITY—A characteristic of an asset, referring to the facility with which it may be exchanged for money and the resulting loss in value, if any, incurred by the owner. The liquidity of a bond is greater than that of a house, mainly because of the competitiveness of the markets in which they are sold.

LIQUIDITY PREFERENCE THEORY—The theory posits an inverse relationship between the quantity of money demanded and the rate of interest. Individuals in the aggregate desire to hold more cash when the interest rate is relatively low than invest the cash in less liquid assets, such as bonds, whose prices are expected to fall.

LOANABLE FUNDS—Money capital available for investors. The supply of loanable funds is determined by changes in the money supply, by savings and by changes in individuals' desires to hold cash. The demand for loanable funds is determined by the availability of profitable opportunities for investment. The *Loanable Funds Theory* says that the supply and demand for loanable funds determines the rate of interest.

LOCKOUT—The counterpart, for employers, of the strike. The employer "locks out" some or all of his employees in an attempt to influence the outcome of a wage negotiation.

MONETARY POLICY—The control by government, acting through the treasury and/or central banks, of the money supply and credit in an attempt to achieve such objectives as price stability, full employment, rapid growth, etc.

MONOPOLISTIC COMPETITION—A market structure composed of many small firms, each selling products which are close, but not perfect, substitutes. The real or imagined differences consumers see in the products enable each seller to have some small degree of choice in choosing the price of the product.

MONOPOLY—The existence of only one seller of a product. The seller is, in effect, the entire industry.

MOST-FAVORED-NATION AGREEMENT—A clause in a commercial treaty in which each member country agrees to extend automatically to the others any favorable treatment or concessions granted to any one country in subsequent negotiations.

OLIGOPOLY—A market structure in which a few firms dominate the industry in the sale of a product which may be homogeneous, such as steel, or in which consumers may recognize differences, such as automobiles. The pricing and output decisions of each firm noticeably affect those of the others; thus, the firms are *interdependent.*

OPPORTUNITY COST—That which is foregone; the cost of doing X is the opportunity to have done Y.

PERFECT COMPETITION—A market structure composed of so many buyers and sellers of a homogeneous product that no one individual trader can influence the market price by his decision to buy or sell.

PRICE-SPECIE FLOW MECHANISM—The idea that international money flows produce a tendency toward equilibrium in international markets where each country is in balance-of-payments equilibrium.

PRODUCTION FUNCTION—A technological or engineering relationship showing, for some time period, the maximum amount of product which can be produced by any given amounts of factors of produc-

371

tion. For example, the production function of a birthday cake is its recipe.

PRODUCTION POSSIBILITIES CURVE—The relationship between the alternative quantities of X and Y which the economy is capable of producing, where the quantities of all other commodities are held constant and technology does not change. The phenomenon of increasing costs is reflected by the shape of the curve.

PRODUCTIVITY—The amount of output or product produced per worker or unit of capital for some given time period. An average obtained by dividing total production by the number of units of labor or capital.

PROFIT—In economic terms, a residual which is the difference between the proceeds from the sale of the product and the factor payments for its production, including interest, depreciation, and the wages of labor and management. To entrepreneurs accrue the profits, or losses, if the proceeds are less than the factor costs.

QUANTITY THEORY—The theory that the absolute level of prices is functionally related to the quantity of money in circulation.

QUOTA—An administratively determined maximum quantity (yards, pounds, etc.) of a good which may be imported or exported, as compared to a tariff which taxes imports or exports but allows the market to determine quantities imported or exported.

SAVING—The postponement of current consumption in order to make an investment.

SAY'S LAW—The idea that long-run unemployment is inconceivable because supply creates its own demand.

SOCIAL OVERHEAD CAPITAL—Durable capital assets, investments in which must be made by government because this type of capital is an indirect input in the process of production but not profitable for private investors. For example, a highway is an investment in social overhead capital made by government which is profitable from the standpoint of the community as a whole. Other examples are canals, harbors, dams, etc.

SUBSTITUTION EFFECT—The tendency of individuals to purchase more of a good whose price has declined because it will yield a higher utility per dollar expenditure than formerly.

SUPPLY—A relationship between the various possible prices of a commodity and the quantities of it which producers will be willing and able to supply. In general, the higher a commodity's price, the more producers will supply it.

TARIFF—A tax levied on the import, export, or consumption of a good in order to raise revenue, discourage consumption, or protect a domestic industry from external competition. *Specific duties* are imposed according to quantity ($.20 per pound, $.05 per yard, etc.). *Ad valorem* duties are computed as a percentage of the value of the product.

TERMS OF TRADE—Refers to the relationship between the prices that a country gets for its exports relative to the prices it must pay for its imports. The terms of trade are said to improve when a country's export prices rise or import prices fall.

TRANSFER PAYMENTS—Any income payments that do not result from current productive activity. An example of a government transfer payment is a payment to a veteran under a GI bill. A business transfer payment might be prize money paid in a contest to publicize a product.

UNION SHOP—A shop or plant in which, as a condition of employment, the hiree agrees to join the union, as compared to the *open shop* (employment in which is not subject to such condition). Employees hiring on in an *agency shop* are required only to pay union dues and may join the union at their discretion. For the above, *prior* union membership is not a condition of employment; in the case of the *closed shop*, management can hire only union members at the discretion of the union.

USURY—An interest payment considered to be unfair or unjust in some sense or which is greater than a maximum established by law.

Biographical Sketches

DAVID HUME (1711-1776)—A philosopher, Hume authored the price specie-flow mechanism of international adjustments.

ADAM SMITH (1723-1790)—Author of the *Wealth of Nations* (first edition, 1776), Smith developed an impressively complete theory of economic development and an explanation of the functioning of the economy in terms of certain economic "laws" which coordinated the diverse activities of individuals to automatically provide the goods and services needed by society.

THOMAS MALTHUS (1766-1835)—Best known for his population theory, Malthus believed that continual increases in population would keep most individuals at a subsistence level of income.

DAVID RICARDO (1772-1823)—A great theorist, Ricardo formalized the Law of Diminishing Returns, a theory of rent, and the theory of comparative advantage.

JOHN STUART MILL (1806-1873)—Mill's major contribution was his *Principles*, a restatement and clarification of the earlier theory. Mill combined his concept of reciprocal demand with Ricardo's comparative advantage theory to explain trade between nations.

ALFRED MARSHALL (1842-1924)—He developed the value theory, which is the basis for today's microeconomic theory. Marshall showed how time was an important dimension in the theory of the determination of value.

JOHN MAYNARD KEYNES (1883-1937)—Keynes developed a theory of recessions and depressions based on the idea that the private sector of the economy, in the aggregate, will not spend enough to buy its own output, causing unemployment. The theory questions the automaticity of the economic system envisioned by earlier economists and the major responsibility for the maintenance of full employment is placed on government.